Saudi Arabia and
the Politics of Dissent

Saudi Arabia and the Politics of Dissent

Mamoun Fandy

palgrave

SAUDI ARABIA AND THE POLITICS OF DISSENT
Copyright © Mamoun Fandy, 1999.

First published in hardcover in 1999 by St. Martin's Press
First PALGRAVE™ edition: February 2001
175 Fifth Avenue, New York, N.Y. 10010 and
Houndmills, Basingstoke, Hampshire, England RG21 6XS
Companies and representatives throughout the world.

PALGRAVE is the new global publishing imprint of St. Martin's Press LLC
Scholarly and Reference Division and Palgrave Publishers Ltd (formerly
Macmillan Press Ltd).

ISBN 0–312–21021–3 hardcover
ISBN 0–312–23882–7 paperback

Library of Congress Cataloging-in-Publication Data
Fandy, Mamoun, 1961-
Saudi Arabia and the politics of dissent / Mamoun Fandy.
    p. cm.
Includes bibliographical references and index.
ISBN 0–312–23882–7
1. Saudi Arabia—Politics and government.   2. Government,
resistance to—Saudi Arabia.   I. Title.
DS244.63.F36   1999
322.4'2'09538—dc21   98–42909
                                               CIP

A catalogue record for this book is available from the British Library.

Design by Letra Libre

First paperback edition: February 2001
10 9 8 7 6 5 4 3 2 1

Printed in the United States of America

To my two intimate friends:
Haj Hamza Fandy and Haja Daifiya Yaseen (my parents)

Contents

Acknowledgments

First and foremost, I wish to thank my wife, Judith Caesar, who repeatedly read and commented upon this manuscript in all its phases. My thanks also go to my parents, who, although they have never understood why I left their world of oral tradition for the world of the written word, have remained loving and supportive.

In addition, I would like to thank colleagues who have commented upon various chapters. Dr. F. Gregory Gause of the University of Vermont has been the most critical and the most helpful. Dr. John Voll and Dr. John Esposito of Georgetown University also provided insightful criticism and suggestions. I also appreciate the kindness of Dr. Sana Abed-Qotob.

Finally, I wish to thank the Saudis of all political persuasions who were so generous in granting me interviews and in helping me to understand the complex political structures of their country.

[I]n order to understand what power relations are about, perhaps we should investigate the forms of resistance and attempts made to dissociate these relations.

—Michel Foucault, "The Subject and Power"

Introduction

Throughout recorded history, it seems stable institutions providing legal, orderly, peaceful modes of political opposition have been rare. If peaceful antagonism between factions is uncommon, peaceful opposition among organized, permanent political parties is an even more exotic historical phenomenon.

—Robert A. Dahl, *Political Opposition in Western Democracies*

On May 31, 1996, four Saudi men were executed for bombing the al-'Uliyya U.S. military mission in the Saudi capital, Riyadh. This was the first time since the takeover of the Grand Mosque in 1979 that the Saudi government had executed its own citizens for an armed attack. This explosion as well as the one that took place in the Khobar Towers on June 25, 1996, were not ordinary local events but global ones. The images of the explosions and their analysis dominated the coverage of the global Cable News Network (CNN) and the front pages of American, European, and Arab newspapers. Because so many of the victims were American, because of the importance of Saudi Arabia as the country that sits on 25 percent of the world's proven oil reserves, and because of the new revolution in global communications, the Saudi opposition became the concern of people far beyond the boundaries of the kingdom. The public pressure resulting from this media coverage forced the Federal Bureau of Investigation (FBI) to get involved. The globalizing new media presented the threat to the Saudi order as a threat to global oil markets and Western civilization. For weeks the American media were busy providing instant analysis and speculating about the stability of the flow of oil, the future of the American presence in the Persian Gulf, and the implications for Western civilization of the rise of "Islamic fundamentalism." Events in countries that once seemed distant now flash across our television sets and computer screens. Although these are mediated events, we feel that we are witnessing them as they unfold.

Globally, the Riyadh bombing led to speculation about the size and capabilities of the Saudi opposition. Locally, the bombing was blamed on foreigners. But the Saudis, government and citizens alike, were shocked to realize that those who committed the act were not foreign mercenary forces following Iranian or Iraqi orders but Saudis from the heartland. On television, the Saudi public saw four Saudi men confess to the crime: Abdul Aziz al-Mi'thim, Khalid al-Sa'eed, Riyadh al-Hajri, and Muslih al-Shamrani. All of the men had recognizable Saudi tribal names and spoke Saudi Arabic. They confessed that they had smuggled explosives from Yemen and timed the device to explode outside the training mission of the Saudi National Guard, killing five Americans and two Indians. Since the bomb went off during the noon prayer, when no Muslims were expected in the area, apparently it was designed to kill only "infidels." No sooner had Saudis recovered from the shock of this event than another blast killed 19 U.S. servicemen in Khobar, a small city in Saudi Arabia's oil-rich eastern province, an area where the "infidels" are most concentrated because of the oil industry and the U.S. military presence. It is also an area inhabited by local "infidels," Saudi Arabia's Shi'a minority. These two bombings highlighted the existence of a home-grown opposition movement in Saudi Arabia, consisting mainly of Islamists of various orientations. In the past, neither Saudi Arabia nor smaller events captured the attention of news networks for that long. Now it is a different story. The Saudi government has to deal with two problems: the actual threat of the opposition on the local level and its global virtual image as a possibly unstable country. Both the state and the opposition are globalized.

One day after the four Saudis were executed, Saudi newspapers published their confessions, confessions that might have been extracted under intimidation and coercion.[1] Nonetheless, one cannot discredit them totally if only for one reason: the statements contradicted what the Saudi government had previously claimed, namely, that outside forces, such as Iran or Iraq, were behind the attack. The confessions undermined the official story and confirmed what the government feared most: that the bombing was a local conspiracy.

Except for 28-year-old Muslih al-Shamrani, all the bombers were 24 years of age. These were not old renegades clinging to the traditions of the past, but men who had grown up in the era of oil wealth and all the social welfare benefits that oil money had brought to Saudi Arabia. Furthermore, with the exception of al-Mi'thim, all of them had fought in Afghanistan.

One, al-Shamrani, who had been part of the Frouq Brigade in Afghanistan,[2] had fought in Bosnia as well. All four men came from modest backgrounds and began their activism with the Tabligh group, an Islamic missionary movement entirely legal within Saudi Arabia. They later went to Afghanistan, a mission not only legal during the 1980s but actively encouraged by both the Saudi and the U.S. governments. Some royal princes ran charity organizations to support both the Afghan jihad and the Bosnian Muslims. It is obvious from their confessions that the ideologies of these men were shaped by the years they spent fighting in Afghanistan alongside members of radical groups from various Arab countries, especially from Egypt and Algeria. The Afghanistan experience was central to the radicalization of many group leaders and activists, leading them away from preaching their own brand of Islam and pursuing peaceful change, and toward taking up arms to enforce their vision of a just Islamic society. All four men claimed to have links to other radical leaders, such as Muhammad al-Mas'ari, leader of the Committee for the Defence of Legitimate Rights (CDLR), and the Saudi millionaire Usama bin Laden, head of the Advice and Reform Committee (ARC). The use of postmodern technological means is also central to these groups. Riyadh al-Hajri stated: "I had a fax machine and received the publications of Mas'ari and bin Laden and the periodicals of the Egyptian Islamic Group, which I distributed to other youth." If indeed these movements and organizations have the ability to mobilize young men into action against either the U.S. troops in Saudi Arabia or symbols of the state, then they deserve special attention. This is the purpose of this book.

Central to the Saudi oppositions' vision is the idea that "Islam" and its values are under attack both globally and locally and that the Saudi government has failed to protect Islam and Muslims. The opposition is involved in globalization through both the means and the issues. According to al-Shamrani, the group used to meet and discuss whether the Saudi state conformed with Islamic teachings, how the state followed "secular law and supported the United Nations, and how the 'ulama such as bin Baz and bin Otheimein were conspiring with the state to undermine Islam. We were also reading the publications of Mas'ari, bin Laden, and other Islamic groups that consider Saudi Arabia an infidel state." The focus of the four convicted men was similar, and indeed they sounded as if they had read the same books and discussed similar material, if we exclude the possibility that they were simply coerced into signing similar confessions. One of these influential books was *al-Kawashif al-Jaliyya fi Kufr al-Dawla al-Saudia* (The obvious evidence of the apostasy of the Saudi state), published in Denmark by someone using the pseudonym Abu al-Bara' al-Najdi. Later, in 1995, a better-organized and improved version of the book was published by the Committee for the Defence of Legitimate Rights (CDLR) and edited by

Muhammad al-Mas'ari. This book, as I will show in chapter 4, selectively uses evidence from the Quran and Hadith to support the idea that the Saudi state is un-Islamic. Most striking, however, is the fact that these activists rely on the teachings of Sheikh Muhammad bin Ibraheem, grandson of the eighteenth-century reformer who established the Wahhabi branch of Islam. Abdul Aziz al-Mi'thim, one of those convicted of the bombing, echoes the book's claim that "the Saudi state allies itself with non-Muslim countries and abides by the anti-Islamic laws of the United Nations and the International Court of Justice," and he further accuses the Saudi 'ulama of "twisting Islamic teachings to support the policies of the state." The attack on the United Nations and the Saudi state's alliance with non-Muslim states, especially the United States, is also a recurring theme in the teachings of Sheikh Safar al-Hawali and Sheikh Salman al-Auda.

However, to focus on the causes of the two bombings alone is to miss the complexity of the Saudi opposition and the roles played by various structures and agents in the making of this opposition. Our mediated perceptions of these acts in the age of globalization and the world of television and satellite dishes are also important to consider. This book is an inquiry into the politics of dissent and opposition in a broad sense. Within this context, the book focuses on the various "Islamic" opposition groups in Saudi Arabia, discussing their leadership, their ideologies and discourses, and their networks and organizations. The interconnectedness of these elements and their mediation is of equal importance. This book looks at the phenomenon of resistance and the various forms of mediation that shape our perception of this resistance. This is an inquiry into the politics of resistance in the context of the globalization debate. Saudi Arabia is an ideal case to explore the connections between the local and the global and their implications for both state and opposition because it seems, on one hand, to be a closed society with its own unique values, while on the other hand it is deeply involved in international politics media, and finance. Of course the analysis leads me to draw conclusions from the Saudi context that might apply to other movements in the region and have implications beyond the Arab world. I also use Saudi opposition as a case to theorize the global-local connection. I view globalization neither through the lenses of modernization theorists, as a positive expansion of capital flow and markets, nor from a nativist and postmodern perspective, as a homogenizing impulse that has to be resisted. Instead I focus on what happens to both state and opposition in the context of the global-local dialectic.

Simply put, I focus on the local conditions that gave rise to the opposition, the impact of global forces on it, and how the interaction between the global and the local enhances the position of leaders locally and/or exaggerates the power of the group globally. For instance, because they are a minority in Saudi Arabia, the Shi'a may not constitute a threat to the dominant order unless they are linked to external forces, such as Iran. Their marginality also limits the cohesiveness of the Saudi opposition. Because they are Shi'a and the larger opposition is Sunni, the Shi'a may prefer the existing regime to the Sunni opposition. Other opposition groups are marginal in a different sense. For example, both Muhammad al-Mas'ari, the leader of CDLR and Usama bin Laden, the leader of the Advice and Reform Committee (ARC), are nontribal. Many Saudis consider Mas'ari to be khadiri, a group that does not possess any tribal lineage and has a lower social standing. Bin Laden's family is originally from Hadramawt in Yemen, which makes his Saudiness suspect in the eyes of many. Sa'd al-Faqih, head of the Movement for Islamic Reform in Arabia (MIRA), is probably the only Saudi dissident who can claim to be from within the center's Sunni and Najdi hegemony. But even he spent most of his life in the Zubair region in Iraq and thus also can be classified as marginal. These marginal figures were contained within Saudi Arabia when the state could shield itself from global exposure and before the coming of the satellite dish, the Internet, and, above all, the 1991 Gulf War.

However, new communications technologies allowed marginal groups to elaborate a new transcript or a cultural paradigm, to construct new identities, and to rewrite the story of Saudi Arabia. As I show in chapter 4, Muhammad al-Mas'ari reconstituted his identity abroad to present himself as a local leader. The new means of communications, whether CNN, the BBC, or the World Wide Web, have allowed marginal figures to elaborate their political programs without any domestic interference. When the message bounces back to the local setting through CNN or the Internet, it gains legitimacy because it seems to have international credibility. The Shi'a also were able to elaborate their argument in London and Washington, where their human rights newsletter became so influential that the Saudi government was willing to compromise with them. Moreover, since a period of radicalism in the 1960s (see chapter 1), the Saudi opposition has been either an extension of or a reaction to global forces. In this period, Egyptian, Iraqi, and Syrian governments backed by the Soviet Union instigated the labor unrest against foreign control of Arab oil. The protestors were mainly Saudi communists and Arab nationalists. In 1979 Iran used the local Shi'a to instigate a protest.

The main argument here is that Saudi opposition cannot be understood without looking at the linkages between the global and the local factors. Outside powers traditionally have manipulated these groups to their own ends, and in turn the internal opposition has made use of global movements to enhance their local standing. The current Islamic opposition is not influenced by any outside ideology—indeed their message is indigenous—but they make use of global forces and technologies and are obliged to adopt a global discourse in order to propagate their ideas. Therefore, the new forces of globalization and the new sites of opposition require special attention.

Saudi Opposition and the Global-Local Nexus

Globalization is not a value-free concept, and it is construed in various ways. There are those who see it in terms of a capitalist war that has been brewing for decades, those who see it as a false concept, and others who see it as a theory that has its own internal logic but does not describe any event in the real world.[3] This book is not concerned with globalization as a contested concept or with its ideological baggage; rather it focuses on the linkages between the global and the local. This global-local connection is indeed "in-here" and "out-there" simultaneously. The local and the global are constantly interacting, defining and redefining each other.

One way of thinking about the interplay between the global and the local is to realize that in Saudi Arabia different times and different places exist at once. Saudi Arabia is both a premodern and a postmodern society. In analyzing the opposition's relations to the state and to the global relations, I sometimes utilize concepts that have their roots in how local people perceive their human condition, namely the work of the fourteenth-century historian Ibn Khaldun. His ideas of the badu-hadar (nomadic-sedentary) dialectic, 'asabiyya (solidarity and group feeling), and ghalaba (perseverance and hegemony) are relevant to this analysis for various reasons. First, like Mas'ari, Ibn Khaldun has also been globalized.[4] He has been rediscovered in the metropolitan sites of higher learning and has been mentioned in the speeches of U.S. presidents as the champion of "supply-side" economics.[5] This global factor has influenced the local to the point that Saudi Islamist Salman al-Auda makes Ibn Khaldun's ideas central to his critique of the Saudi state. Furthermore, the global nomads of migrant workers and the mobile professionals are so different from anything Ibn Khaldun conceived that he must be mentioned here with the idea of rethinking his ideas and their mediation. Intellectual nomadism (generally referred to as interdisciplinary approaches) has come into vogue. Thus Ibn Khaldun is doubly relevant, in the sense that he provides insights into Arab society and politics and also into how these societies and polities have been conceived by both the local advocates of change and the global intellectuals in search of alternative method and theory. But central to my discussion is not just Ibn Khaldun but concepts drawn from the globalization literature such as distanciation, embeddedness, disembeddedness, and the postmodern conception of new global spaces. Only through an understanding of the premodern and the postmodern, the indigenous and the

Western, can we grasp this moment of hybridity in which both the Saudi state and its opposition operate.

To address the opposition's postmodern world, we also have to be cognizant of the local setting. To be aware of old, indigenous sociologists and historians such as Ibn Khaldun as well as contemporary Western sociologists such as Anthony Giddens simultaneously is essential. I use local concepts to show that elements of the past exist in the present, just as elements of tradition exist in modernity and postmodernity. To deliberately conflate these concepts is to miss the whole argument in this book. We can say that the regime of modernity created an iltiham—"connectedness"—between the dominant global and metropolitan space in the first, second, and the third worlds. Only in this sense does this segment of this world order represent a global hadar. Opposition groups outside the country may be part of the world of immigration and the ethnoscape of global nomads. But this neither implies group solidarity ('asabiyya) nor that the groups will take over the cities, although sometimes they do in inner cities. The point is that new analytical concepts need to be devised to deal with these new developments.

Central to the debate about Saudi opposition is the fact that a group such as the CDLR can capture world attention with a fax machine, a Web page, and an e-mail list. This new world opens up new spaces that were not available to earlier opposition groups and greatly reduces the distance between exiled opposition leaders and their followers. Offices, Web sites, and e-mail lists have replaced the secret meeting places where opposition groups met to discuss their plans and form their ideologies. These "virtual communities" are the direct result of the proliferation of new information technology. All of this raises new questions about the study of the opposition. It is difficult for ordinary observers to tell whether what seems to be a movement is a one-man operation or a large, well-organized group. Who is behind the computer screen, a movement or an individual? A Saudi or a non-Saudi? Can Saudi Arabia afford to deprive its citizens of these technologies because a group is using them as a means for attacking the state? Where does the Saudi state end and global space begin? The postmodern world of late capitalism and globalization raises serious questions about tidy categories through which the world has conventionally been understood. Resistance, the subject of this book, is one of these categories.

The proliferation of means of communication, such as the satellite dish and the Internet, has added new dimensions to our world. Messages move faster and reach around the world in a matter of minutes. As time shrinks so does the distance between places. In the early twentieth century, traveling from New York to London by ship took days. With the coming of airplanes, this time was reduced to few hours. Moreover, physical distance is no longer as important as access to modern technology. The distance between the

Egyptian cities of Cairo and Luxor is 11 hours by train; yet the distance between Cairo and New York is ten hours by plane. An e-mail message can travel the same distance in minutes. As we invent faster machines and reduce time, space automatically seems smaller, and thus we speak of the global village.[6] But this perception of space is also agent specific; that is, who has access to these spaces is also of paramount importance. These changes in time and space liberate events from their local markers.[7] As space shrinks, people in different places experience the same events at the same time.[8]

Against this backdrop of compressed time and space, the world seems beset by the paradox of homogenizing and fragmenting impulses. Someone watching television in Riyadh, for instance, can see an animal rights demonstration in London (a homogenizing experience) and feel outraged that Westerners seem to care more about their pets than the malnourished children in Gaza (a fragmenting experience). "Otherness" is not limited to other places; the media[9] bring world events to our homes, giving us the illusion that we have been taken there to witness these events. In this heavily mediated world, the signs of the real, text and image alike, seem more real than the real itself.[10] Saudi Arabia has felt the impact of globalization at least as intensely as anywhere else. Indeed, it can be argued that, even before the impact of satellite and Internet, Saudi Arabia felt globalization more profoundly than other states, by virtue of the global nature of the haj (pilgrimage), which it hosts yearly and which brings people from every country of the world to Mecca.

The importance of these new spaces, especially the worlds of television screens and finance, was made very obvious during the Gulf War. The occupation and subsequent liberation of Kuwait has shown that in the age of globalism, a state can survive even though it is physically occupied by another country. If the state can change the passwords it uses in computers and the world of finance, and if it exists on television screens, that state can continue to function. When a territory is occupied, the state can become diffused in the financescape[11] and the mediascape, or be transformed into what might be called, following Jean Baudrillard, a "hyperreal state," a state that exists on television screens more than in reality.[12] Thus these spaces are open not only for opposition; they also are open for states. A comparison between the state and opposition usage of these new spaces will further enhance the discussion.

These postmodern developments are not irrelevant to the world of the badu (nomads) and hadar (city dwellers) of Saudi Arabia. In his *Muqaddimah,* Ibn Khaldun depicted society as a dynamic tension between the badu (the original noble savages, who were brave and independent but lacked the technology and large-scale social organization of the city dwellers) and the hadar (the civilized city dwellers who had developed arts and sciences but were too specialized and compliant to defend themselves successfully). The badu could attack and defeat the hadar when civilization was degenerating; but the badu rulers would then become hadar themselves, and the cycle would repeat itself. Ibn Khaldun uses the model to explain not only the Arab world but the fall of so many sophisticated ancient civilizations to more primitive but warlike peoples—the Persians to the Arabs, the Byzantines to the Turks, the Eastern Arab caliphates to the Tartars. Can we speak of global badu and global hadar? In our world, for instance, we see greater correspondence between postmodern cities such as Seattle and Osaka than we do between, say, Corry, Pennsylvania, and Seattle, or, on the other hand, Okinawa and Osaka. The difference is not so much their respective sizes as much as their degree of interconnection with global technologies. Riyadh, Jeddah, and Khobar would have more in common with Western cities such as London and New York than they would with a Bedouin settlement inside Saudi Arabia. Thus we can speak of a global hadar of the big cities New York, London, Cairo, Taipei, and Tokyo versus global nomads of unskilled migrant workers coming from the villages of Mexico, the Philippines, Pakistan, and Egypt. In his formulation of a world composed of five distinct spaces, Arjun Appadurai would refer to the global badu as an ethnoscape of global migration.[13] However, there is a major difference between the postmodern global nomads and the desert nomads of the past. The new global nomads are part of a world order and its law. With the possible exception of terrorism and drug networks, the global nomads have given up their group feeling and solidarity ('asabiyya) to carry passports and identity cards that limit their power. The current dominance of the state system and the new spaces that have emerged within it make these global nomads less threatening than the badu were to the hadar in Ibn Khaldun's terms. Ibn Khaldun's badu-hadar dialectic and the difference in the modes of living (Subul al-Ma'ash) can be broadened to have relevance to the globalization literature. Thus global space can be conceived of as containing premodern global nomads, modern cities and towns, and postmodern cities. The last two correspond to Ibn Khaldun's notion of the hadar. The 'asabiyya of the metropolitan cities is cemented by modern and postmodern modes of material and cultural production, international law and treaties, and the world of passports and identity cards that marginalize the nomadic segments of this world. Of course, Saudi opposition in London is not completely within the world of global nomadism, but it is at the mercy of the British state and its laws. No serious study of the politics of dissent can ignore these conditions.

But these are not the only issues with which we have to deal in order to have a more comprehensive understanding of Saudi dissent. Other issues such as how Saudi Arabia has been studied traditionally, the nature of the intellectual communities in the United States and their closed discourse, and the impact of all this on how we perceive Saudi Arabia and its politics are central to my presentation. Additionally, I address the shortcomings of some approaches that have been utilized thus far in the study of Saudi Arabia, such as modernization, class analysis, and interpretive theory. It is to these approaches that the rest of the introduction turns.

Understated Saudi State?

The complexity of Saudi state and society usually is understated and stereotyped. Saudi Arabia appears in most Western writings as a "traditional" society, a misconception that must be dispelled before we can examine the highly complex and sophisticated structure of Saudi resistance. Saudi Arabia is a very complex mix of the "traditional," the various forms of modernities,[14] and the postmodern, depending on the region and the sociocultural formation.[15] For example, the Eastern Province is dominated by a Shi'a population, an oil industry, and an obvious U.S. presence. Highways, shopping malls, and expatriate communities give the impression of an American city, especially with the number of U.S. soldiers and civilians in Dhahran, Damam, and Khobar. Except for the Saudi customs of closing shops for prayers and veiling women, these cities are a microcosm of global creolization. They contain at least as many foreign workers as Saudi citizens. Saudi children are raised by Asian and European nannies and are frequently bilingual. On the local level, hijabs and abayahs (local dress) are made in Taiwan and Hong Kong, and designer abayahs are made in Paris and London. Prayer rugs with a compass indicating the direction of Mecca are made in Japan. The holy places in Mecca and Medina are by definition part of global culture. Almost all religious icons sold outside the Prophet's Mosque in Medina are made outside the country and sold to foreigners as if they were Saudi-made.

Saudi culture also varies from one region to the other; liberal Sunni cosmopolitan in the Western Region, Shi'a liberal and Western in the east, and conservative but Westernized in the center, to give but a few examples. The local Shi'a identity transcends Saudi boundaries and extends into states such as Bahrain, Lebanon, and Iran. Moreover, like Kuwait, Saudi Arabia is diffused financially and informationally in the various global scapes, with investments and media holdings all over the world.

Because of the limited channels for formal dissent in Saudi Arabia, movement in intermediate spaces—between the local and the global, the state and civil society, and the formal and the informal structures—is central to the politics of both the state and the opposition. The following discussion shows not only that domination and resistance have moved from real to virtual space, but that the Saudi political struggle has relocated to a different site, namely London. Currently the British capital is host to resistance leaders such as Dr. Muhammad al-Mas'ari and Dr. Sa'd al-Faqih. Yet London is also the base for Saudi establishment newspapers, such as *al-Hayat* and *al-Sharq al-Awsat,* weekly magazines such as *al-Majalla,* and the Middle East Broadcasting Corporation (MBC), all of which are completely or partially owned by members of the Saudi royal family.[16] Saudis play a role in this global "Islamic" culture as custodians of the holy places, but their relation to the production of associated religious imagery and symbols is ambiguous. Anthony Giddens's idea of disembedding as the "'lifting out' of social relations from local contexts of interaction and their restructuring across indefinite spans of time-space"[17] gains special significance in the case of the Saudis, as do many concepts associated with the globalization literature.

The new global spaces also give the state a chance to be more than one thing to all people. As it appears from London, through the MBC television and the various newspapers and magazines, the Saudi state is centrist and liberal. Conservative state 'ulama are not given the same space or regularity in *al-Majalla,* for instance, as the moderate Egyptian Muslim Brotherhood intellectual Fahmy Hiwaydi. He receives two pages in this Saudi-owned weekly, space that has not been accorded to the state's own religious scholars. MBC television is more mainstream and moderate than many established state television stations in the region. Its only competitor is The Qatari al-Jazerah Television, which is almost completely free from any state control. Furthermore, all these channels speak to the Saudi audience. Although the channel is Saudi, it is accorded more freedom because it is broadcasting from outside. Similarly, *al-Hayat* newspaper, owned by Prince Khalid bin Sultan, the chief commander of the Arab forces during the Gulf War, is one of the best and most reliable newspapers in the Arab world. Its opinion pages are full of controversial articles, yet this paper is permitted inside Saudi Arabia, and it is generally considered a Saudi paper. The same goes for *al-Sharq al-Awsat* newspaper, which is owned by Prince Ahmad bin Salman. A more liberal Saudi state thus exists outside the national boundaries even as the other, conservative state exists inside.

Moreover, Saudi Arabia is unusual in that the state usually presents itself as the defender of the faith in the face of a cultural and religious onslaught from the West. Thus, in macropolitical or global terms, the state presents itself as an inherently oppositional entity. If we imagine the world as one global entity, as many opposition groups do, Saudi Arabia takes on the character of an oppositional state that attempts to preserve Islamic values and Islamic beliefs in the face of ever-encroaching secular and Western trends. The state allocation of resources to take care of the holy places and its insistence on being an Islamic state that applies Islamic law further confirms Saudi

Arabia's image as a country at the forefront of the global struggle against perceived Western corruption. Moreover, Saudi opposition groups are different from opposition groups in other states both because of the extreme limitations on conventional expressions of dissent within the country and because of their access to cash and the global flow of information. They are the first such opposition groups in the Middle East to make extensive use of new technologies in communicating their message to their followers. Of course, the Ayatollah Khomeini used cassette tapes to undermine the Shah of Iran, but the Saudis are the first among Middle Eastern opposition groups to use the Internet and the fax machine as tools of political communication.

In this context, it is no longer analytically useful to think of Saudi Arabia as a closed system. New technologies and new means of communication have provided opposition groups and the state with an intermediate space and a new means of disseminating information in a "virtual space" beyond their limited media and physical spaces. But more for the opposition than for the state, the Internet and other technologies and media, such as fax machines, cellular phones, satellite dishes, and cassette tapes, provide a new space for airing grievances while assuming minimal risk. Absence of risk is not the result of what James C. Scott, in his influential analysis of resistance, refers to as an offstage discourse of whispers and rumors in safe zones inaccessible to the ruling elite.[18] Sites of resistance are no longer the secret nooks and crannies within Saudi society, but essentially public media, such as Internet nodes, Web sites, and offices outside the country that transmit information to sympathizers inside. Neither the hidden transcripts nor the social sites of resistance conform to earlier formulations concerning resistance literature. The transcript of resistance, especially on the World Wide Web, is hidden only to those who choose not to read it or who have no access to the language.[19] Furthermore, the opposition shares this space with the government on an equal footing. The transcripts of both the opposition and the government allow for multiple discourses depending on the language used and the audience targeted. Thus the binary formulations of hidden transcript/public transcript require reformulation in light of the new means of communication, the new relations of mediated social phenomena, and the local/global dialectic.[20]

Political Opposition Studies

Thus far political opposition and dissent have been a poorly researched area in the discipline of political science, in the subfield of comparative politics, and more so in the area of Middle Eastern studies. In the larger discipline, Robert A. Dahl seems to be the only one studying opposition, beginning with his edited volume *Political Oppositions in Western Democracies* (1966).

Seven years later Dahl edited another volume entitled *Regimes and Opposition,* which considered opposition in non-Western countries. A few studies have been published on Eastern European and Asian opposition,[21] but in the area of Middle Eastern studies, examinations of opposition have been rare indeed. With the exception of two journal articles, one by Lisa Anderson and one by Jean Leca, very little has been done.[22] Of course, there have been many articles and books about the Islamic movements, but very few can be considered systemic inquiries into the politics of dissent. Anderson's article was the first to outline this area of inquiry. Although she did not include the Gulf states in her discussion, her attempt to refocus the study of the opposition from a society-centered approach to a state-centered one is nevertheless useful. She suggests that we have to look at opposition in terms of what they oppose on various levels, namely, whether the opposition group is against the person of the ruler, the regime, the policies, or the state. Anderson believes that regimes get the opposition they deserve and that the opposition is a mirror image of the regime. However, there are two problems with her approach. First, she dismisses culture as irrelevant to the analysis of opposition. Second, her definition of the Middle East or the data on which she based her argument exclude the Gulf states and focus mainly on North Africa and Israel. In her quest to avoid being accused of orientalism, Anderson excludes culture from her analysis of opposition. She argues against political culture as a useful concept of studying Middle Eastern political phenomena in favor of an approach that emphasizes political economy.[23]

In his attempt to rectify Anderson's approach to the question of opposition, Jean Leca brings culture back into the discussion. The culture he brings, however, is both essentialized and reified. In arguing against Anderson's approach, Leca asserts that the emphasis on political economy may have to do with the "received knowledge," according to which we are led to believe that "Arab citizens are as rational as anybody else and keen on bread-and-butter issues." This received knowledge, according to Leca, is inaccurate because Arab citizens actually are "much more sensitive about the implementation of the sacred prescriptions. Nothing else is expected of politics."[24] This ethnocentric attitude aside, his main argument suggests that opposition in the Arab world is modeled after the national struggle, in which outsiders constitute the main enemy. Although Leca's article is broader in scope and includes some Gulf states, such as Oman and Saudi Arabia, his data about those states are anecdotal and dependent on secondary sources. Although both articles are informative, they concentrate on analyzing the state as a closed system without exploring the linkages between both the state and the opposition to outside forces. Anderson justifies avoiding culture in order to stay clear of charges of orientalism; yet such avoidance often, in fact, has nothing to do with orientalism as much as it does with competence and the researcher's ability to comprehend the subject matter fully. Unfortunately, even those who champion the importance of culture very rarely use Arabic sources. The problem with culture is that the debate is between those who know nothing about Arab culture and project onto Arabs the worst traits of their own culture and those well-meaning scholars who know very little about Arab history but broadmindedly suggest that Arab culture is important, whatever it is. Both of these viewpoints are dangerous not only for the study of Arab culture but for the study of *any* culture. Furthermore, the question of culture and its relation to social action and social structure has been problematized by various outlooks and schools of thought: Marxism, Weberianism, Durkheimianism, functionalism, semiotics, dramaturgy, and poststructuralism. The fact that these debates are not settled is not enough justification either to fully embrace culture or to throw it away altogether. Culture is a process that requires intimate knowledge of the shifts and the content in particular contexts. It confers meaning to social action, and without this frame of reference we have very little to go by to understand the meaning of events.

Islam, Social Theory, and Dissent

Generally speaking, current social theory has limitations in dealing with religion and politics and, more specifically, Islam and politics. Some of the dominant social science schools have even more limited approaches to Islam. In spite of living almost half of my life in the Arab world and the other half studying the Arab world in the United States, I am always struck by what little relevance Western theory has to the world of the Arabs. I am always left pondering the question of to what degree the "Arab" in Arab and Middle Eastern studies in the United States corresponds to the "Arab" in the Arab world. Two schools that have dominated Middle Eastern studies—modernization theory and dependency theory—bear little resemblance to actual events in the Middle East. Whereas Western scholars enthusiastically espouse modernization theory, dependency theory provides the central model for much indigenous Middle East scholarship. Each contains its own particular flaws. A third approach, interpretive theory, also has limitations, but it has not caught on in Middle Eastern studies.

Modernization theorists present tradition and modernity as opposite poles on a universal development spectrum where modernization is seen as desirable, positive, and something that must be attained; tradition, on the other hand, is seen as undesirable, negative, and something to be transcended.[25] Progress is defined as a linear movement along a predetermined path, whereby all societies are expected to abandon tradition and embrace modernity. Successful completion of this process is envisioned as a leap from one pole to the next, allowing room for neither coexistence nor synthesis. The theory dismisses the possibility of the existence of tradition within modernity or modernity within tradition. Moreover, the theory treats religion and religious forces as traditional obstacles to overcome in the pursuit of secular democratization (read Westernization). According to this theory, as societies move from traditional to modern, religious authority is weakened and is replaced by rational secular authority. The rise of a theocracy in Iran in 1978 and the contemporary growth of religious movements in the United States certainly suggest a different outcome from that predicted by this theory. This school came under attack in the late 1970s from Latin American scholars and some scholars writing about the Middle East.[26] However, some assumptions of the modernization school currently are being transferred to the globalization literature, where globalization and homogenization are seen as positive and fragmentation and the local politics of identity are seen as negative.

Dependency theory also has failed to address the complexity of political phenomena in the Gulf and the wider Middle East, especially in dealing with the relationship between religion and politics. World system theory privileges the material world over culture and religion. However, unlike modernization theory, which looks at countries as closed units, world system authors see social changes in the Third World as part of global patterns of capital penetration and the involvement of exogenous variables that disrupt and distort the developmental path of these societies. In other words, the theory blames Western interference in the political and financial affairs of Third World countries for many of these countries' problems. Through its focus on the material world and its concern with the struggle against imperialism, world system theory has a built-in bias that is hostile to the inclusion of religion as an important factor in understanding social and political change. Dependency theory contributes to the study of the Middle East by providing a counterbalance to modernization theory and raising new research questions.

Even those who wanted to bring a balance and move us away from the pro-American/anti-American debates of these previous schools (such as Jurgen Habermas and other interpretive theorists of the Frankfurt school) consider religious movements to be a response to the incursions of modernity. People may turn to religion when the sudden changes in their society make them uncomfortable, but this return is temporary.[27] With few recent exceptions, interpretive theory has not been applied in the study of the Arab world.[28]

If social theory is inadequate to deal with the question of religion and politics in general, it has been disastrous in dealing with Islam and politics. This is due to various factors. First, many who have written on Islam have very little knowledge of Arabic or other Middle Eastern languages. These are tools that we expect beginners to learn in any other area of study. Lacking these tools, most researchers have depended very heavily on validating theories based on secondary sources. This is one reason why I want to steer clear of secondary sources and focus on primary sources and original material.

The current state of social theory aside, Middle Eastern political studies generally has been poor in explaining or predicting political change in the area. American scholarship has oscillated among various terminologies without any significant contribution to theory. In a seminal article in the *Middle East Journal,* James A. Bill summarized the deficiencies of the field:

> American analysts continue to explore their political empty quarter in search of the oases of knowledge necessary to explain political development in the Middle East. Eventually, these analysts all seem to end up at the same old watering holes, believing they have discovered new oases and giving them different names each time. In the 1950s and 1960s, the signs at the oasis read "liberal democracy and Westernization;" in the 1960s and 1970s, the search focused on "political development and political participation;" in the 1970s and 1980s, the jargon was "legitimacy" and "the state and society" dichotomy; today, the words on the weather-beaten old signs are "civil society" and "democratization." We have come full circle.[29]

Indeed this has been the case for some time. Bill is not the only analyst stating this fact, but he seems to have summarized a consensus on the state of the field that has been building since the 1980s.[30]

If the study of Islam and politics and political studies in the Middle East has been poor, the study of Saudi Arabia has been a disaster. With few exceptions,[31] most political science research on Saudi Arabia in general and political opposition in particular has been grounded in speculation and conjecture. Specialists who have never been to the country depend on archival material and let their imaginations supply them with a fictional setting that conforms to "stereotypical Saudi Arabia" taken from the world of the *Arabian Nights* or, worse, from the American popular media.[32] Fortunately, I had the opportunity to live in Saudi Arabia for two years and visited it twice after the Gulf war. Every time I visit it or any other country in the Arab world, I return to the United States feeling how removed Middle Eastern studies are from the realities of the region.

The conceptual frameworks and terminology used to describe what is taking place in the various Middle Eastern countries have been almost as misleading as the social theories. Even the least pejorative of the concepts used, such as "Islamic revival," do not reflect the area's social reality. "Revival" implies that Islam was nearly dead and is now being restored to life. It also implies that the revived Islam is somehow the same Islam that was dying and that the passage of time has had no influence on either the nature or the discursive interpretation of Islam.[33]

Clearly, there is a need for a refined, if not entirely new, approach to the study of the Middle East. Here I hope to contribute substantively to the development of such a new approach. While researchers thus far have regarded the opposition within the closed system of the modern nation-state, I intend to look at opposition in a macropolitical and global sense. Thus I focus on the internal dynamics of Saudi Arabia, the external global dynamics, and the relationship between the two. Only in this way can I focus on the process and see Saudi opposition within the context of the dialectic between the local and the global. Only then can I claim that this book has implications for disciplinary questions concerning the study of the politics of dissent.

These are issues that concern students of politics. But this book is not written solely for scholars. Certainly there are many important questions that interest both scholars and general readers. These questions include, for example, the relationship between religion and politics in non-Western social formations. Moreover, the world has experienced many changes that have bearing on dissent in Arab states. For instance, with the collapse of communism and Arab nationalism, will Islamism become the dominant ideology in most Muslim states? Furthermore, the Saudi Islamist protest is of particular interest because it arose in an already Islamized society. Given the intense involvement of Islamists in Saudi society, the rise of opposition based on Islam suggests that even if an Islamic state is to emerge, this may not be the end of the phenomenon of Islamist dissent. Other questions of interest to both academic and general readers include: given that Saudi Arabia has about 25 percent of the world's proven oil reserves, what would happen to the oil markets and the Western industrial societies if Islamists come to power? Or perhaps the real question should be whether Islamists can indeed come to power. Is there anything in their ideology indicating Islamist aspirations to control the state apparatus? What is their view of surrounding cultures and states and of other civilizational blocs? Are they, as many claim, a response to the Western challenge confronting a decaying Arab and Muslim political order? Or are they a response to an Eastern rather than Western threat? That is, is the Arab world worried that Iran's Islamic Republic has moved the seat of Islamic power away from Sunni to Shi'a Islam and from the Arabs to the Persians? If that is the case, the West may not figure very prominently in this thesis. Indeed, the rhetoric of some Saudi Islamists suggests that they are responding to both Western and Eastern developments.

One aim of this book is to provide a map of the Islamist opposition in Saudi Arabia at the level of leadership, discourse, and organization. This is useful to both academics and policymakers alike. First, I will profile these dissidents, their backgrounds, and the reasons that led them to risk imprisonment and exile to oppose a regime that would have provided them and their families with a comfortable degree of material security. Safar al-Hawali, Salman al-Auda, Muhammad al-Mas'ari, Sa'd al-Faqih, and Hasan al-Saffar are all intelligent men who are well trained in their own fields and who would like to see a more inclusive form of government in Saudi Arabia; but there the resemblance ends. As an examination of their writings reveals, their knowledge and views of the West differ, as do their ideas about Saudi relations with the West. They differ in their motives and with regard to their bases of support. I examine these clerics and their organizations one by one, looking at their public statements and the ways in which the regime has responded to them. To what degree do Islamic opposition groups have legitimate grievances? To what degree do misunderstanding and xenophobia fuel them? Do they have the potential to be any more than an embarrassment to the Saudi regime? Can and should these clerics' demands be accommodated? What role, if any, should the U.S. assume in this debate? My purpose here is to consider the extent to which these groups pose a threat to the Saudi government as it is now constituted and to current U.S. policy in the region. I will outline the context of the theoretical part of this study in the following pages and address policy implications in the conclusion.

Shifting the Gaze

Although they set the stage for this introduction, the bombings in Khobar and Riyadh might have passed almost unnoticed had the victims been of a different national origin. Thus some of my emphasis on this subject does not come entirely from the fact that there was an explosion but from the fact that Americans were killed. This analysis is taking place at a time of U.S. hegemony on a global scale. The questions evoked by the global power balance may not remain central if a hegemonic shifts take place. I do not claim that the questions and language of this study are not influenced by the dominant discourse shaped by the current hegemony. Furthermore, this study is not a final statement about Saudi society, culture, and politics, but a snapshot of a late-twentieth-century moment of both capital and cultural flux. This analysis is situated among various communities with differing attitudes toward a country like Saudi Arabia. Various discourses dominate in different circles, according to the agenda of those doing the analysis. Economists have focused on the discourse of the rentier state, an analytical framework that frequently has a built-in bias based on the Protestant work ethic, whether its users are aware of it or not. According to this framework, wealth should be the product of work; since Saudis have become wealthy without work, they are thus undeserving people who should not be in control of oil, a lifeline of

Western civilization. I will elaborate this point further in the next chapter when I discuss the political economy of signs. Another discourse has focused on the exotic components of Saudi Arabian culture, namely the veiling of women and other cultural practices that seem most different from the dominant practices in the West. Edward Said has already eloquently expressed the more general points concerning the limitations of Western theories and methods and their bias when dealing with the world of Islam and the Arabs in his famous books *Orientalism* and *Covering Islam*.[34]

It is important to remember that our intellectual production is taking place within a political economy of writing in which scholarship is tied more to political programs than to research programs.[35] The current established discourse on Saudi Arabia is frequently tied to specific political agendas, and what is funded and published tends to support the ideas and approaches sponsors of the research wish to propagate. Publications even tend to predict outcomes that specific groups would like to see. Thus the popularity of various books proclaiming the impending fall of the house of Saud.[36] Other books take the other extreme of "everything is perfect." In this study, I attempt to steer clear of these agendas and instead to examine as objectively as possible how the Saudi system of governance functions and the causes and effects of the Islamist opposition to the Saudi regime. I begin from the premise that the fact that Saudi Arabia differs from the West in its culture, political system, and economy does not necessarily mean that it functions poorly. It may or may not be an unstable structure. I have no a priori assumptions concerning what the Saudi state should be. This may make this study disappointing to those who wish scholarly confirmation of what they believe to be the moral errors of Saudi governance.

For this project I wanted to come closer to the reality of the opposition; thus I moved away from dominant ideas in Middle Eastern studies to focus on primary data that I collected over the years. I have collected, translated, and analyzed over 150 taped sermons of Saudi opposition leaders, and I have interviewed most of these preachers. I hope that this heavy focus on primary sources will take us a step further from the dominant paradigm.

The book begins by further clarifying, in chapter one, some important concepts, such as Islam as a social text, 'a'liyya (Islamic familialism), and the political economy of signs. It then describes both the formal and informal structures of the Saudi state. It summarizes the "Letter of Demands" and the "Memorandum of Advice," which represent the core demands of the opposition. Subsequent chapters trace the genealogy of these ideas in the sermons of the Saudi preachers. Chapters 2 and 3 discuss the taped sermons of, respectively, Safar al-Hawali and Salman al-'Auda, two religio-political preachers who dominated the Saudi scene during the Gulf War period and who depended mainly on audio and video technology to communicate their messages. These sermons set the cultural tone for the other groups. In chapters 4 and 5 I examine the Committee for the Defence of Legitimate Rights and the Movement for Islamic Reform in Arabia, respectively. These Sunni groups have made extensive use of the World Wide Web and other technology to elaborate an oppositional discourse both inside and outside the kingdom, thereby engaging in what I refer to as cyberspace resistance. In chapter 6 I discuss the Advice and Reform Committee, a group led by the radical Saudi Islamist Usama bin Laden. Finally, in chapter 7 I discuss the Shi'a Reform Movement, a group that depends on various media, including cassette tapes, faxes, and a limited use of electronic mail. I describe how these groups have circumvented the state's institutional control through the use of modern technology. Thus I show the degree to which the nature of resistance has changed as well as the practical and theoretical implications of these new forms of resistance beyond the Saudi case.

CHAPTER ONE

Context: Concepts, Parameters, and History

To understand the complex dynamics of Saudi dissent, we must understand the context in which this oppositional politics takes place. This chapter provides such a context. Explaining some central concepts such as Islam or islams, the qabila (tribe), 'a'iliyya and qaraba (tentatively translated as familialism and closeness in both spatial and social relations, respectively) is an essential first step of mapping the sociocultural terrain. I also link this cultural sphere to both the economics and the politics of dissent by focusing on "the political economy of signs," an approach that can give us new insights into the politics of dissent.

The ideology of 'a'iliyya (familialism) and the qaraba (social relations) system are at the heart of the Saudi polity and bring all the previous elements into a unified whole, making the political economy of the Saudi system more than a matter of understanding classes and economic indicators. The qaraba relations transform this from an ordinary political economy in the classical sense to a political economy of signs. This approach takes us away from the notion of the economy of state and traditional measures such as the GDP to a notion of an economy that includes the household and the family. On shortcoming of those who study the economics of the Arab states and the relations between the economy and politics is their failure to recognize the role of this familialism and the household economy and the relationship between this system and a particular economy of signs. To clarify, I describe the structure of authority and governance in the Saudi system, then focus on historicizing Saudi dissent. Next I consider the origin of the current opposition movements in terms of their immediate history, namely the rise of a new political language of Islamic resistance in an

Islamic state during the 1990–91 Gulf War. This includes the cultural debate that preoccupied Saudi society during 1988–89 and the intensification of this debate during the war and thereafter. Incidents that occurred during the Gulf War period are also relevant, such as the women's drive-in protest in Riyadh. Finally I explain and summarize the Letter of Demands and the Memorandum of Advice, two political initiatives that forced the government to respond. Derived from the teachings of various Islamic sheikhs, these two documents are at the heart of opposition politics of Saudi Arabia.

Introducing and/or Rethinking Basic Concepts

This section focuses on three main concepts: (1) "Islamism" and "familialism"; (2) the ethos associated with their interaction as social texts; and (3) the political economy of signs or a critique of the rentier model as a framework for analysis. As a first step toward establishing a context for the discourse of the opposition, the conceptual narrative as well as the dominant models have to be reconsidered. For instance, a critique of the dominant usage of the term "Islam" as a hegemonic concept and the rentier model as a hegemonic model has the potential to lift this study from a stultifying and stagnant discourse and to insert it afresh into a different discourse. Here I try to avoid the dominant story about the gulf states and societies in the U.S., a story that verifies and reaffirms itself by narrative detours rather than by observation and empirical findings.

"Islam" and "Islamism"

"Islam" is at the heart of both the Saudi political culture and social science discourses on Saudi Arabia and "Islamic" societies. Given the problems associated with "Islam" as a term in the dominant Western discourse and in the discourse of the "islamic" activists, I have opted to use "islam" and "islams" rather than "Islam." The reason that I do not capitalize the word "islam" is that islam as a social text is drastically different from Islam as a religion, as a written text, and as an imagined and assumed essence; I use the plural because of the many different interpretation of islam even as a social text. The islams that I am interested in and that I think have analytical utility are those incorporated in the lives of the individuals, not the ideal. Certainly not all Muslims are knowledgeable about all aspects of Islam. To assume that ordinary Muslims possess full knowledge of the holy text is to essentialize and reify both the social relations and the text. Muslims follow certain "islamic" ides that guide their lives and provide them with a stable world outlook. Moreover, interpretations of islam vary from one person to another, from one 'alim (religious scholar) to another, and from one culture to another. Islam as a social text is a language which has its own system of symbols that contribute to the multiplicity of interpretation. Thus islam is not a static text; it is interactive and both "in-here and out-there" simultaneously. Society is the ideological arena where these multiple interpretations compete using various strategies to legitimate themselves. Each and every interpretation evokes a different era of "Islamic" history and a different school of jurisprudence to anchor its discourse and confer legitimacy on the spoil practices of the group. Thus the islam of Saudi Arabia and how it is integrated within the larger social system and customs is different from the islams of Malaysia, Indonesia, Egypt, or the Sudan. The most stable interpretation is the one that can reproduce itself through various agents and instructions in the society. In Saudi Arabia, the dominant interpretation of Islam is based on the teachings and ideas of sheikh Muhammed bin Abdul Wahhab, an eighteenth-century religious reformer who allied himself with the Saud family during the formation of the fist Saudi state (1744–1811). Here the dominant interpretation is linked to the larger hegemony of the dominant group and the state. The islam of the Sunni opposition is also based on the teachings of Muhammed bin Abdul Wahhab, minus the elements that legitimize the current political order. The hegemony of the royal family and its world outlook in Saudi society is not made of islam alone, but islam mixed with 'asabiyya (solidarity or group feeling) and the dominant ethos of familialism ('a'iliyya) within the larger context of qaraba (closeness both in space and social relations) society.

Familialism ('A'iliyya)

Familialism, not family, is central to this analysis. Various studies of Saudi society have focused on the tribe, not the 'a'ila (family). I try to avoid using the term "tribe" or use it with extreme caution, due to the pejorative connotations the term has acquired and to problems associated with analytical utility. The segmentary model dominant in anthropological analysis limits our understanding of Saudi Arabia. Furthermore, the term was used to explain simpler social relations. Saudi Arabia is a very complex society in its local and global networks. For the purposes of this discussion, I prefer to use 'a'ila (tentatively translated as extended family) instead of the term "tribe." One reason for this is that contemporary Saudis see themselves as part of 'ai'las rather than part of tribes. For example, although the Saud family is part of the 'Aniza tribe, no member of the royal family or any Saudi citizen use this tribal name to refer to Al Saud or any member of the family. Although tentatively translated as "family," the Arabic connotation of the 'a'iliya encompasses far more than genealogical bonds. Derived from the verb ya'ul, which means to protect and support, it connotes relations based on protection, interdependence, and accountability,[1] lending a sense of purpose and an identity. Further, it also implies the notion of pride and household in connection with both people and animals. The reputation of the family is something beyond monetary value; it is something that cannot be lost without losing oneself. This is an ambiguous term that can be understood only within its own specific and historical evolution of a specific political economy of signs.

Focusing on 'a'iliyya (familialism) rather than the tribe and tribalism offers an escape from the misleading connotations associated with the term "tribe" and provides a more accurate model for understanding identity construction and organization of interests and relationships. Whereas the "tribe" connotes a clearly defined unit wherein lineage is the ultimate determinant of membership status, 'a'iliyya relations are more inclusive both in terms of membership and organizational cohesion. This familialism, in the sense of sponsorship, accountability, and interdependence, runs through the whole political system, where a foreign worker cannot work in Saudi Arabia without a kafil or 'a'il (sponsor). "Islamic" teachings also center on the family more than on the tribe.[2] Women cannot leave the country without an 'a'il, or a companion or guarantor of safety. Small families who enter the world of business usually have a sponsor from the royal family. Thus it is not only the royal family that espouses familialism; the ethos of familialism saturates the whole political system. By familialism I mean the concept that the private domain is what matters most. Doing good means doing good for one's family, nuclear and extended alike, but it also suggests responsibility. For example, even the king is referred to as wali al-amr, which literally translates as "the one who is responsible," suggesting a continuity in the patriarchal, familial organization of society. Furthermore, the discourse of 'a'iliyya permeates the Saudi public discourse. When the king appointed his new cabinet, *Al Riyadh*, the main Saudi daily, focused both the editorial and the lead articles on "the renewal of the concept of Saudi Arabia as one family." The writers conclude that "the concept of family is what governs Saudi Arabia."[3]

Ambiguity is central to Saudi politics, and conflation of concepts is dominant. One example of the convergence of familialism and Islamism is in the common Saudi saying "al-shoukh abakhas," meaning "the sheikhs know best." The word "sheikh" is used here to refer to multiple identities: the sheikh of the qabila, or head of the tribe; the sheikh of the family, or the family elder; the sheikh in the religious sense, or the 'alim or man of religion; and the political rulers. This phrase is central to understanding Saudi politics, because without a context, the word "sheikh" means very little. Only in a specific context can we recognize whether it refers to a worldly or religious leadership. Given the ambiguity and multiple connotations of the word, the royal family can use it to establish its identity and authority on multiple levels. By intentionally blurring or hiding the contextual referent, the state thus can exploit the word's association with various sources of power and authority.

Saudi religious opposition must be contextualized in the history of the relationship between islam and the various 'ai'las (families) that dominated Muslim history. With the exception of the da'wa (missionary) state in Medina under the leadership of the Prophet, Islam historically has been secondary to the 'a'ila; its main function has been to support the cultural hegemony of the ruling tribe/dynasty. This interaction between state and Islam brought about certain adjustments to Islam rather than the other way around; the state was not adjusted to become Islamic; rather, Islam was adjusted to support the state. In this arrangement, the state has used the 'ulama to justify the policy choices of the ruling elite. The function of the 'ulama is thus to establish the hegemony of the ruling amir and his family. The 'ulama solidify the hegemony of the amir and his family because the interpretation of the Shari'a principles has traditionally been their exclusive domain. The 'ulama perform this function with the assumption that the Shari'a regulates all human activities. The 'ulama have devised the system of qiyas (analogy) and ijma' (consensus) to address modern-day problems in relation to the centuries-old codes. In both qiyas and ijma', the 'ulama's personal or class interest may dictate the new laws adopted. Here the 'ulama stratum corresponds to the intellectual strata in the Gramscian scheme where the relationship between them and the world of production is "mediated" by the whole fabric of society and by the complex of superstructures, of which the intellectuals are precisely the "functionaries." The intellectuals are the dominant group's "deputies" exercising the subaltern function of social hegemony. Thus the intellectual functions as an instrument to prepare the masses for consent. Of course, in the Muslim world, intellectuals of the state have interpreted Islam differently within the frame of reference of various madhhabs (schools). The various schools of Islamic jurisprudence, the various cultures where Islam took root, and the various styles of governance led to the emergence of varieties of islams at the sociopolitical level that are significantly different from an ideal static and literal Islam. This is why for the purpose of social analysis, I find it more analytically useful to speak of islams rather than Islam.

Oil, Resistance, and the Political Economy of Signs

In addition to problematizing dominant concepts such as Islam and the tribe, a dominant approach to the study of "oil states," namely the rentier model,[4] requires examination before we discuss the analysis of political opposition and resistance in Saudi Arabia. Currently this model dominates the discussion of the possibilities for democracy and political change in the Gulf states. The central concept of rentier state theory is that assets accrued from oil rent represent the bulk of the economy of these states and that this economic dependence on oil frees the states from being accountable to their citizens. The model assumes state autonomy, that is, that the state is not accountable to its citizens, although some native scholars have shown that this is not the case in Saudi Arabia.[5] Indeed, had the state been free to do what it wanted with total disregard for the power of society, we would have witnessed large-scale human rights abuses or the state would have ignored opposition demands instead of responding by forming the Shura Council. In spite of its flaws, namely its economic determinism, the rentier model dominates the literature on the Gulf states. The model links the "authoritarian" character of these regimes to state autonomy at the economic level. According to this model, "state-society relations seem predicated on the principle of 'no taxation, no representation.'"[6] That is, because citizens do not pay taxes and yet receive generous social welfare benefits from the state, they have no right to participate in government decision making. This model focuses heavily on oil and ignores the roles of indigenous cultural structures.

According to the rentier model, protest is positively correlated with the decline of oil prices. Citizens protest and revolt when their economic interests are affected, that is, when their social benefits are cut. Indeed, according to this theory, political change can be predicted according to oil booms and oil busts. The more oil prices increase, the more the rent (money to be distributed to citizens in social welfare benefits) and the lesser the resistance; whereas when prices fall, resistance increases. However, this has not been the case in Saudi Arabia. Indeed, if we look at a plot of oil prices (figure 1.1) between 1970 to 1997, we would expect the mid-1980s to signal a shift in the political equilibrium in Saudi Arabia in light of the downward trend in oil prices and the severe contraction in public revenues and outlays that have been forced on Saudi Arabia and other oil exporters in the region. However, there was no significant protest. Furthermore, looking at the same data, we cannot explain the protest activities of 1979, when the Shi'a of the Eastern Province rioted and Juhaiman al-'Utaibi and his Sunni followers took over the Grand Mosque, since oil prices were rising then. In 1978 the state oil revenues were $32,234 million and the price of a barrel of oil was $12.90. In 1979 the price of the barrel of oil increased to $18.60. The price of the barrel of oil increased steadily to reach $26.50 in 1985. Then in 1986 the price declined sharply, to $13.70, and the government deficit in the two years that followed increased from 52.3 to 60.9 billion Saudi riyal. Had the assumption of the rentier model been sound, this period should have witnessed political turmoil. Because of the relative stability of the Saudi polity during that pe-

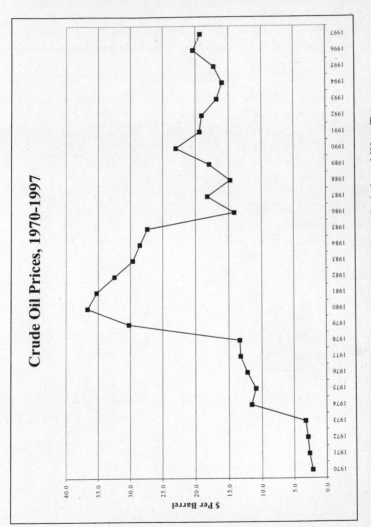

Crude Oil Prices, 1970-1997

Note: Crude prices are the average spot price of UK Brent, Dubai, and West Texas.
Source: International Financial Statistics, International Monetary Fund.

riod and the rise of opposition at times of greater increase in oil prices, we must look beyond the rentier model when analyzing Saudi resistance.

Figure 1.1 plots crude oil prices in absolute terms. Were we to deflate the price of oil by that of imported manufactured goods to get a sense of the purchasing power of oil exports, the story would become even more pronounced given the upward trend in manufactured goods prices during this period. Thus, oil and the purchasing power of oil have been on a downward trend since 1980, when oil prices reached their historical peak. Saudi Arabia, among other oil exporters, has seen gradual erosion in the price and purchasing power of its chief export commodity, the biggest contributor to its budget and foreign exchange earnings. Did this downward trend in prices, revenues, and expenditures by the Saudi government after 1980 coincide with increased systematic political resistance to the state or an intensified weakening of its structures and perceived legitimacy? Conversely, did the boom of the 1970s lead to concentration of state power and the marginalization of the political opposition? Clearly not, since examples and counterexamples may be cited to support or refute the rentier model.

A look at figure 1.1, summarizing the Saudi case, and a more general look at other oil-producing states serves to further discredit the universal assumptions of the rentier model. Although the decrease in oil prices coincided with protest in Algeria, different patterns surfaced in Venezuela, the republic of Gabon,[8] Nigeria (trends there are much more complex), and Iran. Furthermore, the model has little utility in explaining the strength of the Kuwaiti parliament, where the Islamist parliamentarians have been challenging the government on various issues since 1996 and forced the resignation of one cabinet and the formation of another in 1998.[9] All these examples suggest that it is not enough to cleverly invert common American slogans into "no taxation, no representation" and "ask not what you can do for your country, but ask what your country can do for you," and use them as substitute for theory or analytical frameworks. Furthermore, the rentier literature provides very little explanation in terms of either resistance or governmental human rights abuses. Although the Saudi government did not respond to Shi'a demands during the 1970s and 1980s, it has responded in the 1990s. It responded with grand steps to the demands of supposedly marginal figures, yet it also ignored the demands of women. The question is where we locate our explanation of resistance.

To have a better explanation of resistance, we need a more nuanced understanding of the Saudi political economy. First, the system is not merely one of use value and exchange value alone. It is also a political economy of signs and exchanges.[10] The Gulf War shook the signs system and symbols of the "oasis of peace," revealed the vulnerability of the watan (homeland), and replaced it with the signs of "the land of Islam," under attack both regionally and globally. The fluctuations in the world of production in Saudi Arabia are not as threatening as fluctuations in the cosmology of the community of believers. Many of these signs relate to notions of honor, lineage, and authority. While oil has been a very important factor in solidifying the rule of Al Saud, it has not been the only factor. Likewise, oil is also another reason for great power interest in the region, but it is not the source of these powers' hegemony. However, the Sauds ruled Saudi Arabia for 66 years (1745–1811) in the first Saudi state and for 22 years (1843–1902) in the second without oil. The third Saudi realm started in 1902, became a consolidated state by 1932, and has continued since. Thus while oil gives the modern state more flexibility, the state does not rest on oil alone. Given that the state existed before oil and that many describe it as distributive, the money coming from oil rent is distributed to enforce the earlier qaraba hierarchy. In this argument oil becomes a downstream variable while social relations and structures are upstream variables. The rent coming from oil is distributed to consolidate an already existing hierarchy of qaraba relations. Thus families loyal and close to Al Saud were given a bigger share than those whose loyalties were suspect. The families that dominated the commercial scene in Saudi Arabia—the Jufali, the Aliriza, al Rajhi, al Khashoqji, al-Uliyan, and bin Laden—have all benefited from the largess of the royal family.

Thus the Saudi society is not just based on oil wealth but is a society of qaraba, dominated by what I call Islamic familialism.[11] By Islamic familialism I mean the dominant ethos that results from the interaction between general Islamic values and familial and qaraba customs, habits, and values. Even the nascent class formations are intersected by these qaraba elements. To understand the cleavages within the society, we have to look at the structure of this Islamic familialism and its system of inclusion and exclusion. At the top of the Saudi society are the royal family and its allies, namely the Sheikh family. They make up the elite circle. A wider circle that follows includes the aristocratic families with tribal bases. The third tier of circles involves commercial families with limited tribal bases. A final circle and the most remote from governance are ordinary Saudi families who are not wealthy and who lack tribal standing and thus cannot intermarry with tribal families as a way of gaining political power. Outside these circles of power are 4.9 million foreign workers, Muslims and non-Muslims alike. This "proletariat class" is both functional and disposable. It serves as an element of identity consolidation that differentiates Saudis from non-Saudis. Wahhabism, or Saudi islam, serves to separate the Saudi Wahhabis from the non-Wahhabi foreigners and from the Shi'a of the Eastern Province. These cultural signs are central to inclusion and exclusion from power, and in many cases are the main criteria. Thus what can be conceived of as "corruption" and nepotism in a discourse where meritocracy and legalism are the dominant criteria can be construed as another form of wealth distribution in a qaraba-centered discourse. Qaraba

relations can also include those who merit inclusion through marriage relations. Thus familialism is an expansive system that benefits from those outside it who exhibit exceptional qualities that merit inclusion in the qaraba
system. Ending this system of the allocation of values on the basis of qaraba
means ending political and economic participation, as most Saudis know it.
This is not to condone corruption; rather, I merely seek to explain how
money and power are allocated within the Saudi system.

To understand this value system, the political economy of signs must be
uncovered. When a senior member of the royal family asks the Saudi elite,
"Do you want to be governed by a Ghamidi (i.e., Safar al-Hawali)?" this says
something about the currency and value of the Ghamid tribe and its exchange value in this context of social relations. In an interview, some Saudis
referred to a rule by the Ghamidis as "the equivalent of devaluating the Saudi
riyal."[12] Regions and tribal values are reflected in Saudi slang, which catego-
rizes citizens according to their telephone area code and electrical voltage. In
the area code slang, the lower number indicates the most prestigious region;
in the electrical voltage slang, the highest voltage indicates the most powerful tribe. The Ghamedis are 07 in the area code slang and 110 on the voltage scale, whereas the Sauds and other Nadji families are 01 and 220,
respectively. These local markers are important in a coded language of signs.

The reputation of the family and the place of tribal origin are worth more
than money in the Saudi social context. Disgrace brings shame to a whole
family and is the worst possible punishment, because it can mean a family's
exclusion from power for generations. Both the exchange and the use value
of commodities are used to enforce a political economy of signs rather than
the other way around. We may hear of a Waleed al-Ibraheem (non-royal but
related to the king by marriage qaraba) or Prince al-Waleed bin Talal, famous
entrepreneurs in Saudi Arabia, but not many non-tribal or non-loyal families. The lineage and the kin-ordered mode of production (qaraba) and the
relations of production contribute to the making of a superstructure of islamic familialism in the Saudi state. Contrary to the underlying implications
of the rentier model, oil wealth does not allow the royal family simply to de-
tach itself from the other circles of power in Saudi society. Rather, wealth is
filtered through and reinforces a preexisting system. Without paying special
attention to the political economy of signs underlying this system and its
qaraba context, the substance of Saudi politics could be missed easily. I believe what is necessary is a political economy approach that is sensitive to the
local context of signs and qaraba relations. Clearly, such an approach is essential to understanding the existence of protest within Saudi society as well
as the state's response to different sources of dissent. Integrating these elements into existing models can only increase their explanatory power, jeop-
ardizing neither the elegance nor the parsimony of these models.

The Country and Its People

Saudi Arabia is a vast country (2,240,000 square kilometers) with a population of 16.9 million people. Not all of those are Saudis; 4.9 million are foreign nationals working in the kingdom. Saudi Arabia is a very rich country by regional standards. In addition to controlling 25 percent of the world's proven oil reserves, the country's gross domestic product (GDP) exceeds $100 billion. Administratively, it is divided into 13 emirates, officially called provinces. Two of these provinces constitute the Saudi heartland, Najd; they include Riyadh, the capital of the kingdom, and Al-Qaseem, an agricultural and commercial area where the recent unrest in Buraydah took place. The western region of Saudi Arabia includes the province of Mecca, the first holy city in the kingdom where the Grand Mosque and the main site of the annual Muslim pilgrimage are located, and the province of Medina, the second holy city, which contains the Prophet's tomb and mosque, the second holiest shrine in Islam. The other regions include the Eastern Province, Al-Hasa, and the southern region, which includes three provinces, Asir, Jizan, and Najran. The other provinces are Tabuk, Hael, the Northern Frontier, al-Baha, and the Jawf. According to the statute of the provinces, each province has a governor and vice governor who are appointed and dismissed by the king at the recommendation of the minister of interior.[13] Each province is ruled by a council composed of the governor, the vice governor, the managers of regional government agencies, and at least ten prominent members of the region nominated by the governor and approved by the minister of interior. They serve for a term of four years, which can be renewed.[14] Each region has a governor or amir (prince) and deputy amir, and each imara (region) has a council of local notables that helps the governors in running the affairs of the state. The laws for these governorates were codified in 1992 as part of a government response to the Letter of Demands and the Memorandum of Advice submitted to the king. Before that time, there was no written law.[15]

According to the Basic Statute of Governance, Saudi Arabia is an Arab Islamic state. Islam is the religion of the state. At the top of the government is the king. The king appoints the crown prince and can dismiss him. However, Abdullah, the current crown prince, is exempted from this by a royal decree, since these laws were established after he was already a crown prince. The laws of succession link the royal inheritance to the sons and grandsons of the late king Abdul Aziz.[16] Beyond this point the statute does not specify any mechanism for the transfer of power. Although it has been traditionally acceptable that the second deputy, currently Prince Sultan, be appointed crown prince as soon as the crown prince becomes king, some members of the royal family state clearly that this is not automatic since there is no specific law concerning this. Thus the family must meet to decide the future crown prince.[17] A mechanism for succession satisfactory to all branches of the family has yet to be devised. Thus far the system is not one of seniority, but the state specifies that all those who are fit among the sons or grandsons of Abdul Aziz can be considered. Age may be a factor, but certainly it is not the only one. Given this ambiguity about the rules of succession, it appears that the Saudis may face a greater problem in the coming 20 years from within the family than from other social forces.

The people of Saudi Arabia are known for their conservatism. Islam and traditional or familial ethos are central to their social and political dealings, and Islam and familialism provide for the main mechanisms of social control in the society. About 20 percent of the Saudi public are mutawa (very conservative religious people who take it upon themselves to persuade others to be strictly observant of the faith. These mutawa are different from what Americans refer to as mutaween, or morality police in Saudi Arabia. Saudis refer to this as al-Hayi'ah [the Committee], a reference to the Committee for Promoting Virtue and Preventing Vice, a formal organization associated with the state. The mutawa are ordinary conservative people with no official capacity.) Some 20 percent of the Saud public are liberal. According to Saudis themselves, the other 60 percent of society are in between; they are conservative whenever they are around conservatives and liberal around liberals. These are the pragmatic Saudis. Nonetheless, the conservatives have the upper hand, since the basic conceptualization of the state and its political formula is based on the centrality of religion. The royal family can be counted among this 60 percent.

Unlike many Arab countries, Saudi Arabia was spared the experience of direct colonialism. This affected the process of state building and made the political structure indigenous. Certainly, the Hashimites ruled on behalf of the Turkish sultan in the Western Region (Hijaz), where the holy sites of Islam are located, and people in the Eastern Province (Hasa) also were nominally under Turkish control at various times. Arrangements in the northern part of Hail and Jabal Shammar were under the control of a local amir, Ibn Rashid, who was loyal to the Ottomans. Yet these Ottoman influences had very little affect on how the Arabs ruled their people. The Najd region, where the drive for state building started, was not colonized at all. Later on Ibn Saud, the founder of the kingdom, allied himself with the British, but he was never an agent of Britain in the Gulf. The British signed treaties with him to ensure that he would not expand beyond the domain known as Saudi Arabia and to keep him away from Iraq, Kuwait, and many of the Trucial states.

Saudi Arabia was also spared the process of decolonization, which was a mixed blessing for other Arab states. The departure of colonial powers from other Arab countries left a legacy of laws and institutions and a great deal of distortion in Arab societies. None of this took place in Saudi Arabia. With the exception of the Hijaz region, where the Hashimites used to have a Turkish and British administration, very little in Arabia was formally structured. Indeed the ethos of familialism, tribal customs, and religion were the law and the informal institutions were the functioning ones. State building in the Saudi case was an indigenous process. King Abdul Aziz was a Bedouin amir who ruled according to laws that were a mix of religion and tribal customs. He also had the advantage of having learned from his predecessors. These events contributed to the making of a society and a state that is difficult to understand and requires more nuanced thinking at the levels of theory, method, and data gathering. This indigenous process led to the emergence of a different form of participation and structures of authority and power.

Political Authority and the Structure of Governance

To understand the opposition, we have to understand the loci of power and seats of authority in Saudi society and the structure of governance. Here, I describe four important institutions—the royal family, the 'ulama and the Islamic institutions, the Council of Ministers, and the Shura Council—in an attempt to map out the power configuration of the Saudi system and provide a context for the opposition and its activities.

The Royal Family Between the State and Society

To analyze the legal-formal structure of the Saudi state and society is to miss the essence of how politics actually function. Formally, the government consists of the royal family, the bureaucracy, and the 'ulama. The important question, however, is where the state ends and society begins. The royal family is the largest and most cohesive group in the kingdom with 5,000 members who are related to almost all the important tribes of Saudi Arabia through marriage. The marriage connection is central to rule, since familialism as an ideology is an important part of governance in most Arab states. Like the rest of the Saudis, members of the royal family work primarily to maximize the gain of their own family first and their other relatives second. The relatives of the Sauds inside Saudi Arabia are part of a web of social relations that could include most of the tribes. In this domain of civil society, the royal family is important at the domestic level. The formal structure, it could be argued, works well only in terms of the Saudi state's dealing with the outside world. The formal legal structure exists so that Saudi Arabia can conduct its international affairs.

Domestically, however, the royal family exists within both civil society and the state simultaneously. The Sauds may be hated as bureaucrats, regional governors, or heads of particular government agencies, yet they are loved as a magnanimous family at the level of civil society. It is that liminal nature of the royal family that makes it inside government and civil society at the same time. This is the secret of the Sauds survival and their stability in dealing with crises. If we consider the house of Prince Salman, the governor of Riyadh, these issues become obvious. Prince Salman has five sons: One is Prince Abdul Aziz, the deputy minister of energy and oil. The second is Prince Ahmed, the owner of the Saudi publishing group called al-Saudia lil Nashr wa al-Tawzi'. Prince Ahmed thus is both a businessman and part of the Saudi government by being the son of Salman. What is important is that each of these princes has his own small bureaucracy that works for him and mediates his relations with both the state and society. At the level of society each amir has his own "mini-majlis," as one young prince called them. It is not as grand as the majlis of the governor, but it is a meeting place where he brings his friends, usually young technocrats, businessmen, and colleagues from his university days. A patronage system is established in the form of a shella as well as a following. Each amir also takes care of the 10 to 20 families that work for his office. Thus at least 200 people are associated with each young prince. The prince's office is there to help them whenever they are in trouble with the formal structure, and in turn they are dependent on him. This circle around each amir shields him from other would-be beneficiaries of his largess. Thus the role of the so-called middle class is not to compete with the royal princes but to limit other people's access to them. This is why Prince Salman has an open majlis, where those who are traditionally prevented by his second tier of bureaucrats from seeing him are given a chance to meet with him and be heard. Usually people leave the majlis praising the royal prince and cursing the non-royal gatekeepers who prevented the amir from hearing their cases earlier. Of course, some of the dissidents I discuss are outside this system and thus have revolted against it.

The liminality of the Saudis makes their job easier and complicates the life of the opposition. For instance, as we will see in chapter 7, the Saudi state entered into negotiations with these groups and answered one of their demands by giving them passports and allowing them to return to the country to look for jobs. However, if they played by the formal rules, very few of these returning opposition figures were likely to get jobs, because they would have to compete against better-connected people in the marketplace. Although Saudi Arabia is a capitalist free-market society, people rely on the informal structure to get a job. In essence, a job-seeker has to find an amir who believes in him, brings him into his sphere of influence, and offers or finds him a job in his office or with another agency that he does business with. Thus the government could respond to all the demands of any members of the opposition without doing anything to change their actual situation; the question remains whether it is important to have formal legal rights, if the system rarely works according to these rules. In a sense, at the domestic level, the state's formal structure is a far less important than its informal structure. The network of power is a web of family and tribal relations that ensure both the rights and the safety of most Saudi citizens within an ideology of familialism and a network of patrimonial politics. Another element that adds to the power of the royal family is its ability to transcend the question of regionalism. Although Saudis acquire part of their identity from their regions, and they view each other in those terms, the Saud family has managed to be above these regional loyalties. They do not present themselves as a Najdi family but as a symbol of national unity. Of course, their position of power has allowed them to monopolize these symbols to their advantage. By using various strategies, the royal family succeeded in making itself indispensable to the maintenance of unity.

The 'Ulama and the Maintenance of Hegemonic Islamic Discourse

Saudi politics cannot be understood without understanding the role of Islam at the level of formal and informal structures. The Saudi state started with an Islamic mission. As stated, it is not an alliance between a secular tribal leadership and a religious family, as it is conventionally perceived, with the Saud family representing secular power and the Sheikh family representing religion. The fact is that both families are religious, although the religious credentials of the Sheikh family are stronger, and both of them are prominent tribal families, although the Sauds have long been more powerful. The Sheikh family owes its prominence in part to being the descendants of Muhammed Abdul Wahhab. However, there is nothing in Islam to suggest that piety is inherited. Those members of the family known for their piety and religious learning have been appointed to religious positions, but others occupy secular positions that they owe to their family's tribal prestige. Some members of the Saud family have been known for their piety, such as King Faisal, whose mother was from the Sheikh family,[18] Prince Ahmed bin Abdul Aziz, and the current crown prince, Abdullah. Thus the relationship between the Sauds and the Sheikhs is not a tribal-religious alliance between two families; rather both families are a part of the tribal and religious 'asabiyya of Saudi Arabia.

Institutionalization of these ideas, coercion, and other means of social control have maintained the hegemony of Islamic familialism as an outlook for both state and society. One of the institutions that maintains this hegemony is the Council of Higher 'Ulama. This council produces fatwas, books, and sermons designed to legitimate the political order. It was established in 1971 by a royal decree. The king appoints its members. The function of the 'ulama, as the decree specifies, is "to express opinions on the Shari'a regarding matters submitted to them by Wali al-Amr [the king]." It is also entrusted with advising the king on policy matters and with issuing fatwas to guide Muslims in areas of belief, prayers, and worldly affairs. The 'ulama themselves assert that they are an independent body accountable only the teachings of the Shari'a; however, their fatwas very rarely contradict the views of the royal family. For example, the fatwas issued to execute those responsible for the take-over the Grand Mosque in 1979 came at the request of the royal family. During the Gulf crisis in 1990, the 'ulama issued a fatwa permitting foreign troops to defend Saudi Arabia. In its statement, the Council of Higher 'Ulama asserts that "It is necessary in a situation like this that 'ulama clarify the Islamic ruling on the matter so that the people of this country and elsewhere may be aware of the correct standpoint on it. The Council of the Senior Ulama approves, therefore, of the steps taken by the ruler, may Allah lead him to success, in inviting some forces equipped with arms that frighten away anyone who thinks of invading this land."[19]

Generally speaking, the traditional 'ulama support state policy, both internal and external. Even their views in dealing with Western powers usually provide legitimacy to the state's foreign policy. Using various media, such as publications, radio, and television, they propagate this hegemonic discourse legitimizing the state. This is in sharp contrast to the junior or younger 'ulama whom this book deals with.

Other official religious agencies include the Committee for the Promotion of Virtue and the Suppression of Vice; the religious supervision of the Holy Mosque; the Ministry of Pilgrimage; the Directorate of Religious Research, Religious Decrees, and Promotion of Islam; and the General Department of Women's Education. Through, among others, the Committee for the Promotion of Virtue and the Suppression of Vice, hereafter referred to as the committee, and the Directorate of Religious Research which includes the Council of Higher 'Ulama, the regime makes use of religion to control society; through them also society makes use of religion to limit the power of the state.

Little has been written about the committee, primarily because its finances are secret and its members tend to respond to questions about their exact function by merely elaborating on their full name. In essence, its members are a group of public employees and volunteers whose task is to chastise or arrest those who violate these members' perception of what is Islamically appropriate—men who are not in the mosque during prayers, women who are inadequately veiled, people hosting parties at which men and women guests mix freely or at which alcohol is being served, and so on. In a rare interview in *Alyamamah* magazine, the head of the agency, Dr. Abdul Aziz al-Said, stated, "We only arrest those who do wrong. After finishing the preliminary procedures, we hand them to the special branch of government that deals with their case."[20] He also said, "Our men raid the homes of evil and corruption, but of course we do it in coordination with other agencies." Two interesting facts emerge from these statements, first that arrest carries the assumption of proven guilt, and second, that while the committee arrests, the civil police have the ultimate authority. This creates an atmosphere of fear and intimidation that is a very effective means of social control, particularly of foreign workers, who are unlikely to have a network of friends and relatives in official positions to intercede for them. Although this organization seems indigenous and exotic, it functions like earlier American models such as the Charleston (Virginia) Association for the Reformation of Morals and the Alabama Society of the Suppression of Vice and Immorality. The main function of these organizations was to promote adherence to their own version of religious morality—that is, observation of the Christian Sabbath and prohibition of the sale of alcoholic beverages, blasphemy, and gambling. In the future, some students may be interested in comparing these societies in the early American period and modern-day Saudi Arabia.

The Council of Ministers

Established in 1953, the Council of Ministers represents another stage in the evolution of the Saudi state.[21] King Abdul Aziz appointed his two eldest sons, Saud and Faisal, as president and vice president of the council, respectively. When Saud assumed the throne, he appointed Faisal as president of the council. The evolution of the council's power was a function of a power struggle between the king and the crown prince, fiscal crisis, challenges from Nasserism, and the rise of opposition in the Eastern Province. As the situation in Saudi Arabia deteriorated between 1958 and 1962, Faisal used the royal members of the council plus a fatwa from the 'ulama to remove Saud from the throne. Thus more variables were involved in the development of this institution than just money, oil boom, or oil bust. Major ministries, such as the Ministry of Defense, Interior, and Foreign Affairs (with the exception of one year, 1961–62, when Al Suwayil held this position), are always under the control of the royal family. The head of the National Guard is also from the royal family. Other ministries are open to non-royal elements, but certain last names seem to recur. For example, since its inception the Al Sheikh name recurs in the Ministries of Education (1960–75), Higher Education (1975–87), Justice (1995-present), and Municipal and Rural Affairs (1991–95).[22] Members of the al-Khwaiter family held the Ministries of Education (1975–95), Health (1974–75), Higher Education (1987–91), and State (current). Members of the Al-'Anqri family once held the Ministry of Information (1970–75), twice the Ministry of Higher Education (1991-present), and the Ministry of Municipal and Rural Affairs twice.[23] Thus certain loyal families constitute the backbone of the regime and are central to the running of the affairs of the state. Some of these families are tribal and others are commercial and non-tribal. The list of families included in the system increased with the introduction of another 90-member institution, the Shura Council, which I discuss later. Although the Council of Ministers includes non-royal family members, important decisions remain within the royal family. Some ministers do not make any decisions without going back to the royal court. In cases where there is a non-royal head of a ministry, the Saud family uses the innovation of "the Supreme Council of"[24] to ensure royal authority and jurisdiction of this ministry. Whenever an institution has this prefix, two things can be deduced: one, the minister holding this position is non-royal, and two, the real head of the council is a member of the royal family. Thus the Saudis manage to use capable technocrats and confer on them the title of minister while, in fact, the real power remains in the hands of the royal family. This system of complexity and politics of ambiguity is central to the workings of this institution. Thus the governmental structure is both a representative and non-representative institution at the same time.

The Shura Council

In response to the Memorandum of Advice, described later in detail, the royal family has recognized regional notables not only by allowing them to represent themselves in the local councils but also in the new body known as Majlis al-Shura (the Council of Advice). This council was organized to institutionalize an Islamic injunction that says "And their affairs are based on consultation among them." As a concept, this council has the potential for becoming a parliament although thus far it is more of a government think tank. The council does not have the power to legislate, but it does have the authority to question cabinet ministers, study decisions, and then send these decisions to the king to be signed into royal decrees. What is important about this council is that it started as a 60-member body in 1992 and increased to 90 members by 1996,[25] which suggests that it is becoming increasingly inclusive. The members form a veritable who's who list of prominent Saudi tribes. Thus the Shura Council took into account both tribal and regional representations, as shown in tables 1.1 and 1.2.

Table 1.2 shows the regional distribution of the council members. It is obvious from that 40 percent of the council members come from the Najd or the central area (Riyadh, Qaseem, and other central regions). The main reason I put Qaseem in a special category is to show that indeed the government has paid special attention to this region. One of the main Islamic opposition leaders, Salman al-Auda, comes from there (see chapter 3.) The central region is followed by the Hejaz region (31.1 percent), an area where most merchant families are concentrated.

Table 1.1   Tribal Affiliations of Members of the Shura Council (N = 90)

	Number	Percentage
Tribal	60	66.6
Nontribal	15	16.7
Unknown	15	16.7
Total	90	100.0

Table 1.2   Regional Distribution of the Members of the Shura Council (N = 90)

Region	Number	Percentage
Najd/Qaseem	12	13.3
Najd	24	26.7
Hijaz	28	31.1
South	11	12.2
Eastern Provence	4	4.4
North	3	3.3
Other	2	2.2
Unknown	6	6.7
Total	90	100.0

Table 1.3   Highest Level of Education Attained by Shura Council Members (N = 60)

	Number	Percentage
Diploma	3	5.0
Bachelor	11	13.8
Master	9	15.0
Doctoral	33	58.3
Unknown	2	3.3
Total	60	100.0

Table 1.4   Type of Education of Shura Council Members (N = 60)

	Number	Percentage
Western	41	68.3
Non-Western	15	25.0
Unknown	4	6.7
Total	60	100.0

Source: Al-Jazeera, July 7, 1997.

It is also important to note that those who represent the tribes or the regions are not mere tribal men, but university graduates and capable technocrats. As tables 1.3 and 1.4 show, almost all council members have had college training. Of the 60 members of the first Shura term, 68.3 percent were educated in Western universities, mainly in the United States. Note that 58.3 percent of the members hold doctoral degrees.

Faced with accusations regarding the lack of political representation, the government recognized a potential crisis within the growing middle class that could threaten the stability of the system if not accommodated. The Shura Council was designed to accommodate the needs of the tribes, the regions, and the middle class in one large stroke. The council is likely to become the nucleus of a parliament, which members can use to push the government toward greater representation. Saudis claim that with this modest step they are ahead of many republican governments in the region. This is because "unlike the neighboring governments, which learned politics through conspiring in smoke-filled rooms and conducting coups d'etat, Saudis are being gradually socialized into politics."[26] Indeed, Saudis do not expect the step from al-Shura to a parliament to come soon, but no one I talked to had any doubts that the government would recognize the scope and nature of the problem of representation. Although Saudi responses are conservative and slow, no one can say that the system is not responsive.[27] Thus far the Shura Council represents a formalization of the traditional majlis and another channel of political communication. The government uses this forum not only to test policies but also to communicate its successes to the political elite or those who matter most.[28]

Dissent: An Historical Background

The Saudi historical experience can be put on a spectrum that ranges from the total destruction of the realm at one extreme and total stability on the other. While both total stability and total destruction are imaginary points, history has witnessed the disintegration of Saudi dominance in Arabia as well as a intermittent periods of relative stability and continuity of the dynasty. There were also events in between, namely outbursts of opposition and violent acts at various stages of the state's history. This section provides a historical map of those experiences as a necessary context for understanding modern-day opposition.

The Disintegration of the Political Order: The Early Saudi Experiences

The Saud family is no stranger to threats that have sometimes brought the downfall of the state, but that has not meant the end of the rule of Al Saud in the peninsula. The Saudi state has collapsed twice, yet the Saud family re-covered power. Local contradictions may have contributed to the disinte-gration of the first Saudi state (1745–1811), but the main reason for its collapse was the invasion of the central areas by a very powerful force com-ing from Muhammed Ali's Egypt. Internal dissent was a contributing factor. Some tribes refused to pay the religious tax (zakat) because the central state failed to offer them adequate security. Moreover, during the expansionist stage of the regime, some local notables became dependent on the money given to them after they invaded new territories. When they stopped receiv-ing this money from the central treasury, they stopped supporting the cen-tral Saudi state. At the time the Saudis had consolidated a vast realm, bigger in territorial size than the modern Saudi state, including parts of the coast of Oman, Bahrain, and Hadramout in modern-day Yemen. The leaders of those areas paid a tax to the prince in Dir'iya, the Saudi capital. However, as the Saudi state expanded, it confronted the British interests in the Arabian gulf. In addition to these political threats, the Wahhabi religious ideology prohibited trade with infidels (non-Wahhabis), which weakened the state economically. Until 1810, trade with Iraq and Syria was prohibited. Finally, in 1811, the sustained attacks by the armies of Toson and Ibrahim Basha of Egypt further weakened the Saudi state, leading to its collapse.[29]

While external attacks by a powerful neighbor brought down the 66-year-old first Saudi state, internal factors were more decisive in the collapse of the second Saudi state (1843–1865). The rise of the second Saudi state was a result of lack of interference by external forces into the affairs of Ara-bia. However, this state was smaller territorially than the first one and its control was even more tenuous. The Rashidis of the north were more allies of the Saudis than subjects, and there were also problems of control in the central area of al-Qaseem. The two main cities of al-Qaseem, Buraydah and 'Uniyazah, were under the control of two powerful families (al-'Uliyan in Buraydah and al-Zamil in 'Uniyazah) who sometimes allied themselves with the Saudis and at other times with the Saud's enemies. The latter rebelled against the authority of the Saudis in 1845. However, the Saudi rulers reached a reasonable compromise and allowed the head of the rebels, Ab-dullah bin Yahiya al-Zamil, to rule over 'Uniyazah. In 1860 the Saudis were also confronted by the rebellion of the 'Ujman and Montafiq tribes. Al-though Faisal managed to defeat the rebels, the Saudis were confronted by the Qaseemi problem again in the 'Uniyazah rebellion of 1862. Qaseem re-mains a problem in Saudi politics even today.[30] The end of the second Saudi state came as a result of rivalry and infighting within the family among the four sons of Faisal bin Turki, the founder of that state. These sons were Ab-dullah, who controlled the central province; Saud, Abdullah's rival, who con-trolled the southern areas; and Muhammed, who controlled the north. The

Saudi princes had to rally their local constituency and deal with their own rivalries. After the death of Faisal bin Turki in 1865, his son Abdullah succeeded him. He was supported by his brother Muhammed. His other brother and rival Faisal contested Abdullah's authority by using his mother's tribe, the 'Ujmans to fight against his brother. The two brothers faced off in Riyadh, where Saud was defeated and had to flee to the tribal territory of Banu Murra. In 1870 Saud headed an army of the 'Ujmans and Banu Murra and took over al Hasa. In 1871 he took over Riyadh. This led the Ottomans to interfere on behalf of Abdullah and invade the Hasa region; thus the Saudis lost the Eastern Province to the Ottomans due to the rivalry between Saud and Abdullah. In 1874 the youngest son, Abdul Rahman, led a rebellion against the Ottomans in the Eastern Province. Although he later became the ruler of Riyadh, his rivalries with the sons of his brother Saud after Saud's death led to more divisions within the family.[31]

Accelerating the process of disintegration of the second Saudi realm was the Rashidis' attack on Riyadh. The Rashidis, rulers of Hail, took over the Saudi capital in 1890, bringing the second Saudi state to an end. When the Rashidis defeated the forces of Abdul Rahman, which were composed of Qaseemi and Mutairi tribes, Abdul Rahman had to flee to Kuwait, which he reached in 1893. According to Abdul Aziz, the founder of the modern kingdom, the second realm collapsed because his uncle Abdullah failed to include his nephews in the governing system, thus alienating them and enabling them to use the tribes against him. A second contributing factor was Abdullah's misguided policy in Qaseem, where he pitted the powerful 'Uliyan and the Muhana against each other as a way of asserting his power. The third reason for the collapse of the realm was the rise of the power of the Rashidis in Hail and their desire to rule the whole area. Indeed, they ruled for almost 12 years.[32]

From 1890 to 1902, the Saudis faded into the background. In 1902, however, a young Saudi prince, Abdul Aziz bin Abdul Rahman Al Saud, returned with his followers from his hijra in Kuwait to kill the Rashidi governor of Riyadh. The people of Riyadh supported the young prince and his father, and from 1902 the Saudis engaged in wars and alliances until 1932, when Abdul Aziz announced himself king of what is now known as the Kingdom of Saudi Arabia.

Nonreligious Opposition and the Modern Saudi State

The current Saud regime, while free of the external threats that ended the first Saud kingdom, has nevertheless faced internal threats. Looking at some of the earlier protests, moreover, helps to place the current Islamic dissent in perspective. Saudi opposition can be classified into three main categories:

royal opposition, secular opposition, and religious opposition. Although the first two categories are not central to this book, a brief summary may prove helpful in understanding the third type of opposition. Unlike the current opposition, the ideological drive of the opposition to Saudi rule during the reign of King Saud (1953–64) was secular and Arab nationalist. However, the object of the Saudi anger remains to some degree similar to that of the past. Saudis were angered by the U.S. presence in the Dhahran air base or at least were manipulated by Arab nationalists outside the kingdom to use this issue as a symbol of protest. Thus workers in the then joint American-Saudi petroleum company (Aramco) declared a strike in 1953. During Nasser's visit to Saudi Arabia in 1956, Saudi nationalists wanted the king to nation-alize Aramco in the same way Nasser had nationalized the Suez Canal. Most of this protest came from the Shi'a population of the Eastern Province, a province that has changed tremendously since the discovery of oil in 1930 and its commercial exploitation in 1946. The workers' strike also came at time of regime change (after the death of the founder of the kingdom and the ascension of King Saud to the throne). Another workers' strike at Aramco took place in 1956, again it was largely orchestrated by Arab na-tionalist forces in the region. Although he supported Nasser to some extent by cutting off Saudi relations with Britain and France as a result of their at-tack on Egypt in 1956, Saud also embraced the Eisenhower Doctrine. Dur-ing his visit to the United States in January 1957, he supported U.S. policy and also agreed to extend the lease of the Dhahran air base for five more years in exchange for military and economic assistance from Washington. This led to further anti-royal family sentiment. Thus the internal strikes and the general Arab nationalist mood agitated against the royal family. How-ever, this was not the only problem that the Saudi royal family faced during King Saud's reign. It also faced divisions from within.

From 1958 to 1962, Prince Talal Bin Abdul Aziz led a movement to re-form the system and change Saudi Arabia into a constitutional monarchy. This movement is usually referred to as the Movement of the Liberal Princes. Times were not good for the Arab monarchies in general. This was the heyday of republicanism, and monarchies were seen as anachronistic. The Movement of the Liberal Princes coincided with the collapse of the Iraqi monarchy in 1958. Within the Saud family there was an open con-frontation between Prince Faisal, then prime minister, and King Saud. Cau-tious Prince Faisal was the actual manager of state affairs, and many royal family members rallied behind him against Saud's policies. As a counter-move, King Saud drew support from different elements within the royal family and from Saudi technocrats. In June 1960 the liberal princes submit-ted a plan for constitutional reform and proposed a draft constitution that would have taken Saudi Arabia closer to being a constitutional monarchy.

They also proposed a partially elected national council and some measures for the protection of human rights. Faisal rejected this proposal for constitutional reform; even the king himself could not support it. In December of 1960, the king formed a new government, which included Prince Talal as finance minister and Abdullah al-Turaiki as oil minister. Al-Turaiki was a known Arab nationalist, and his appointment along with Prince Talal was a Saudi way of accommodating the rising Arab nationalist feelings in the region. This was the most progressive government in Saudi history. However, the ailing king was criticized by his brothers for the free reign he gave leftists in his court. Moreover, because of economic problems at home and regional pressure from the Arab national trend, Saud had to seek Faisal's assistance. Faisal agreed to join the government only if the king dismissed the leftists from the cabinet. In a press conference on August 15, 1962, Talal accused Saudi Arabia of arbitrarily taking away his property. Three days later Prince Abdullah Bin Abdul Aziz held a press conference in which he chastised Prince Talal for proposing a constitution, saying "Talal knows full well that Saudi Arabia has a constitution inspired by God and not drawn by man." After the press conference, Talal left for Egypt with his brothers Abdul Muhsin, Badr, Nawaf, and Fawaz. They stayed in Cairo from 1962 until 1964, verbally attacking the royal family. When Faisal assumed power in 1962, he introduced what is known as the Ten Point Program. This was a turning point in the political development of Saudi Arabia.[33] Consolidating centralized power, it introduced new social programs to cope with the problems of modernization. The liberal princes, frustrated with the Cairo government and its control of the media campaign, decided to leave Cairo in 1964. Prince Talal was later implicated in the 1969 military coup attempt and has been barred from political participation in the kingdom. This is probably the only incident, other than the 1975 assassination of King Faisal, that directly indicates divisions within the royal family. However, these differences have not proven fatal to the survival of the regime. Thus the royal family can claim to have one leg in the opposition and another in the government. The liberal princes' demands were for as major an overhaul of the system as the 1992 Memorandum of Advice, if not more so. The only difference is that the liberal princes wanted the rule of law and the memorandum wants the rule of Islamic law, the Shari'a.

The secular opposition included the Saudi Communist Party and the Ba'thists, who advocated Arab unity and socialism. The most important of these groups was the Union of the People of the Arabian Peninsula, established in 1958 and active until the 1960s. This group was headed by Nasser al-Sa'eed, who advocated Arab nationalism and Arab unity as the ultimate solution. His demands focused on constitutional reforms and an elected parliament. This movement died down with the general collapse of Arab nationalism following their defeat at the hands of the Israelis in 1967. It is very difficult to identify any organized secular opposition in contemporary Saudi Arabia similar to the movements of the 1960s.

Other threats to the royal family have come from ad hoc coup attempts conducted by the officer corps. Secular ideology inspired some officers to emulate other military regimes. For example, in 1955 senior army officers attempted to kill King Saud and Prince Faisal and establish a government similar to that of Egypt under Nasser. U.S. intelligence reports considered 1956 the year in which the military was most likely to challenge the royal family. In 1963, 9 Saudi pilots defected to Egypt, and in 1969, the government arrested 63 officers along with civilians for plotting against the government. In 1969 some Hijazi officers also attempted another coup. Fewer incidents were reported during the 1970s, 1980s, and 1990s. According to rumor, officers loyal to outside powers plotted one coup attempt but escaped to Libya when their plot was discovered. The only organized group that has forced the Saudi government to respond to its demands is the Islamic movement, the focus of this book.

Religious Opposition and the Saudi State

The relationship between the religious forces and the royal family are part of every aspect of the Saudi society. This relationship is apparent in the Saudi Arabian flag: The color of the Saudi flag is green (a symbol of Islam). On it is written the Proclamation of Faith, or what Sheikh Muhammed bin Abdul Wahhab referred to as Kalimat al-Tawheed (unity). Under the Proclamation of Faith is a sword (a symbol of the tribe and the secular power of the Sauds). This alliance between the royal family and the religious forces in Arabia has been central in the maintenance of the political order. Nonetheless, this alliance has never been free from tension. In Saudi Arabia, religious forces have questioned the hegemony of the ruling elite, but with very few consequences to the power of the royal family. In 1929 the Ikhwan (the brothers) of Najd who had been instrumental in establishing Ibn Saud's power wanted to invade other countries, such as Iraq, to form a greater Islamist state; Ibn Saud's vision of state building focused only on Saudi Arabia. Moreover, the Ikhwan considered Ibn Saud to be their imam (leader) only as long as he followed the teachings of Bin Abdul Wahhab and worked for that vertical order. In their eyes, Ibn Saud clearly had violated the Islamic codes on two counts: he declared himself King of Arabia and he signed an agreement with the British, Islam's enemy in the eyes of the Ikhwan. These violations provoked the Ikhwan to revolt. After expanding his territory, Abdul Aziz had to choose between the expansionist impulse of the Ikhwan and the political constraints imposed on him by major powers with interests in the surrounding area, namely Britain.[34] Like modern-day major powers concerned about the Islamists of Saudi Arabia, the British then were concerned about the Ikhwan. The British warned against the dangers the Ikhwan movement might pose to Abdul Aziz's authority in Arabia. John S. Habib states: "Very early in the reporting of British political agents, the warning that Ibn Saud was losing, or had lost control over the Ikhwan became a regular theme, and the warnings increased in number directly in proportion to the Ikhwan military strength."[35] Nonetheless, the local leader handled this issue with very little damage to his control, although his power was significantly less than that of the modern Saudi state. Realizing that the Ikhwan may provoke a confrontation with the British, he decided to rein the Ikhwan in. Thus in 1929 Ibn Saud fought the Ikhwan at Sibla. The battle lasted only a few hours and ended in total defeat of the Ikhwan army. Thereafter Ibn Saud destroyed the Ikhwan camps, declared that religious issues would be decided only by the 'ulama, and banned all meetings for any purpose without his prior approval.[36]

The destruction of the Ikhwan forces liberated Abdul Aziz from the bargains he had made with particular members of that group and consequently made religion again subordinate to secular power, although it cannot be claimed that Ibn Saud was secular himself. Like his followers, he was a religious man, or at least a mixture of religious and secular. Later on the position of the 'ulama was routinized. "The 'ulama lost whatever limited autonomy they had enjoyed; they became paid civil servants whose status, income, and general activities were governed by state regulations and objectives." In this the Sauds are not unusual in the larger pattern of Islamic history. Islam has been subordinated to the tribe or the ruling dynasty since the Umayyads (661–750) and the Abbasids (750–1258).

The second religious challenge to the Saud's authority came in 1979, when two major events took place in Saudi Arabia: the takeover of the Grand Mosque and the riots in the Eastern Province. The first occurred on November 20, 1979, when Juhaiman al-'Utaibi and a few hundred of his followers took over the Grand Mosque in Mecca and remained there for three weeks. The fighting that followed caused heavy casualties among rebels and government forces alike. That year another incident took place in the Eastern Province, a region dominated by Saudi Arabia's Shi'a minority. The Shi'a, perhaps inspired by the success of the Islamic revolution in Iran, rioted but were quelled by National Guard forces. In both cases the challenge did not come from the mainstream religious 'ulama of Saudi Arabia or even from the dominant tribes, but from the margin of Saudi society. In Islamic history, the Grand Mosque had been taken over twice before. In A.D. 693 Abdullah ibn al-Zubair laid siege to it in an attempt to revolt against the Ummayyad dynasty. That revolt lasted for eight months and ended with the surrender of al-Zubair and his followers. The second time was when the

Qaramatians revolted against the second Islamic dynasty, the Abbasids.[37] However, in both cases tribal loyalty defeated contenders who couched their revolt in Islamic terms. With the Sauds as well, tribal alliances have always been more powerful than Islamist forces.

The 1987–88 Cultural Debate: Modernism and Islam

Although the voices of opposition became more pronounced during the Gulf War, the debate between the Islamists and the liberals in Saudi society has been fermenting since 1987 around the issue of modernity and Islam. Central to this debate was Sheikh Awad al-Qarni's book *Al-Hadatha fi Mizan al-Islam* (Modernity on the scale of Islam) and two audio-taped lectures by the conservative Dr. Sa'eed al-Ghamidi. All these works confront the liberal forces of Saudi Arabia and accuse them of undermining the Islamic foundations of Saudi society. The government is accused of allowing these "secular" forces to control all the major publications and the media outlets in the country. By controlling the media, the liberals are able to shape the minds of the new generation and spread Western ideas, which are, in the eyes of these Islamist authors, inherently anti-Islamic. The Islamists also feel that the Marxist ideas that dominated socialist circles in Egypt, Syria, and Lebanon have found their way to Saudi society through these secular writers. According to the Islamists, by replacing religious discourse with Western or Marxist narratives, secular writers are trying to undermine the language of the Quran. Moreover, the liberals are portrayed as agents of modernity, which itself is considered tantamount to the destruction of traditional and religious values. The Syrian poet Ali Ahmed Sa'eed (Adonis) has been accused of contributing to this anti-Islamic trend and consequently has been called an infidel. Indeed, Adonis is suspect because of his Shi'a background and his daring ideas. In fact, in the late 1980s the literary pages of the Saudi newspapers were among the best literary publications in the Arab world and were open to a range of ideas. Some female poets openly criticized the way women are treated within their society. Female poets such as Khadija al-'Amri rejected the notion of veiling and attended conferences outside Saudi Arabia unveiled, according to the Islamists, who view the increase in female columnists in the Saudi press as part of this secular conspiracy to undermine Islamic values. The Islamists were disturbed when authorities interfered with the distribution of tapes by al-Ghamidi among the young at universities. By that time, the fault lines between the liberals and the Islamists were clear.

The Gulf War and After

The Gulf War has been a watershed in Saudi politics, or at least in the changing political language that enveloped that polity. Daring demands have been put forth before the king and the royal family. This section focuses on some of the major events that brought about this change in both attitude and political language. These events include the women's drive-in in the Saudi capital, the Letter of Demands, and the Memorandum of Advice.

The Women's Drive-in

The confrontation between the Islamists and the liberals crystallized when some 45 women drove their cars in Riyadh in a demonstration, asking for the right to drive. Some of these women reportedly took off their veils and stepped on them. To the Islamists, these acts epitomized the secular conspiracy. According to the Islamists, these liberals, almost all of them American-educated Saudis, were emboldened by the presence of the U.S. troops and wanted to further their own interests and undermine the foundation of the society. Supposedly the women wanted to turn Saudi Arabia into America and wanted women to have complete freedom, in defiance of local custom and law. To the Islamists, these women were infidels who deserved to be killed. In their leaflets attacking the female drivers, the Islamists accused the women of being "communist whores." The leaflets listed the names of the women, their husbands' names, and their professions, and urged the Saudi public to take action. The Islamists also wrote to the king, Crown Prince Abdullah, and Prince Salman, the powerful governor of Riyadh, asking that these women, and those behind them, be punished. Although nothing in Islam would prevent women from driving cars, both the regime and the Islamists were disturbed by the women's protest because of the centrality of women in the kinship system of qaraba. Women maintain the purity of tribal configuration and keep a specific hierarchy of relations in place, but women who are free to drive might select their own mates. Perhaps one reason why the Islamists insist on the control of women is that they fear that if this stable category of social relations of who intermarries with whom is undermined, the very basic formula of familialism could collapse. This fact also explains why so many Saudi men want to keep women out of politics. Women are guarded by tribal honor and the ideology of familialism as well as by Wahhabi teachings.

Moreover, the perception that these women were emboldened by the presence of American troops in Saudi Arabia further intensified the attack on the alliance between the United States and Saudi Arabia. The fatwas of the young 'ulama against seeking the help of non-Muslims in a war against Muslims were a part of this debate. Saudi Islamists felt that if the Americans stayed longer, they would further erode the authority of Islam in the kingdom. Thus a worst-case scenario about how the Americans would eliminate Islam in Saudi Arabia gained momentum. The taped sermons of

'Awad al-Qarni, Safar al-Hawali, Salman al-Auda, and Nasser al-Omar circulated in the kingdom, criticizing the presence of the foreign troops and
advocating greater roles for the 'ulama in the public life of Saudi Arabia.
They also urged the government and the public to weed out the secularists
from all the Saudi media because of their danger to society. As we will see
in the detailed discussions of Hawali and Auda in chapters 2 and 3, these
tapes and the criticism of the internal and external behavior of the Saudi
state provided the springboard for both the Letter of Demands and the
Memorandum of Advice, the two documents that represent both the plat-
forms of most Saudi Islamists and their demands for reform. It is very important to understand them before we delve into a detailed discussion of
the various opposition leaders and groups.

The Letter of Demands and the Memorandum of Advice

Emerging as a result of various discussions in Saudi Islamist circles, the
Memorandum of Advice represents the core document of the Islamists' consensus (ijma') concerning the kinds of reforms they expect of the Saudi government. Some elements of these conversations were fragmented and
delivered by different means, including the taped sermons of preachers.

The Memorandum of Advice focuses on a critique of the Saudi system
and its specific sectors, including: (1) the role of the 'ulama and preachers;
(2) laws and regulations; (3) the judicial system and the courts; (4) the rights
of those who submit to God (Huquq al-'ibad, not necessarily human rights);
(5) public administration; (6) the economy and finance; (7) social institutions; (8) the army; (9) the information system; and (10) foreign policy.
These issues are included in the Memorandum's introduction under the
heading "Big Issues."[38]

This introduction reveals a great deal about the orientation and basic assumptions of these groups. It starts with Surat al-Nas, which states that with
the exception of those who do good in this world, believe in justice, and are
patient, humans are likely to be a confused mass of impulses. The second
verse states that what distinguishes the Muslim nation from others is that it
enjoins good works toward eliminating evil, and that its members are true
believers in God. Then the memorandum uses one of the Prophet's sayings,
"Advice is the core of religion." This advice should be for all Muslims and
their leaders.

After it provides an Islamic rationale to justify its purpose, the memorandum outlines the current state of affairs in the world, which is characterized by confusion and change. It also states "the citizens of this country
are given the honor of having the holy places in their land and thus they are
responsible for this trust in the eyes of God." Because of these religious re-

sponsibilities and teachings, this group wanted to present the leaders of Saudi Arabia with a list of problems that could be corrected in light of Islamic teachings. Thus this memorandum fulfills its authors' Islamic duty. They say: "We pray to God that this Reformist advice will fall on receptive ears and that it will be accepted by the rulers of the Muslims."

The Memorandum of Advice was first sent to Sheikh Abdul Aziz bin Baz, the Grand Mufti of Saudi Arabia, for endorsement before being sent to the king. In the letter to the sheikh, the authors write:

> This advice is the result of the tireless efforts of your sons, students of Islam, preachers, and university professors. More than a hundred individuals signed this. Many 'ulama have read it and corrected it. It was also endorsed by many trusted ulama such as Sheikh Abdullah bin Jibreen, Sheikh Safar, al-Hawali, Sheikh Salman al-Auda, and Sheikh Abdullah al-Jilali. . . . Our purpose is to follow the teachings of Islam that requests advice and consultation. We would like you to read it and add what is missing and improve on it. This advice is of course an effort that is likely to have mistakes and we would want you to correct these mistakes. Whatever good in this advice is a gift from God and whatever is wrong is our responsibility and we stand corrected. Finally we would like you to endorse it and submit it to the Custodian of the Two Holy Mosques.[39]

It is obvious that the authors have tremendous respect for the sheikh and are deferential toward him as well as toward the king. The letter from Sheikh Salman al-Audah that endorses the memorandum states that he has read the document: "I found it to be a very serious effort offering a realistic treatment for many of the social ills of this society."[40] Hawali's letter states that he has read the memorandum and finds it worthy of the attention of all officials and every responsible individual.[41]

The 'Ulama and the System

With regard to the position of the 'ulama in Saudi society, the memorandum identifies six areas for criticism and suggests seven ways for reform. The activists claim that the role of the 'ulama and the religious institutions in public life is minimal and marginal: "The fact that the various ministries do not consult the 'ulama in conducting their policy could eventually lead to separation between politics and religion, which defeats the very purpose of the establishment of the Islamic State." Moreover, the bureaucratization of the 'ulama limits their independence. The sensitivity of state institutions toward the involvement of religious people limits their role in society. The Islamists are also distressed by what they feel is the lack of exposure of the 'ulama to the state media and the absence of any kind of media censorship to control the dissemination of material contradicting the teachings of Islam. They say that the government limits the role of the mosque and imposes restrictions on preachers who dare discuss salient issues[42] and that the role of religious preachers in state institutions, such as the Ministry of Information, educational institutions, and embassies, is limited.

How do these activists want to rectify this situation? Their answer is divided into two main themes: by solidifying the position of the 'ulama in society and by making sure that the state follows the teachings of Islam. The memorandum suggests lifting all restrictions on the activities of religious activists and preachers. The state should allow greater freedom in forming civil society associations, and the religious establishment should be able to regulate these associations. The selection of the Council of Higher 'Ulama should be based on merit, and members should be nominated based on their knowledge, piety, and sincerity; their membership in this council should not be subject to dismissal, unless there is an Islamic reason for it. To ensure the Islamic nature of the state, all treaties and arrangements should be subject to the Council of Higher 'Ulama for approval. The activities of religious associations and their finances should be run by an independent group of 'ulama and should be delinked from state budget. The government should issue a policy statement to all agencies to allow the religious people the right to promote Islamic teachings. Finally, the government should allow 'ulama from outside the kingdom to come in and conduct seminars, thus making it easier for them to exchange ideas with the 'ulama of Saudi Arabia. It is also the duty of the state to have religious people in all of its embassies to make sure that all activities conform to Islamic teachings. There should also be radio and television stations for the preaching of Islam. This point is the core of many of Hawali's taped sermons, because the main threats to Islam, according to him, are the television channels of the American Christian fundamentalists. The group also requires the state to strengthen the Committee for the Promotion of Virtue and the Suppression of Vice. In essence, the group wants the equivalent of a religious supervisor in all state agencies and wants the 'ulama to have an equal, if not a greater, share of power with the monarchy.

Laws and Regulations

The section on laws and regulation begins with an introduction that emphasizes the supremacy of Islamic law, which should govern the relationships between the individual, the family, and the state as well as the relationships between the state and society and the state and other states. The Islamists see it as a good sign that Saudi rulers have repeatedly stated that they would review and codify the laws and regulations, getting rid of all laws contrary to

Shari'a. This is why the Islamists feel it is their duty to point out the areas in which the political system does not correspond to the Shari'a and to suggest ways of reforming it.

After a theological introduction, the memorandum describes eight areas in need of reform. Some of these points seem to be variations or specific examples of earlier points. I have kept the original organization to convey the style of the memorandum and well as its content, since the two cannot be separated. The writers appear to repeat points they feel are important, and list together specific points that they feel are less pressing. The eight areas are as follows:

1. Many of the laws are derived from other legal traditions, either Western or secular Arab traditions. Some examples of this are commercial laws and those governing the relationship between employers and workers, which are derived from international accords in which the Shari'a is not the frame of reference.

2. In the area of commercial law, laws concerning corruption, military law, and civil law concerning the privileges of public officials, the rules of specific agencies and bureaus are not derived from Shari'a law but from international jurisprudence.

3. The Gulf Cooperation rules concerning the treatment of foreign workers is not based on the Shari'a, yet Saudi Arabia is a signer of this agreement.

4. Commercial banks in Saudi Arabia allow the charging of interest, although the Shari'a prohibits usury. Moreover, non-Saudi Muslims are not permitted the same rights as Saudis, which violates the idea that Islam is one nation and that there should be no discrimination among Muslims on the basis of nationality. The idea that there should be a statute of limitations on bringing complaints in disputes between workers and employers is also contrary to the Shari'a. To use wiretaps, informers, and violation of private homes in order to obtain evidence against suspected criminals is in violation of the Shari'a, which presumes innocence.

5. Some laws have limited things that God has permitted and legalized that which God has not permitted. For instance, to prevent banks from engaging in various sorts of business, such as agriculture and industry, and to limit their incomes to usury is un-Islamic. Requiring employers to give employees medical insurance and retirement benefits is also un-Islamic, since these matters do not concern the state but are private contracts between the employer and the employee. That is, individual employers may give these benefits if their employees wish, but the state has no right to demand this.

6. Some laws allow monopolies of certain facilities and permit no competition. Companies like the Saudi national airline control all the air
routes with no room for other commercial airlines.

7. Some taxes, fines, and levies are inconsistent with Shari'a laws. These
include customs taxes on Muslims, tolls for roads, fees for passports
and licenses, and many similar instances of taking money from the
people in a way that is not prescribed by the religion.

8. The disciplinary practices of the state, such as imprisonment and
fines, ignore other Islamic methods. For example, a fine as a punishment can be a deterrent to the poor but does not serve a similar purpose for the rich.

To eliminate these problems, the signers advise the following: (1) review
the laws and eliminate the non-Islamic laws and replace them with Islamic
ones; (2) establish a higher court to look into the compatibility of the laws
with the Shari'a; and (3) require academic institutions to focus on the study
of Islamic teachings and teach Western traditions only to graduate students
with the sole purpose of undermining and discrediting these traditions.
They conclude by stating that the frame of reference for Saudi laws should
be Islam, not the laws and traditions of other countries. The formation of
committees to study these laws should include only theologians who are
known for their knowledge and sincerity. For every law there should be a reference concerning how it was deduced from the Islamic tradition and showing that it does not contradict the Shari'a.

The Judiciary and the Court System

After a long introduction about the legal tradition in Islam, the memorandum makes four points describing the current system: (1) The country has
a dual system of justice, for in addition to the courts there are more than 30
committees that base their judgment on the state's laws and not the Shari'a.
This dual system has led to many violations of Islamic law. (2) The courts
are not independent, which violates the notion of the supremacy of the
Shari'a above all other authority. The governors impose the restrictions and
the ministry of interior is involved in the works of the courts. (3) Shari'a
courts in certain provinces are underdeveloped and require more support to
improve their performance. And (4) the execution of certain rulings issued
by the ombudsman against state agencies has been delayed. To reform these
problems, the following are suggested: All the committees that have the
power of the court should be eliminated, and all judgments in disputes and
crimes should be under Islamic law. The ombudsman should deal only with
cases against the state and its agencies. Other functions should be added to

the Shari'a courts. Judges should be elected by other judges or by the Council of Higher 'Ulama. No judge should be removed for any reason except the violation of Islamic teachings.

People's Rights

It is obvious that the Memorandum of Advice does not address the issue of human rights as a universal concept, but rather focuses on Shari'a rights for Muslims only. First, it states that all rights are derived from Islamic law and, second, that all rights included in the Shari'a are rights that must be granted by the state. No violation of these rights is permissible from a religious standpoint. The Islamic state is responsible for guaranteeing these rights. Next the memorandum follows the previously established pattern by identifying what is wrong with the current system and then suggesting reform or advice to the ruler in keeping with Islamic teachings.

The memorandum lists the following complaints: Some government workers, university professors, teachers, and judges were suspended from their jobs and did not receive their salaries or were transferred to other regions without any trial. Many religious preachers were prevented from delivering their sermons and were banned from travel with no Islamic trials. Moreover, members of the police spy and search private homes, sometimes beating and torturing the accused in violation of the teachings of Islam. Equality before the law is lacking. There are no government agencies responsible for the rights of citizens. Some government regulations prevent citizens from marrying non-Saudis or forming companies and importing and exporting goods. These violations should be reformed by canceling all government regulations that contradict the Shari'a, by eliminating all behavior that leads to torturing citizens, and by ordering government agencies and police not to arrest citizens for periods of time without trial and by ordering police not to search homes or prevent anyone from freedom of movement. The government also must allow conduct that is permissible according to the Shari'a, such as freedom of opinion and freedom of association, must make sure that the accused has a fair trial, must eliminate all laws that discriminate among Muslims, and must educate the police concerning the rights of citizens according to the teachings of Islam.

Public Administration

Again, the group states that according to Islam, there are three major criteria for a good administration in the Islamic state: (1) honesty, knowledge, and power should be the main criterion for government posts; (2) administration policies should be based on efficiency and striving for perfection; and (3) there must be a system of investigation to ensure that public officials conduct the affairs of the state honestly.

According to the group the current situation is characterized by the following problems:

1. The system of administration does not cope with modernization.
2. The centralization of power in a few individuals even in simple matters is inefficient, for it wastes the time of the senior officials.
3. The criterion for replacing officials is not based on merit and competence, as evidenced by the fact that there are aged and infirm officials who have been occupying their positions for decades despite the abundance of younger and more capable Saudis.
4. There is no reason for honorific titles for officials.
5. There has to be a fair distribution system for appointing officials that takes into account regionalism and various other categories.
6. Corruption must be exposed and nepotism eliminated.
7. The system must be reformed so all regions in the kingdom benefit from the same level of services.

In this section few Islamic sources are quoted; instead the demands for administrative reform seemed primarily political, the demands of younger Saudis who would like to be given the chance to move up the social ladder.

The Economy and Finance

Money is a trust to the Muslim nation. It belongs to God and should be administered in ways that fulfill God's teachings. Money should not be squandered, because there are very clear verses against tabtheer (extravagance). Money should be also preserved in ways to ensure that the next generations are not left in poverty. The economy is a very important pillar of the Muslim community, and its development should be treated as such. Some of the violations that the memorandum lists concerning the Saudi economy and its compliance with Islamic teachings include:

1. Violations concerning the sources of the money, which include usury, imposition of unlawful taxes and fees, and adding the zakat (charity) money to the treasury.
2. Violations concerning spending, including money spent on political parties and states that violate Islamic teachings. This money is given as grants to support non-Islamic causes.

3. Some agencies and ministries do not have enough money to spend on necessary things such as health, transportation and educational issues.
4. The depletion of oil and water resources as a result of the lack of strategic planning in using them.
5. The absence of any religious oversight over how money is being levied and spent.
6. The disappearance of money as a result of kickbacks and corrupt practices.
7. The monopoly of certain individuals over various kinds of commercial dealings in the kingdom.

The document signers advise that the economic system be brought closer to the teaching of Islam by stopping aid to un-Islamic governments and organizations and stopping all forms of monopoly, usury, and extravagant spending. They also urge the king to separate zakat money from the treasury and to use it benefit the poor.

Social Services

The writers open this section with verses from the Quran and sayings of the Prophet and the caliphs, particularly Omar ibn al-Khattab, the second Muslim caliph. Here the group makes it clear that the poor have an absolute right to the money of the rich and that this money should be given through the zakat system. It is also the duty of the Islamic state to take care of the poor, the sick, and the aged using funds from the public treasury. Thus in an Islamic state, citizens' basic needs should be satisfied in a way that protects Muslims from the humiliation of need. Wealth in the Islamic state should be distributed fairly. Money is for God, and Muslim leaders should administer this money. Furthermore, the Islamic state should build educational and health institutions to save the Muslims from ignorance and disease.

The memorandum then describes the state of welfare in Saudi Arabia and finds it lacking. Thus the authors advise the government to change the laws concerning social welfare to guarantee the rights of citizens and residents to housing, health care, food, and other basic needs no matter where the people live, whether in towns, villages, or the desert. It also recommends that the government study the ways other nations have dealt with the issue of unemployment. The government should make it easier for those who want to get married to borrow from financial institutions, and it should increase spending on health and education, transportation, and mosques to meet the pressures of a growing population. The government should also work hard to reduce the imbalances among the various classes of society.

The Army

The authors of the memorandum contend that the Gulf War exposed the general weaknesses of the Saudi army. This is why the kingdom relied on foreign troops to defend its soil. The main function of an Islamic army, according to the authors, is to protect the Islamic state, its faith, and its people. The group criticizes the state for the disjunction between the budget allocated to the army and the general lack of readiness of the Saudi forces. According to the memorandum, the numbers are small, the equipment is not advanced, and the training is weak. Furthermore, a country the size of Saudi Arabia requires a larger army to protect its boundaries and ports. The memorandum also notes the absence of military and jihadi education in Saudi society. The authors advocate that the Israel army should be the model for the Saudi army. That is, all Saudis should be trained for mobilization. The government should recruit Muslim experts and build a military industry. The group also advises the king to end all military alliances with non-Muslim states. If there is any need for external support of the Saudi army, it should come from Muslim countries. All Saudi nationals should be required to undergo military training. In essence, "Prepare yourself with whatever will impress the enemy of God and your enemy." Thus Saudi Arabia should allocate more money and resources to build an impressive army.

The Information Sector

The authors start their advice by emphasizing the importance of information and media to the propagation of the faith, because Islam is a global message and not limited to one race, language, or ethnic group. Thus the content of the Islamic media should reflect the purpose and the teachings of the faith. These purposes include dissemination of facts, reforming public opinion, and the building of an "the Islamic person." Thus far the Saudi media and information system is inadequate in certain areas. To start with, the Saudi media propagates lies and creates images of leaders that elevate them to a godly status, things explicitly forbidden by Islam. Sometimes the media gives a wrong impression about basic concepts of the religion. The religious programs are limited in the Saudi media, while secular programs that undermine rather than build the Muslim person are common. Censorship also undermines the dissemination of facts. The absence of a censorship system on the direct broadcast may undermine the morals of Muslims. To reform this, the rulers should start by putting together a new media policy that reflects the Islamic nature of the state: prohibiting what is wrong and enjoining what is right. The government should allow preachers greater time on television radio and in print media. It should have special programs for women and children that conform to the teachings of Islam. The government should also allow for private media with as few regulations as possible. The only system of censorship should be conformity to Islamic law. The government should ban the programs that show unveiled women and present an un-Islamic image. The people at the helm of the information ministry should be men of religion known for their piety and sincerity. This section is a direct response to the taped sermons of Hawali and al-'Auda.

Foreign Affairs

In this area, the authors open by stating their notion of Islamic international relations, which includes three principles: the global propagation of Islam, the unity of the Muslims, and the need to aid Muslims and support their causes. The thrust of the memorandum's critique of Saudi foreign policy is the state's lack of support for Islamic movements, such as the Algerian Islamic Salvation Front, and its support for states that fight Islamists; the Syrian state is cited as a prime example. The authors also criticize the relationship between the United States and Saudi Arabia, which continues "in spite of America's general hostile policies toward Muslims." The memorandum also criticizes Saudi foreign policy for its support of peace with Israel, Saudi embassies abroad for their failure to propagate the faith and for employing females who dress offensively, and the government for buying off journalists and political parties and allowing these groups to exploit Saudi Arabia.

The memorandum counsels the king to support all Islamic states and groups and to cut off the kingdom's relations with states hostile to Islam. The kingdom should develop a wise policy in dealing with blocs of non-Muslim states, especially Western ones. Islam should be central to Saudi foreign policy at the bilateral level as well as in the international arena. The government should reorganize its embassy to eliminate all elements that do not conform to the Shari'a.

One hundred nine men signed this memorandum,[43] almost all of them Islamists. Although most of the signers come from the Saudi heartland, Najd, many come from other regions in the kingdom. The authors apparently wanted to convince the king that these reforms were supported by a wide spectrum of Saudi Islamists regardless of regional and tribal affiliation; indeed, the demands in the letter and the memorandum come from diverse preachers and opposition groups. However, while these various dissidents agreed on these basic principles, they disagreed on how to pressure the government into implementing these reforms. Some wished to concentrate solely on arousing Saudi public opinion, whereas others wished to enlist the moral support of Islamists outside the country. Still others sought to persuade Western governments to pressure the Saudi regime to reform. Others advocated violence as the most effective way to bring about change. Threatened by the letter and the Memorandum of Advice, the Saudi government arrested and interrogated the key activists, although most were later released or allowed to leave the kingdom. However, many dissidents continued to agitate for reform, making use of new technologies to convey their ideas when it became obvious that traditional peaceful means, such as written petitions, were counterproductive. Preachers working within the kingdom relied on cassette tapes to convey their message, while those in exile used more advanced technologies. Thus the opposition splintered into several groups, each of which used different methods and technologies to propagate their message.

A thorough analysis of contemporary power relations and the politics of dissent in Saudi Arabia necessitates a reexamination of dominant frameworks and concepts, an effort to find new, more meaningful tools of analysis, and a placing of the current trends and events within a wider political and historical context. In a departure from both the pervasive rentier model and common misunderstandings of the tribal unit, I will present the politics of dissent as part of a preexisting network grounded in familialism, social relations, and various interpretations and applications of Islam. Collectively, the various elements of this network constitute a political economy of signs that serves as an underlying force guiding relations and interactions among individuals, opposition groups, the wider Saudi society, and the state. This force is reflected in the structure of authority and governance within the Saudi system and requires analysts to look beyond oil wealth and tribal divisions to understand power relations and resistance in Saudi Arabia. The chapters that follow examine the leaders and groups associated with contemporary Islamic resistance as well as the responses and role of the Saudi government within this overarching analytical framework.

CHAPTER TWO

Sheikh Safar al-Hawali, Geopolitics, and Islamic Dissent

What is happening in the Gulf is part of a larger Western design to dominate the whole Arab and Muslim world.

—Safar al-Hawali, "You will remember what I say to you," taped sermon, 1991.

Introduction

The epigraph presents a minority opinion during the 1990–91 Gulf War. Now, however, it has become a common view throughout the Arab world. Safar al-Hawali's (henceforth Hawali) name came to prominence during a global and media event, the Gulf War, when his books and taped sermons galvanized public debate inside Saudi Arabia on a range of domestic and international issues of major concern for both the Saudis and the Muslim world. However, because most Western writings on the Islamists' discourse have depended on secondhand material, Hawali was presented as a Saudi sheikh who opposed the royal family, even though this was not his central issue. Hawali's opposition is not limited to the Saudi government but to a hierarchy of opponents. This hierarchy starts with the West in general, followed by the United States, the American religious right, secular Arab regimes, and finally the Saudi government. Apparently his criticism of the Saudi government has been limited not only because it would be politically dangerous for him personally, but because he sees that government as part of a larger web of global relations that must be criticized as a whole, not in isolation. Hawali is currently imprisoned in Saudi Arabia for his views. Here I attempt to give a more complete picture of the man and his discourse through an analysis of 20 randomly selected taped sermons and two of his most important books. This portrait will reveal that Hawali believes that a critique of the Western/American core culture is central to any serious critique of the Saudi State, because what concerns him is not the problems of the Saudi state itself as much as its subordinate position to the United States, whose culture he sees as extremely hostile to Islam. Thus one of Hawali's targets is the American Christian right. His discourse about this movement seems very informed, although he seems to believe, correctly or not, that the Christian right is not a peripheral movement in American politics but a central movement that plays a major role in the future of any conflict in or with the Middle East. In another sense, his target is not precisely the U.S. government but the right-wing Christian opposition to that government. The interplay between the discourse of the American fundamentalists and that of Hawali highlights the importance of the global-local dialectic. Hawali's views of the United States appear very close to being a mirror image of the views of the Christian right concerning the Arab world.

Hawali's next layer of criticism focuses on the secular Arab states, particularly their Western-influenced constitutions and legal systems. Finally he moves toward criticizing the Saudi government in the context of this complex interplay among metropolitan hegemony, the right-wing opposition of this metropolis, the regional setting, and Saudi liberals and their influence on the current Saudi government. As we begin to understand the complexity of his narrative in which both Islamic and nationalist impulses shape each other, it would seem that America's foreign policy in the Middle East may be more dangerous to the stability of the Saudi regime than is Hawali's critique of the Saudi government. The argument that I will advance throughout is that the Saudi oppositional discourse is determined more by exogenous variables, such as the Gulf War and America's role in the Middle East, than it is by domestic variables. Obviously these variables are not isolated from each other, and the internal and external forces interact constantly. However, the effects of these external influences, from U.S. foreign policy to the rhetoric of the American Christian right, seem to have been seriously underestimated.

Before I begin the analysis, let me start with a few biographical remarks about the man. Sheikh Safar bin Abd al-Rahman al-Hawali was born in 1950 in the al-Baha region, which lies south of al-Taif. He comes from a minor but reputable tribe, which, along with his credentials as an Islamic scholar, makes him the most mainstream of all critics of the Saud regime. As a young man, Hawali attended the Educational Institute in al-Baha and later studied for his bachelor of arts degree at the Islamic University in Medina. After finishing his bachelor's degree, he continued his Islamic studies at Um Al-Qura University in Mecca, where he received his master's of arts degree and graduated at the top of his class. Hawali's master's thesis, which focused on al-'ilmaniyyah (secularism), exhibited strands of thought that continue to dominate his thinking today. His lectures and debates show a profound mistrust of the influence of secular thought in Arab society and reveal his belief that secularism is a Western way of undermining Islamic society from within. Alone among the Saudi dissidents, he did not receive his doctorate from a foreign university, but from Um Al-Qura University (in 1986). Hawali became a teacher in the Department of 'Aqida (Belief) at the university and later became head of that department. The main focus of Hawali's work has been to defend Islam against the onslaught of secular Euro-American traditions.[1]

Hawali and The Western Politics of Domination

The theme of resistance to Western domination is not unique to Hawali's thought; it has been a part of Muslim and Arab discourse since the time of anticolonial movements in the first half of this century and the postcolonial Arab nationalists of the 1960s. In fact, some sources Hawali uses to make this point are published by Arab nationalist centers, namely the Beirut-based Center for the Study of Arab Future.[2] This relationship between Arab nationalist discourse and the current Islamist discourse and the synthesis that results are at the center of the language of political Islam today.

The centrality of nationalism to Hawali's thought cannot be overstated. He is not a traditionalist who favors a retreat into a premodern past, as some Western analysts have portrayed him. His concern is protecting his country and his culture from foreign domination. Hawali's fear of Western dominance over the Arab and the Muslim world is evident in his cassette tapes, sermons, and published books. Unlike many Islamists, whose khutbas (sermons) are articulated in a specifically Saudi context, Hawali's speeches and writings include the larger Islamic world. According to Hawali, the most pernicious threat facing Saudi Arabia (and the rest of the Arab-Islamic population) is "the imposition of Israeli and American hegemony over the whole area."[3] Like Samuel P. Huntington, Hawali views the world as a clash of civilizations, especially between the West and the Islamic world. Although he does not specify exactly when this conflict will take place, he repeatedly emphasizes that "blood is unavoidable" and that the army which will carry out this conflict (a conflict that he describes as the

"the new phase of the Crusade war") will be the Muslim youth. This, he believes, will be the starting point for the renewal of Muslim societies and the confrontation with the West.[4]

Hawali considers the Arab and Islamic world to be unprepared for this impending confrontation between the Muslim and the Western worlds. He identifies two main weaknesses of the Arab and Muslim world: political disunity and military and economic dependency. These two themes clearly inform Hawali's internal critique of contemporary Islamic societies.

Unlike other Saudi preachers, Hawali's critique does not make the unity of the Muslim states or the caliphate his goal; he seems satisfied with a certain level of coordination of policies and an agreement between Muslim states on what they have in common. He uses the West both as an example and as an enemy. "Nothing can be achieved," he insists, "if not by means of unity under the rule of the Book of God."[5] He contrasts the disunity of the Muslims with the unity of the West against Islam. He tells his listeners that in spite of the tensions that exist between the various Western states, the West acts as one in confronting the Islamic world, citing the West's support of Israel against Palestinian Arab and Muslim interests. In a series of taped sermons (later published in book form) on Palestine, *Filistin Bayn al-Wa'd al-Haq wal Wa'd al-Muftra* (Palestine between the real promise and the false one), he singles out the unwavering support of the Christian fundamentalist movements in the United States for Israel and the "Zionist crusade against Islam."[6] In light of the unwavering solidarity of the enemies of Islam, the disunity of the Islamic world in the modern age is a severe handicap. Thus for Hawali, it becomes vital to "mobilize all the energies of the umma [Islamic community] against a vicious enemy."[7] In this call for a united Arab front, Hawali is in essence reverting back to the discourse of Arab nationalism that Gamal 'Abdul Nasser popularized in the 1950s and 1960s. As the West has made clear, unity is one of the main components of success. Although Hawali sees the Western world as a dangerous enemy that the Muslim world should reject, it is nonetheless an example to be emulated in its unity against one cause: the Islamic cause. In response, Hawali emphasizes the need for unity among Muslims and Arabs in order to counter the Western threat.

The economic dependency of the Arab-Islamic world on the West informs several of the core tenets of Hawali's discourse. He explicitly calls for the withdrawal of all assets from Western financial institutions and their reinvestment in Islamic countries.[8] This is as close as he gets in criticizing the Saudi and the Gulf states regarding their dependence on the Western capitalist system. It is toward this end that Hawali returns again and again to the Islamic prohibition of usury (riba). According to Islamic law, any money return should be based on shared losses as well as shared profits. Thus any bank that gives fixed interest on money is Islamically prohibited. It becomes permissible only if investors share in the loss as well as the gains of the investment.

The military dependency of the Arab-Islamic world and Saudi Arabia on the West came under scrutiny during the Gulf War, when the Saudi government was obliged to permit the deployment of military forces from the West inside the kingdom. The ninth "necessary" reform contained in the May 1991 Memorandum of Advice (Muthakerat al-Nasiha), signed by Hawali and 108 other Saudi Islamists, entailed the construction of a strong indigenous military and a domestic capability for weapons manufacture. In this regard, Hawali chastises Arab societies for using a Western military force to protect them, rather than turning to God for such security. Unless there is a serious attempt to break away from this dependency, Hawali argues, very little can be done to counteract the growth of Western military and economic hegemony over the Islamic world. He believes military dependency is followed by economic and cultural dependency, which are far more dangerous, for they pose a direct threat to the Islamic faith. Hawali claims that the spread of Western secular ideas into the region has weakened the integrity of the Islamic faith; thus an awakening (sahwah) that alerts the Muslim world to the importance of the return to God is urgently needed. Internal reform is required before relations with the outside world can be reformed and restructured. "The first war should be against the infidels inside, and then we will be strong enough to face our external enemy."[9] By the "infidels inside," Hawali means the liberals and the leftists of the Arab and Muslim world. Although in this cassette-taped sermon Hawali does not cite his sources, the theme of liberating the Muslim world from its internal problems first is a very common theme of Hizb al-Tahreer (Liberation Party), a clandestine pan-Islamic party originating in Jordan. This is probably why Mohammed al-Mas'ari, a committed member of Hizb al-Tahreer, has found Hawali's tapes useful and continued to distribute them through his London-based Committee for the Defence of Legitimate Rights (CDLR). Chapter 4 is devoted to the discussion of CDLR.

Hawali warns that the process of globalization is accelerating the intrusion of Western secularism into the region. He considers the spread of new means of communication, such as the satellite dish and the Internet, to be part of a Western conspiracy to subvert the Islamic faith. Hawali advocates strict censorship of the media to prevent the spread of un-Islamic ideas. Like most Islamic activists, he is ambivalent about the issue of freedom of expression. Even though he criticizes the Saudi government for silencing his voice and those of his colleagues, Hawali demands that some form of control be exercised on global networks to preserve the integrity of the Islamic faith. Therefore, Islamic criticism should be allowed, but non-Islamic views should be censored. The main point of Hawali's argument is that Muslims will suffer under this irreversible process of global communication since they will watch and read items that they are not supposed to see or read. Thus, in a way, Hawali contradicts himself; he suggests that the spread of global communication is a product of the West and needs to be controlled but simultaneously acknowledges that this spread is inevitable.

New advances in air travel have particularly disturbed Hawali. AirBus and McDonnell Douglas talk of cutting flight times by half, thus reducing flight time between, for example, Jeddah and New York to six hours, and between Jeddah and Bangkok, "the city of prostitution," to three hours. "In light of the dominance of desire among our youth and the retreat of Islamic values, these changes are likely to have great implications for our society and the Islamic world at large," he suggests. Hawali goes on to reject the idea of turning Jeddah into a tourist city, saying that this is a clear effort to transport what takes place in Bangkok and graft it onto Jeddah, and that instead of preventing evil, the government would be bringing evil home. According to Hawali, the best solution to deal with this problem is to go back to taqwa [faith] and belief in God. "If we ignore God and choose the West we are the losers."[10]

Hawali reveals some contradictions, however, when he talks about the modern world. He criticizes the fast transportation system that takes Muslims from their local communities to places of corruption, yet he criticizes his own community for its inability to move forward. What is really appalling to Hawali is that while the rest of the world is changing so dramatically, the Islamic world is stagnant. He criticizes many aspects of Muslim life. Very specifically, the sheikh mentions that one can go for years to the Grand Mosque in Mecca to listen to the lectures of the great 'ulama and invariably hear the same thing over and over again. He also feels that Muslims spend most of their time asking the 'ulama about marginal questions instead of larger, more prominent issues affecting the world. Though Hawali's stance is clear regarding Western domination, he seems nonetheless confused as he is constantly pushing for the advancement of his community while at the same time criticizing Western technology and advancement. Apparently he does not reject either change or technology as such but is deeply disturbed by the fact that technology can be used to subvert Islam and that change too frequently has meant a change for the worse, that is, a change away from Islam. However, he never states this clearly.

The contrast between a world that changes by the minute and a reality that seems muted through the years is poignant. Not only is the rest of the world moving at a speed the Muslims do not remotely try to keep up with, but all that takes place in that world is going to affect them most closely and most directly, regardless of their indifference to it. How is it possible then to imagine a future for the Islamic world? Hawali argues that the answer already lies in the hands of the Muslims, since they are the ones that have inherited the Book, and since Gabriel gave to Muhammad a message that is still as valid today as it was centuries ago.

"We are the nation (umma) of the good and of the victory," he reminds his audience; therefore the solution to any problem is to be found in the Quranic verses (ayat), and its spirit can be summed up in one word, namely piety (taqwa). He also points out the importance of unity for the Muslims; the West moves toward an institutional unity by regulation; Muslims need to take practical steps to improve the situation of the Muslim world. The only way to unite is to start with the youth while appreciating the differences among them in terms of their socialization, upbringing, and regions.[11]

These are the general points Hawali makes about the West, including the United States. Then his discourse focuses primarily on the United States and its policies in the Arab world. In his assessment of the Gulf War and America's role in the Middle East, Hawali's religious discourse gives way to a discourse of national security and geopolitics. Religion may be behind it, but the critique is certainly based on a different language.

The United States and the Muslim World

Hawali's distrust of the United States and the West is most clearly articulated in his 1991 book, Haqa'iq Hawl Azmat al-Khalij (Realities behind the Gulf crisis). This book was so popular that several editions were published in different countries, including one in the United States bearing the title Wa'd Kissinger wa al-Ahdaf al-Amrikiyya f'l-khalij (Kissinger's Promise and the American objectives in the Gulf). Both books summarize many of the tapes Hawali circulated during the Gulf crisis and are central to understanding his thinking and the security dilemma of Saudi Arabia. Hawali explains the dilemma in the Gulf as one that should concern all Muslims, not just the Arabs of the Gulf. In spite of this pan-Islamic claim, Saudi nationalism represents the heart of this book. The introduction is addressed to Sheikh Abdul al-Aziz bin Baz, the head of the High Council of Saudi 'Ulama. Hawali contends that Iraq's invasion of Kuwait in August 1990 and the ensuing Gulf crisis were instigated by the Western powers in accordance with their global strategic objectives:

> I'm of the opinion that what took place [in the Gulf] was not a random event, but part of the larger Western design, a position that I stated publicly in front of many sheikhs and 'ulama. Many who objected to my opinion had misinterpreted it. I'm writing this because of the encouragement I received as a result of a dialogue between myself and the Deputy Minister of the Interior

[Prince Ahmed bin Abdul al-Aziz] on the one hand, and between you (Sheikh bin Baz) and the minister of the interior on the other. You have recommended a further study of the subject with the results presented as an advice to the nation. I'm sending my advice to you, in hopes that you will read it and recommend whatever you consider right to the government, while advising me on what you consider to be wrong. You should pay special interest to this, for it is a major crisis that would be followed many others. We will be accountable to both God and the coming generations concerning how we handle this crisis. Here I present to you a summary of the roots of this crisis, an analysis of the larger international designs, and finally some policy recommendations.[12]

It is clear from the introduction that Hawali is writing as a strategic thinker rather than a theologian. His first chapter establishes the context by emphasizing the history of Euro-American interests in the Gulf and the importance of Gulf oil to the industrialized economies of the West. Western and American interests in the Gulf, according to Hawali, are not new; they are part of a larger plan. "Western Crusaders" led by the United States have been drawing up long-term plans and strategies concerning the Middle East, especially the Gulf and the Arabian Gulf region (p. 10). Hawali believes that the West's complete dependence on oil for its economic prosperity has made the Arabian Gulf the "most important region in the whole world" for the West, and he cites figures to support the decline of Western oil reserves and the rise of these reserves in the Gulf region (p. 7). Thus for the past three decades the West, headed by the United States, has been devising strategies to occupy the area under the guise of the Gulf security. According to Hawali, this is the essence of Richard Nixon's plans for the region outlined in his book.[13]

The United States and the Gulf Region

Hawali starts his discourse on the United States and the Gulf region by placing the question in a historical context. Although in many of his accounts Hawali appears very well informed, what is important here is not his accuracy as much as how he frames the issues. This framing and the construction of a particular narrative is central to how Islamists view the U.S. role in the region. Halwai starts off by explaining that the U.S. alliance with Iran and its dependence on the Shah was within the overall framework of the Cold War and the importance of Gulf oil in that strategy. This, he explains, became more obvious during the 1973 war between the Arabs and the Israelis, when oil was used as a strategic weapon. The 1973 October war intensified the West's sense of economic vulnerability to the growing political independence of oil-exporting Arabian Gulf countries; "During this war, King Faisal showed that Saudi Arabia can challenge the West, although partially" (p. 13).

With the fall of the Shah in 1979, the United States began devising other strategies to secure its interests in the region. According to Hawali, the United States was wary of depending on local powers to ensure regional stability and looked more and more toward a direct presence for U.S. troops to carry out such a role. He cites the "Carter Doctrine" regarding the oil wells of the Gulf and the various plans the Pentagon devised for rapid deployment of troops in the region. Hawali considers these strategies and plans to have been a "clear and practical translation" of the United States' earlier plans "to secure U.S. interests in the region" (p. 29–30).

Hawali believes that, following the fall of the Shah and the emergence of revolutionary Iran as a threat to vital American interests, the United States orchestrated the entire Gulf War in order to secure for itself a direct military presence in the area. Toward this end, the U.S. government strengthened ties with the Gulf states, particularly Saudi Arabia, enabling itself to set up air bases throughout the Arabian peninsula. In effect, Saudi Arabia replaced the Shah's Iran as the client of the United States. The power vacuum that revolutionary Iran had created by losing its status as the policeman for the area served as "a cover for the West's direct hegemony over the region"(p. 38). Hawali reminds the Council of the Higher 'Ulama and Sheikh bin Baz in particular that the force sent to Saudi Arabia in 1990 was the same "rapid deployment" force created under the Carter administration, ostensibly to deter Soviet designs in the region.

The advent of the Iraq-Iran war in 1980 led to the creation of a strong alliance between Iraq and the Gulf states. Hawali criticized the clear "coordination" of Iraqi and Saudi policy, calling it a major blunder in Saudi foreign policy. He argues that the "atheist" regime of Iraq was an unfit ally for an Islamic nation like Saudi Arabia. The billions of dollars that the Saudis gave to Iraq were a waste of resources in support of a regime that treated those who read the works of Sheikh Mohammed bin Abd al-Wahhab as criminals. Hawali chastises the Saudi media for its earlier praise of Saddam Hussein and its inability to see through the Ba'thist regime's animosity to men of religion and the basic doctrine that guides the life of Saudi society.

Following his discussion of the U.S. role in shaping the politics of the region, Hawali continues by discussing the "New World Order" that emerged out of East-West conciliation—a reconciliation that is characterized by its fear of the "Islamic revival" in the Middle East. According to Hawali, the New World Order is nothing but a cover for the West's control and domination of the world. The West has experience in this, he says, as represented in the League of Nations and the mandate system, which allowed the West to control the Middle Eastern countries under the excuse that these countries were not yet developed. He says this was nothing more than enslavement, although it may have been called a mandate system or colonialism. After the reality of this situation became clear to the world, the colonized countries desired to break free from this enslavement, leading to World War II.

Following the war, the Western powers raised a new global banner that emphasized the idea of self-determination. However, self-determination for the Third World was conditioned on subjection to the international system and the so-called legitimate international order of democratic systems, of which the United States is now the sole policeman. When the power of Islam became clear, the West looked for a new system to provide a cover for its intervention into foreign affairs and its domination of the world, especially the Middle East. The only beneficiaries of this system of so-called international legitimacy are the Jews of Israel and the United States, the latter through its ability to control the resources of the region and to force its culture upon the rest of the world.

In the late 1980s, with the East-West realignment, the West shifted its focus from Eastern Europe and the Soviet Union to the Middle East—a region that now poses the greatest danger to the West's security (p. 60). Not only was this region exploding demographically, but it had also witnessed the growth of militarily strong states that posed threats to the West's hegemony there. However, the military strength of a Middle Eastern country is not as ominous to the West as the strength of Islam. Still, Islam has proved to be (at least for the West) a never-ending threat; sometimes the phrase "the clash of civilizations" between the West and Islam is used. Thus Islam has forced the West to find alternate ways in order to preserve and maintain its security.

To meet this new Islamist challenge, the West has followed two strategies. The first one was the creation of alliances between the United States and the "moderate" Arab and Islamic regimes such as Jordan, and between Israel and Arab regimes as a "defense perimeter" against the expansion of Islam. The second strategy includes the increased U.S. military presence in the region—a strategy that Hawali refers to as the "new Christian crusade of the twentieth century." Toward that end, the U.S. government has created a "core" of diplomatic, military, and intelligence expertise to study and work to "enforce complete Western hegemony on the Islamic world and to eradicate Islamism" (p. 67).

After Saudi Arabia refused to accept a formal military alliance during the early 1980s, the United States looked for other ways to establish itself militarily in the region. The decline of the Soviet Union and Iraq's invasion of Kuwait opened the door for U.S. troops to flood into the area. Hawali believes that the Iraqi invasion of Kuwait was orchestrated and planned as part of a grand strategy to gain a foothold for Western troops in the region (p.83). With that invasion, the United States was able to shift military bases and personnel from Western Europe to the Middle East, with the help and support of other Western powers.

The reason for the rapid deployment of U.S. and Western troops into the Gulf region, Hawali contends, was not to "liberate Kuwait" but to subdue any regional power that opposes the West and to tie the region's states into a new security arrangement that would extend from Pakistan to Egypt and perhaps even to Israel (p. 87). "Do you think that the West came to this region to defend us?" Hawali asks. "By God, no! They have never wanted any good to happen to us. Whether it is we who are destroyed or Iraq, it is our Nation that is destroyed."[14] Hawali believes that the purpose of this war was not oil, as many claim, but the humiliation of Islam through the subjugation and destruction of the Islamic movement. For example, in November 1989, when newsmen asked an American administrator, "Are you afraid of Iraqi power in the region?" He answered, "No, Iraq is the only force in the region that can be used to suppress the Islamic movement that we are afraid of."[15] In addition, in *al-Hayat,* a Saudi newspaper published in London, the British foreign minister was asked in an interview why the British had earlier supported Iraq. His answer was: "Because Iraq was fighting fundamentalism [and] what disturbs us is the alliance between nationalism and fundamentalism supporting Saddam."[16] Hawali declares that Saddam is not the Saudis' problem; when Islamic forces sided with Saddam, the West fought against him. Isn't it clear what the West is after? he asks. It is after Islam. However, the sheikh also blames Saddam for being greedy and power-hungry. According to Hawali, after the Western powers had refused to give Saddam the role of their new policeman, Saddam, knowing their plans to draw up a new map for the Middle East, decided to take the initiative and to share in the spoils by a "preemptive" invasion of Kuwait. This invasion, though risky, would have minimized the losses as far as Saddam was concerned. Thus he attempted to rally the Arab masses to his cause.

Today these views are becoming popular among the elite of the Gulf states. Although many people I interviewed seem restless about the threat posed by Saddam Hussein's continued rule in Baghdad, they are far more concerned and puzzled about "America's reluctance to take him out."[17] Many of the Gulf elite are concerned about the implications of Saddam's continuity and "America's cat-and-mouse game with Baghdad." They claim that this costs them in terms of domestic support among their local constituencies. The popular view in the Gulf now is that the United States is using Saddam as a bogeyman to "shove unnecessary and expensive weapons down our throats."[18] Thus today Hawali's views are more common not only in the Gulf region but also throughout the Arab world. Two factors account for the dominance of this view: the seductive simplicity of Hawali's view of the West and America's role in the Middle East and U.S. foreign policy blunders at the level of both rhetoric and tactics. For instance, it does not boost America's credibility in the region when Newt Gingrich, the speaker of the House of Representatives, visits Israel to declare his support for the anti-Arab policies of the Likud and Benjamin Netanyahu.

Towards the end of his book, Hawali describes his great dismay at the "petty bickering" (over the issue of the legality of inviting U.S. troops to Saudi territory) that has consumed the religious sheikhs and reduced the issue to technical gambits that have obscured the gravity of the situation. He calls for an end to these "useless" debates and makes five proposals:

1. The creation of a panel of competent men to study the question of Saudi Arabia's military capabilities, its strengths and its weaknesses;
2. The creation of a panel to study how Saudi Arabia can and should defend itself and its independence;
3. The formulation of a defense strategy against Western troops in the event that they should turn against Saudi Arabia;
4. The creation of a panel to study the economic impact of the war on Saudi Arabia's economy and society; and
5. The formulation of a peace initiative that would save Kuwait and allow Saddam a face-saving mechanism.[19]

Realities Behind the Gulf Crisis is a study of the geostrategic implications of the Gulf War; very little is concerned with theology or Islam. The only reference to Islam comes at the end, where Hawali emphasizes that it is un-Islamic to allow foreign non-Muslim troops to occupy the holy land of Saudi Arabia. His main concern here is with the implications of the "sinful" and un-Islamic practices that have swept Saudi Arabia as a result of Western physical presence in the country, which is usually coupled with media and cultural influence. The long-term effect of this troop presence is harmful to Saudi Arabia, its culture, and its value system. From this book alone it is very difficult for anyone to detect that Hawali is a religious activist. All that can be concluded is that he is a Saudi nationalist, not merely an Islamic activist.

U.S. Christian Fundamentalism

Central to Hawali's discussion of America's role in the Middle East is the role of American fundamentalists and their support for Israel. He presents a very long story about the role of the American evangelists in undermining Islam and Muslim rights. By focusing on the question of Palestine and Jerusalem, Hawali constructs a convincing narrative that links Israeli's policy of land confiscation, the support Israel gets from "Zionist Christian fundamentalists" in the United States, and America's approval of this policy. His discourse focuses on specific popular evangelists in the United States and their unwavering support for Israel. He refers to this group of U.S. preachers as the "Harmagediyoon" (those whose theology is driven by an apocalyptic vision of the world). Among the Armageddonist preachers Hawali discusses are Jerry Falwell, Pat Robertson, George Otis, and Mike Evans.

Hawali's description of the "Christian Zionists" is heavily based on Grace Halsell's book entitled *Prophecy and Politics* [20] and, to a lesser extent, on Paul Findley's *They Dare to Speak Out*. Hawali informs his audience that these televangelists control the hearts and minds of more than 13 million viewers in the United States. Of course, this number seems threatening to Hawali because it is greater than the combined population of the Gulf states, even though it is only about 5 percent of the American public, a fact he omits from his discussion. He then lists some of the most popular preachers, quoting some of their declarations on the issue of Palestine and Israel's claims to it.

Jerry Falwell leads Hawali's list. Hawali's interest in Falwell stems from the latter's open support for Israel in its occupation of Arab-Muslim land and his hatred of Arabs. Hawali quotes Falwell as saying "[T]he United States must support Israel not simply for Israel's sake, but for America's self preservation."[21] Falwell is also reported to have said that a Greater Israel is necessary to realize the Bible's prophecies, and thus he advocates Israel's "taking portions of present-day Iraq, Syria, Turkey, Saudi Arabia, Egypt, Sudan and all of Lebanon, Jordan and Kuwait."[22] Furthermore, Hawali presents Falwell as someone who has made it very difficult for any American to understand the Muslims and Arab issues. He quotes Falwell as portraying Arabs as anti-American and saying that there is no place for Arabs in American society because of their refusal to recognize Israel. Hawali sees Falwell as a powerful man who shapes the parameters of American politics and makes it difficult for Americans to sympathize with Muslim and Arab causes. Hawali quotes Falwell as saying "Anyone who does not support Israel is in essence standing against God."[23] Thus Falwell and his theology, according to Hawali, are very dangerous, and Muslims should be aware of militant Christian Zionism and its consequences for both their land and their faith. Hawali effectively portrays Falwell as a powerful figure who is capable of ensuring "no candidate unfriendly to Israel be elected to any U.S. office."[24] Hawali also says that Falwell is a close friend of former President George Bush (in fact, Bush is an Episcopalian and his own pastor opposed the Gulf War, although Bush may have had his picture taken with Falwell some time during his presidential campaign) and suggests that both Falwell's power and his theology are directed toward the total annihilation of Muslims.[25]

The second American evangelist to attract Hawali's attention is Pat Robertson, whom he uses to make a point about how ill-treated Islamic leaders are in Muslim countries: "You can see by yourselves which degree of influence this man enjoys, so much so that he was even able to run for president, despite the fact that he is one of the most extremist fundamentalist leaders in the USA. Politics is a forbidden realm only for the Islamic fundamentalists" (p. 48). Using this example, Hawali points out the contradictions between the so-called Islamic Arab regimes that do not encourage men of religion to run for public office and the secular Western states that encourage fundamentalists to run for even the presidency.

Mike Evans is another preacher Hawali considers. Again, it is Evans's position on the Israeli occupation of Arab land and Muslim holy places that forces Hawali to speak. He quotes Evans as saying "If Israel gave up the West Bank, it would bring destruction upon itself and upon the United States. If it gave up the West Bank to the Palestinians, this would mean refusing to believe in the promise made by God in the Torah, which would lead to the destruction of Israel and of America" (pp. 50–51).

The American Fundamentalists and the Peace Process

Hawali displays an astonishing familiarity with individual Christian fundamentalists, their organizations, and their activities. In his taped sermons and books, Hawali describes the International Christian Embassy as an organization that declares itself to be "more Zionist than the Zionists themselves." He tells his audience that these evangelical preachers are the real force behind America's support for Israel. These people, according to Hawali, "believe that if Israel does not continue to exist, the Messiah will not have a place to go back to." He describes the kind of programs these preachers and their followers support. They include support for the Israeli settlements on Palestinian land and a larger educational program that ties Christianity to Judaism (p. 53). Hawali believes that these fundamentalist Christians are a tool in the hands of the Zionists, but they also affect America's perception of the issues. In this regard, Hawali mentions the creation of a fundamentalist evangelical Zionist conference, ironically, in the same Swiss town where Theodor Herzl organized the first conference of the World Zionist Organization in 1897. Hawali reports on the resolutions issued by the conference. First, the conference considers the Palestinian Liberation Organization to be a terrorist organization. Second, it calls on the Organization of World Churches to "recognize the Torah-based tie between the Jewish people and the Promised Land, and the Torah-based prophetic quality of the state of Israel" (p. 59). Since this is what the religion teaches will happen, "Then all that happens in these disgraceful conferences [here he means the Madrid

Peace Conference of 1991] is not tantamount to a step toward peace and reconciliation, but rather it is an affirmation of faith in the false promise and a refutation of the true one, which is the essence of the whole matter"(p. 59).

Since the Christian fundamentalists believe that the fate of Palestine has been decided by God, Hawali doubts that they would accept any negotiated settlement on Palestine. He illustrates his point by quoting Evans as saying: "The word of God is not liable to be negotiated upon. Moreover, we believe that the holy books recognize Jerusalem as the only capital of Israel, and that the Jewish Messiah will come back there"(p. 52).

Hawali is puzzled that "Christians, who believe in the same Messiah as that of the Muslims, support the Jews in their claims to the Holy Land." He is also puzzled by the fact that Jews also trust Christians, given the history of persecution of Jews at the hands of European Christians. The first explanation that comes to his mind is that the Jews took advantage of the fact that Christians believe in the same book, the Old Testament, and manipulated this to gain Christian support. But this explanation is inconsistent, since Christians and Jews also share things in common with Muslims, and harmony has seldom been the result of this shared heritage.

Hawali spends a great deal of time both in his taped sermons and in *Palestine Between the Real Promise and the False One* to show the irrationality of the alliance of Christian fundamentalists and Zionists. While there are points of agreement, there are large points of disagreement between the two. On the level of agreement, Hawali explains that the Jews and Christians both believe that the Messiah will come out of Bani Isra'il and that His reign will be based in Jerusalem. They moreover agree that the date of this advent will be a multiple of 1,000. As the end of the 1990s approaches, therefore, the dream of the Christians who believe that the Messiah (Jesus) will come to kill all non-Christians in the battle of Armageddon meets the dream of the Jews, who believe that a Messiah King will come out of the offspring of David and make all peoples subject to the state of Israel. Hawali explains that in spite of the differences between the Christians and Jews on the Messiah, their hatred of Muslims unites them and makes such an irrational alliance possible.

Another irrational agreement, present at least since the end of World War II exists, between the Muslims and the Christians and Jews. Both during World War II and the Gulf War, Arabs made alliances with the West against their own interests. In both cases the West disguised its real intentions. According to Hawali, after World War II the West used the rhetoric of the Charter of Human Rights and the right of self-determination to achieve widespread acceptance among Arabs, and yet this rhetoric was merely a cover for the creation of Israel. And after the Gulf War, the mask was represented by the New World Order and international law, which served to cover the Christian-Jewish agreement termed "international détente" and to ensure that Christians and Jews would impose an unchallenged hegemony by preventing the Arabs from having chemical or nuclear weapons.

U.S. Presidents and the Christian Fundamentalists

The sheikh continues his discussion by addressing the degree of popularity enjoyed by the millenarian ideas and the belief in the battle of Armageddon among the American leadership, and in particular Presidents Jimmy Carter, Ronald Reagan, and George Bush, whose actions were, in his view, informed by such beliefs. Hawali quotes St. Paul's letter to the inhabitants of Thessalonika and some parts of the Apocalypse as being the basis for Evangelical Christians' beliefs concerning these issues. He further declares that the faith of some American presidents has led them to conceive their relationship with Israel as a special one and to see the Arab-Israeli conflict as one between David and Goliath. He mentions that Reagan believes in an Armageddon that would take place in his own lifetime. Hawali further explicates this point by quoting Paul Findley on the relationship between Reagan and the Israeli Lobby in Washington: "I turn back to your ancient prophets in the Old Testament and the signs foretelling Armageddon and I find myself wondering if . . . If we're the generation that's going to see that come about. I don't know if you've noted any of those prophecies lately but, believe me, they certainly describe the times we're going through."[26] Reagan is not the only American president to support the fundamentalists and the Israeli lobby. George Bush, too, is said to have expressed his sympathy for the Christian fundamentalists (p. 32).

One of the most representative figures in this pro-Zionist trend among U.S. presidents was Woodrow Wilson, who is reported to have declared that "it is the duty of the son of the Church's shepherd [that is, himself] to contribute by giving back the holy land to the Jewish people"(p. 39). In general, there is evidence that American Christians did not want the Holy Land to be in the hands of the Muslims as long as 25 years before Israel was created. The position of such religious presidents toward Islam has been openly hostile. Hawali quotes Richard Nixon as saying: "In the Islamic world, from Morocco to Indonesia, Islamic fundamentalism has replaced Communism as the main instrument of violent change"(p. 34). The sheikh then turns to examine the historical efforts of those who have committed themselves to the realization of the false promise and he argues that it was not Herzl who created Zionism, since "the first ones to give start to the call to reunite the Jews and to make the Torah's prophecies come true were the Christians, long before the Jews, and indeed at least four centuries before the Zionist movement"(p. 35).

Hawali and the Roots of the "False Promise"

Two main events have contributed to bringing about the rise of the powerful force that has committed itself to the realization of the false promise, namely the discovery of America and the rise of Protestantism. Hawali believes that the latter takes inspiration from Islam in its refusal of mediations between God and the believer. He argues that the translation of the Bible into German and other European languages was a major factor in the spread of the false promise and in the evolution of a new notion of the relationship between Christians and Jews—one that is contrary to the traditional Catholic enmity toward Jews. The sheikh writes that the Jews contributed to the diffusion of Protestantism because it was in their interest to do so; thus they tried to reinforce its tendency to believe in the false promise. The direct result of this Protestantism was the emergence of a Christian Zionism which dates back to the mid-nineteenth century.

Another example of this kind of "Christian Zionism" was represented by the special fund established in Great Britain under the supervision of the Archbishop of Canterbury for the "discovery of Palestine." Chaim Weizmann, the first president of Israel, also recognized the impact of this phenomenon, declaring: "Among the main reasons why the Jews succeeded in obtaining the Balfour Declaration from Great Britain concerning the creation of a Jewish national entity was the extent to which the British people were influenced by the Torah"(p. 39).

The relationship between Christians and Jews, however, has not always been so positive. Hawali notes that God cursed the Jews in the Gospel. He argues that the main reason for the presence of some animosity between the Christians and the Jews is the latter's role in killing the Messiah. This made the Jews, in the eyes of the Christians, responsible for the evils of the world; thus various "cleansing" campaigns have been conducted against them in several European countries.

Hawali and the Arab-Israeli Peace Process

Hawali's second book focuses on the Arab-Israeli peace process. This book is an edited version of two cassette tapes entitled "Filisteen Bayn al-Wa'ad al-Haq wal Wa'ad al-Muftraa" (Palestine between the true promise and the false one) that Hawali circulated earlier. The book carries the same title. While this book does not capture the resonance of the spoken sermon and audience responses, the substance of his argument is the same. Thus I will focus here on the edited narrative, which attempts to explain to Hawali's followers the main factors behind Israel's intransigence and how Muslims ought to deal with them. Hawali assumes that the key to understanding the ploys in the peace process is to analyze the American political scene and uncover the alliances between the various forces of American society and their implications for the Arab-Israeli peace process. Thus he devotes a large part of his book to discussing the religion and politics of the United States, focusing on the relationship among Christian fundamentalists, Zionists, and two American presidents and the impact of this relationship on Arab and Muslim issues. In the final section he presents an appendix that includes original documents and news reports from U.S. publications about America's commitment to Israel's security and military superiority over all Arab states combined.

In the introduction, Hawali states that his main purpose in writing a book about Palestine in the aftermath of the 1991 Madrid Peace Conference is to teach Muslims how to return to the right path and to demonstrate how Israel, backed by U.S. support for its superiority in the region, connives against the Muslims as a means to an end. The sheikh attempts to show that the Madrid conference was part of a larger Jewish design to achieve the dream of a Greater Israel. Hawali's contempt for the conference and those who participated in it is the result of "Islam being absent—or made absent—from the conference"(p. 7). The book, Hawali states, also shows the unholy alliance among the Christian Zionists (who he says are "more Zionist than the Jews themselves"), Israel, and the local Muslim governments. Through an elaborate discussion of Christian fundamentalism and televangelists, Hawali tells his audience that these people's theology advocates the destruction of Islam and Muslims.

Hawali's Views of the Peace Process

Although Hawali does not reject the idea of peace, he is very critical of the current peace formula outlined in the Madrid and the Oslo peace talks of 1993. His objections to the peace process are a mixture of serious analysis of what he calls "imperial objectives" of the West and Israel.

Hawali lists what he sees to be some of the main objectives and consequences of the peace process that was initiated in Madrid, the most prominent of which was the intended destruction of the Palestinian jihad in the territories, and the Intifada, which represented the most serious threat to Israel's security. By creating a new Palestinian entity, the wrath of the opposition will be directed against Yasser Arafat instead of Israel. Thus by pitting the Palestinians against their leadership, the power of resistance will lose its legitimacy for it is no longer directed against the occupying power but rather against the Palestinian Authority. Furthermore, Hawali warns that the peace process could lead to obstruction of "the Islamic da'wa" (Islamic mission or propagation of the faith). Hawali also warns that the peace process could destroy the Islamic movement everywhere, perhaps even in the territory stretching from Morocco to Indonesia, as Nixon once sought. The Arab force that surrounds Israel could be destroyed while U.S. and Israeli military hegemony is imposed over the entire area. This new force would prevent the emergence of any regional military power (with the excuse that under the conditions of the New World Order armies are no longer necessary). The implications of the peace process could also lead to "the modification of the local systems of education and information in order to delete all that can arouse enmity towards the Jews"(p. 66). In addition to imposing of military hegemony, Israel could impose its economic and financial hegemony as well. The culmination of the peace process may result in the Christianization and "Judaization" of the region. Furthermore, Hawali claims that the process will lead to the corruption of the region's inhabitants through the development of tourism and archeology; the former could bring drugs into the country, and the latter could encourage efforts to search for "Jewish archeological sites" all over the region, including as far deep into the Arab land as the southern Arabian peninsula. Finally, he sees the peace plan as a way of opening the doors of all the countries in the area to Jewish spies. In a footnote, he makes it clear that this analysis of both religion and politics in the United States or the peace process is not a result of paranoia or Islamists' "conspiratorial thinking," as many Westerners would like to claim. The analysis is based on "facts and figures published in the United States. This analysis is based on published books, which in turn are based on primary sources and interviews. None of this is based on exaggerations or is imaginary"(p. 27).

Hawali provides theological reasoning for his rejection of the current peace process between the Arabs and the Israelis, stating that those who follow this unjust path of peace are followers of the anti-Christ and that they are misled by false promises. Hawali urges all Islamic movements to reject this process. "Our path should be different from that followed by those who were lured by Madrid. Because of the subsequent surrenders that are likely to follow . . . our position should be a sharp rejection. Our rejection of Madrid is not the result of rigidity and stubbornness, but because of our moral and religious obligations"(pp. 56–57).

For the current process to work, Hawali suggests a substantial overhaul of the formula adopted at both Madrid and Oslo. In his appendix, he includes the texts of the Declaration of Principles, the text of the Oslo Accords, and commentary from the American press on Oslo's shortcomings. After reading his analysis and the primary texts he includes in the appendix, Hawali's ten points for reforming the peace process appear very sound, at least to his followers.

As to the suggestions put forth by the sheikh for those who want to commit themselves to counteract this "malicious" plan, the first call is to a complete reform of the Muslim community (Islah of the umma), which requires passing through the following proposals:

1. The diffusion of doctrinal awareness and true beliefs at all levels in the whole of the umma, especially as concerns the principle of companionship and competition (or friendship and enmity). The declaration of the Islamic nature of the struggle, which does not concern only the Palestinians, or the Arabs, or even only the contemporary Muslims, but rather all the Muslims, until the final hour (p. 68).
2. The revival of the message that is spread in the mosques. Since the Muslims' da'wa cannot count on satellites for telecommunication, it has to make the most of the means it has available.
3. The unification of the whole community of Sunni Muslims (ahl al-Sunnah wal Jama'ah).
4. The establishment of Islamic banks to prevent the Jewish system of riba [usury] from penetrating the region and the warning of the community of the threat posed by the will to alter its educational culture gradually. To this end, Hawali recommends teaching children those verses of the Quran and the hadith that explain the Jews' malice in order to prevent the children from ever trusting them. Diffusing in the community the hope in a true promise so that is does not fall into despair.
5. Promotion of the da'wa in the West, especially in the United States, in order to disrupt the anti-Islamic movements active there.
6. Support for the Palestinian jihad in the territories.
7. The withdrawal of Islamic money and assets currently in Western banks and funds, and using them in order to meet the true needs of the Islamic communities at home. "We have to fight against the effeminacy, squandering and emptiness in which this community lives, and mobilize all the energies of the nation (umma) against this malevolent and tentacled enemy. We are before a malicious and dreadful enemy, so that the battle will not be one between winner and loser, but rather one between who will live and who will be doomed to perish"(p. 70).

Many of Hawali's points informed both the Letter of Demand and the Memorandum of Advice.

Western Influence and the Structure of Arab Governments

Despite Arab governments' claims that they are against Western influences, Hawali argues that they have adopted Westernization at their very core.

This, according to Hawali, is but one example of Muslims giving in to Western domination. The prevalence of political systems based on the concept of popular sovereignty rather than the Islamic concept of divine sovereignty and recourse to positive laws in lieu of the Shari'a is a form of kufr (unbelief).[27] He closes the door in the face of those who argue for ijtihad (a modern interpretation of the Islamic tradition) and argues that proponents of Western secularism misuse the concept in order to cloak their political discourse in the language of Islamic reform: "It is not acceptable for them to say that they are mujtahidoun [Islamic interpreters] since they are the most ignorant of Islamic law and ijtihad has clear conditions, which they do not meet. For instead of pursuing the truth of Islamic law with pure intentions . . . they merely pick through the sources of Islamic law that are vague enough to provide justification for their desires."[28]

Hawali views Muslim "modernizers" as agents of Western cultural imperialism that must be rejected. This is because, in his judgment, these groups work to "undermine the basis of Islamic law."[29] Muslim governments should promote "those who are knowledgeable about the principles of the Islamic faith" into positions of political authority.[30] In spite of Hawali's deep misgivings about the Shi'a, this idea is not different from the institutional arrangement and the discourse of Islamic Iran.

Hawali does not contest the nature of governance in Saudi Arabia; rather, he pushes for further application of Islamic law. His critiques are devoted more to other Arab and Islamic governments than to Saudi Arabia. In his taped sermons and books Hawali makes it clear that imitating Western-style democracy or any style of governance is tantamount to accepting total Western hegemony. This for him represents a moment of defeat for Islamic law and indigenous practices. Instead, he advocates an indigenous style of governance in accordance with the Shari'a. He considers the legislative power of parliaments to contradict God's injunctions, especially if parliaments are given the sole power to legislate. He sees no difference between a parliament approving a law that is in agreement with God's rulings or rejecting it, since it is the principle that matters. The crux of the matter is not the practical outcome of this situation but the very fact that God's laws are made subject to man's whims. According to Hawali, the fact that a parliament may be allowed to decide whether to maintain or discard clearly stated injunctions, such as the prohibition of alcohol, is in itself a form of kufr, for it indicates that what exclusively belongs to God is given to man. If the parliament passed a law that prohibited the drinking of wine, it would be respected because it comes from the parliament and not because it reflects a divine injunction. Legislative power (haqq al-Tashri') thus is the domain of man, not God. This is idolatry, according to Hawali. Here Hawali's criticisms are directed to other Arab and Muslim governments; although he is generally seen as an opponent of the Saudi government, he does not criticize Saudi Arabia on this issue. For him, Saudi Arabia still governs according to the rule of Islam and may be the only nation doing so, since Hawali considers the Shi'a government in Iran a form of heresy.[31]

To provide a point of comparison to his audience, Hawali presents an admittedly very simplified description of the way positive law has dealt with the issue of political power (sultah or siyadah, here not differentiated). He explains that prior to the Enlightenment, most Europeans continued to believe that kings and emperors ruled as God's representatives. This made it inconceivable to question the rule of monarchs, whose divine origin was acknowledged even by men of religion. Europeans believed in the concept of rule by divine right. These ideas prevailed until the ideas of the Enlightenment, which in turn led to the French Revolution.

Hawali further classifies other schools of thought that emerged in contrast to divine right. He puts them in the category of schools that emphasized "social right" as opposed to "divine right." As a representative of such a school of thought, Hawali cites Jean-Jacques Rousseau as arguing that politics does not originate from an expression of divine power over people but rather from a contract between individuals and the ruler. According to Hawali, the West regarded the idea of the social contract as a great achievement; nevertheless, this idea has been used to legitimize tyrannical rule. This, he says, was because of the ignorance of the European masses at the time.[32]

Hawali further explains that with the French Revolution, the theory of the social contract dominated. It provided the first example of "attribution of sovereignty to the people, together with the power of legislating [tashri'], prohibiting [tahrim], and permitting [tahlil]." All of this, however, "is against our beliefs and against what was revealed to our Prophet." Here Hawali contends that when Muslim countries import Western laws and constitutions, they also import the principles and assumptions behind them, namely that man can create laws and acquire the right to rule. This implies that even if there is a dictatorship, it is actually the people who have sovereignty, and therefore there is "democracy" in the etymological sense of the word. However, in a democracy, where people are free to choose, the sheikh does not believe that people will choose Islam, for the very fact of making them free to choose goes against the divine ruling that demands the believer's absolute submission to divine law. This is a very important and original point. Unfortunately, Hawali does not elaborate on it in any of his published writings.

In his critique of Arab constitutions, Hawali does not mention Saudi Arabia. Most of his critique is devoted to Arab republican states and Gulf countries. He singles out Egypt as an example of the worst case. First he points to the fact that Egypt's constitution combines the French tradition and the Anglo-Saxon tradition (common law) with some elements of German and Latin American law—a combination that has nothing to do with Islam. What makes Egypt's case particularly negative, in Hawali's opinion, is the fact that most Arab countries have followed its example. He reserves some particularly harsh words to describe the cases of Lebanon (where, according to the constitution, the president has to be a Christian) and Tunisia (regarded as the country whose government has been most active in the jihad against Allah). He also criticizes the Ba'th party of Syria and Iraq, which he portrays as promoting the interests of Christians against Muslims. He specifically cites Syria; its president is not even a Muslim, in his opinion, but rather a Nuseiri and therefore a kafir (infidel). Hawali lists Kuwait, Morocco, Jordan, Tunisia, Iraq, Lebanon, Libya, Yemen, Bahrain, Algeria, and Sudan as countries in which the ruler rather than God is the source of the law.

To overhaul these systems, Hawali argues that Muslims should start with da'wa (Islamic mission and the propagation of Islamic principles) to socialize Muslims into the new system and continue with jihad (struggle) to bring Islam into government. He also counsels that the making of the first Saudi state is the model for how to build a Muslim community. Unlike other opposition leaders who would like to return to the Prophet's state in Medina, Hawali wants to return to original Saudi state of Dir'iya and the ruling coalition of Imam ibn Saud and Sheikh Mohammed bin Abdul Wahhab (1744–1811). This makes it difficult to claim that the sheikh is against the Saudi rule; clearly he exonerates the regime he is supposedly opposing. In his mind the "Islamic" Saudi state is the model that all other Muslims should follow. It is for this reason that he supports the struggle of the Islamists in Algeria against both the socialist system and the military government.

Hawali and "Jihad" against Arab Governments: The Case of Algeria

Hawali uses the case of Algeria to illustrate how the seeds of successful jihad can be cast in a society, thwarting Western domination of the political system. He believes the strength of the Algerian reform movement lies in the fact that the Algerians were able to rally a generation of 'ulama sharing the same convictions, thus forming a united body that enabled them to move the hearts and actions of the nation. "Goodness is present in every nation, but it takes united people of religion ['ulama] and patient preaching [da'wa] to bring it to light." According to Hawali, this is possible only if the 'ulama do not aim to become government officials, but rather make Islam their only goal.

Hawali sees the present wave of Islamism as a Salafi phenomenon (a return to the beliefs of the Muslim ancestors); thus it is a positive movement deserving the support of all Muslims. However, by repressing this movement, the government of Algeria has acted as an infidel (kafir). It has been helped in achieving that goal by other foreign infidels (kuffar)—those Western forces that fear the resurgence of Islam. He thus criticizes those who accuse Algerian Islamists of being only after power. Part of his criticism is directed toward the Saudi newspaper *al-Sharq al-Awsat*. This kind of unfair reporting, according to Hawali, serves only to arouse fear of Islam even among the Muslims themselves.[33]

Hawali makes a particular point of Algeria because it was a society that was once highly Westernized. Before the Algerian revolution (1954–1962), French was the language of instruction in schools and to be educated meant to be Western educated. Even the government that ruled after liberation was a secular state based loosely on Marxist ideologies and certainly committed to the idea that progress meant Westernization. That Islamists could have been poised to win an election in such a country strikes Hawali as particularly heartening, since it shows the triumph of Islam over secular values. And of course throughout the Middle East, "Western secular values" have not meant democracy and human rights but vulgar popular culture and mindless consumerism.

The Effectiveness of the Message

It is difficult to assess how many Saudis have read Hawali's books and listened to his sermons and still more difficult to assess how many agree with his position. We know that his books sold many copies, but we cannot know whether they were passed around to many readers or if they were bought but remained unread. We cannot even know the number of the tapes that were sold, much less how many people actually listened to them. However, it seems unlikely that a person would risk buying a banned tape if he were not going to listen to it, and most of the people whom I interviewed after the Gulf War had heard at least parts of Hawali's message and knew his basic arguments.

Hawali ideas, moreover, are likely to seem reasonable to most Saudis. His thorough knowledge of Islam would make these ideas seem more credible to a Muslim audience. Psychologically, people are more apt to trust new information and opinions when they come from an established authority on a subject about which they do know. This is the rhetorical device known as "appeal to authority." In addition, Hawali's message is likely to be effective both because of who he is as well as what he is saying. After all, he is a tribal Saudi who was a respected member of the religious establishment before he began criticizing the Saud regime's alliances with the West. His knowledge of the West, moreover, is likely to seem impressive to an Arab audience for three reasons. First, he provides answers to questions that many people throughout the region have pondered for many years: why the United States supports Israel when in their view both justice and wealth lie on the side of the Arabs, why the United States came to the aid of Kuwait, and why the American media is so unrelentingly anti-Muslim and anti-Arab. Many Saudis who have been abroad or discussed politics with Americans know that the commonly held explanations are inadequate. Hawali provides more complex answers. His analysis of the Christian right, for instance, provides a far more nuanced explanation of American support for Israel than the idea that "The Jews control the media." Second, his ideas are supported at times by verifiable facts. He does not just say that Westerners hate Muslims. He quotes specific influential people, from evangelists to former presidents, to prove that many important Americans have indeed publicly expressed extremely anti-Muslim sentiments. He refers to specific historical events and documents that readers and listeners, especially educated ones, would be familiar with. The power of Hawali's ideas comes from their being a synthesis of various ideas and beliefs held by Arab nationalists since the early 1960s. Of particular importance is the belief that the West, particularly the United States, is vehemently anti-Muslim and anti-Arab. And of course, everything—from the image of Arabs in American films to the remarks of prominent American legislators—confirms this view. Many Arab leaders also assume that the West is hopelessly opposed not only to Arab culture but to Arabs as human beings. We may disagree with this assumption, but we cannot ignore its local effectiveness. For instance, the "Jewish factor" in American policy in the Middle East looks different in the Arab world than it does in Washington. In the Arab world, you do not need Hawali to tell you that Bill Clinton's foreign policy advisors are primarily American Jews. Arab television and newspapers repeatedly list the names of Madeline Albright, William Cohen, Samuel Berger, Dennis Ross, Aaron Miller, and Martin Indyk as American Jews who are formulating U.S. Middle Eastern policy. The fact that these ideas are mainstream in the Arab world makes Hawali's discourse all the more effective, because he seems to have been proven right.

And finally, even the educated among his audience would be unlikely to catch Hawali's errors about European and Western history, since they would not have studied European history in detail and certainly not from a Western perspective. Thus he can, for instance, say that the anticolonial movement led to World War II without his audience being aware of the complex economic and cultural factors that led to the rise of fascism in Europe. In fact, Hawali does seem to know much more about the West than many popular Western "Arab experts" know about the Arab and Muslim worlds.

Conclusion

Sheikh Safar al-Hawali's opposition clearly is not limited to local conditions. His main grievances are actually not at all based on a direct criticism of the Saudi government and the royal family, although the Western media has often portrayed him in this way. In fact, most of his criticisms consist of external components—such as Western domination and U.S. neocolonialism—directly affecting local issues—such as the Saudi government and the royal family. Hawali's main goal is not to harshly oppose and criticize the Saudi government. He is more concerned with warning and advising the Saudi royal family about the dangers of collaborating with the West—whether it is in military dependence, as was seen with the advent of the Gulf War, or with Western imperialism and influence imposed on many parts of the Muslim world. Preventing corrupting external influence is central to Hawali's main argument about maintaining a well-defined Islamic culture. He believes that external factors, such as Western domination and influence, are directly related to local issues, such as resisting the secular liberals and the leftists within the Muslim world and specifically Saudi Arabia. Resisting foreign influences, particularly America's imposing role in the Muslim world, is the core of Hawali's call for a Saudi state "purified" from such evil and foreign influences.

What is important to Hawali's mission is not the failure of the Saudi state but the continued subordination of the kingdom to "its enemy," the United States. The weakness of the Saudi state to give in to Western influences and demands is first a problem in the character of an aggressive and evil West and second an issue to be criticized concerning the Saudi state itself. What is important to note is that Hawali's criticisms of the Saudi government are interrelated to a set of global factors that need to be addressed in totality. Whether his discourse targets such external forces, such as the American Christian right, Western domination, or American foreign policy, his arguments explain the subordination of the Saudi state not by focusing on domestic variables but by connecting the issue to external ones—such as American presence during the Gulf War and Western domination of the Middle East. Thus in a way Hawali's many sermons and speeches conclude by pointing to the West as the main problem from which other smaller problems arise and have continued to intensify locally.

Hawali is distinguished from other Saudi Islamists in that he does not question the political or religious authority of the Saudi state. While excoriating other Arab states and their constitutions for lacking solid Islamic credentials, Hawali exonerates Saudi Arabia. He chastises the Saudi elite not for its lack of religious propriety but for its failure to confront adequately the challenge of Western "cultural and moral pollution." Indeed, Hawali's belief in the impeccability of Saudi Arabia's Islamic credentials underlies his criticism of the Saudi state. Because of these unique religious credentials, Saudi Arabia bears primary responsibility for spearheading resistance in the Islamic world against Western cultural imperialism. For Hawali, the Saudi state is not doing enough to propagate Islamic faith and preserve it from the onslaught of secularism. In his taped sermons, Hawali seeks not to criticize the Saudi royal family so much as to warn it of "American and Jewish designs" in the region.

Given the international focus of Hawali's sermons, it is overly simplistic to typify him as a local opposition leader. This discussion illustrates that Hawali is not only a religious preacher but a global actor with an agenda that transcends Saudi Arabia. One of the sources of Hawali's fear is the growing global influence of American Christian fundamentalists, whose activities in the Middle East, he believes, "should be of concern to all Muslims." It is ironic that Hawali—or what he represents—also represents a major worry for Western fundamentalists. In spite of the globalized interplay between Islamist and Christian fundamentalist movements, there is an asymmetry to the relationship. Hawali and his group listen to and watch the Christian fundamentalists, but the American evangelists are unaware of the specific demands of the Islamists, much less their larger cultural context.

Hawali's views were a minority view during the Gulf War, but over time they have acquired legitimacy and popularity. When his views were a minority opinion, they may have been dangerous, especially when Saudi Arabia was facing a threat from Iraq during the Gulf War. Now that such views appear in newspaper columns all over the Middle East, apparently confirmed by America's continued support for the Likud in Israel, continued sanctions on Iraq, and insistence on Iraqi disarmament, as well as by the widely quoted anti-Arab and anti-Muslim statements of prominent Americans, Hawali no longer represents an extreme view. While such ideas may be dangerous to U.S. interests in the region, Hawali himself is not, since he is merely saying more eloquently what many people in the Middle East, citizens and rulers alike, now believe to be true. And Hawali never was a threat to the Saudi state itself, merely a loyal if outspoken critic of a regime unaccustomed to public criticism. Hawali, however, is not the whole story of Saudi opposition. He is merely a voice among many voices that range from moderate to extreme.

CHAPTER THREE

Salman al-'Auda: A Preacher from the Heartland

Brothers: the concerns and issues of the Muslim umma [nation] are not likely to progress unless they become the concerns of everyone of us. The message should be for all Muslims to elevate their thinking and sharpen their focus. These issues should not be the concerns of the preachers alone or one group of religious leaders alone. We are at a moment of transition and an Islamic revival. Our efforts will not bear fruit unless we make these issues the concern of every Muslim.

—Salman al-'Auda, "The Absent Nation," 1992

Salman al-'Auda became a prominent preacher during the Gulf War. His message was both local and global, for it addressed not only Saudi citizens but Muslims all over the world. Al-'Auda presented his message to the broader audience through cassette tapes. At the time many prominent preachers made effective use of tapes. Al-'Auda was aware that he was using a new and important medium, and he used it effectively.

Al-'Auda knew that there were both advantages and problems with tapes as a medium for bringing his message, and that of the Islamic movement as a whole, to the global audience. He devoted a whole sermon to assessing the medium.

The tapes of speeches and messages by Islamic figures are not a minor or an unimportant part of the contemporary scene in the Muslim world in general and Saudi Arabia in particular. Al-'Auda himself estimates that in Saudi Arabia, "One shop specializing in Islamic tapes has a list of 9500 separate tapes. That shops sells 60,000 a month. One popular tape sold 30,000."[1] Popular tapes are made by traditional preachers who do not criticize the state as well as by those who are more critical. Many Saudis collect these tapes just as Americans collect books. In fact, the sermons are treated as books on tape. What made al-'Auda's tapes different, however, is that both the subject and the event, the Gulf War, left people with many unanswered questions and a thirst for information. The state information agencies were silent during the first few days of the war, thus contributing to the popularity of these tapes. However, this popularity brought to al-'Auda the wrath of both the government and secular forces in Saudi society.

Who is this media-savvy and supposedly dangerous Saudi preacher? Is he a Saudi version of the Ayatollah Khomeini, as many have claimed, or is he just an ordinary preacher who has been caught in the storm of both global and local politics that are beyond both his education and his power? Does he have any power base or organization, or is he merely part of a mood of religiosity and native defensiveness that swept Saudi Arabia during the Gulf War? This chapter is devoted to answering some of these questions.

Background: from Buraydah to Riyadh and Back

Salman al-'Auda was born in 1955 in the village of al-Basr, near the city of Buraydah in the Qaseem Province of central Saudi Arabia. He comes from a modest but reputable Najdi family. Al-'Auda began his religious studies at Buraydah Institute and later specialized in religion at Saudi Arabia's religious university, Imam Mohammed bin Saud University in Riyadh (Saudis call it Imam University), where he studied both the Arabic language and Islamic jurisprudence. After finishing his degree there, al-'Auda returned to Buraydah to teach at the same institute where he once studied. After four years of teaching in there, he joined the faculty of Imam University.[2] As the analysis of his taped sermon reveals, al-'Auda's focus is not as much on religion as it is politics, domestic and international. In this regard he is part of the larger phenomenon of politicized sheikhs who are occupying a specific space in Arab politics now and changing the discourse of both Islam and politics.

Qaseem, al-'Auda's birthplace and the center of his activism, is an agricultural area that used to be an important divide between the Hail area and Riyadh. The two major towns of Qaseem are 'Uniyzah and Buraydah. Buraydah in particular made the news when local farmers protested government agricultural policies. Indeed, compared to other Saudi towns,

Buraydah is poorer and less developed than many towns even in the predominantly Shi'a areas in the Eastern Province, towns the Shi'a there feel are neglected due to the fact that those in power in Saudi Arabia are Sunnis. The Shi'a labeled them discriminatory and sectarian. However, when the small towns in the Qaseem region are considered, the discrimination or lack of development seems more a question of rural-urban division than a Shi'a-Sunni one. This point will be elaborated on in chapter 7. Other rural areas surrounding Qaseem include al-Qara'a. It is important to note that local identity in that part of Najd (central Arabia) is very strong, making it very difficult for someone from a different region to claim local identity or to have the same credibility as someone local. One example of this is the imam of King Fahd's mosque, Sheikh al-Qar'awi, who comes from a neighboring village. When he told me that he was from Buraydah, two locals sitting with us contested his claim on the basis that people from al-Qara'a, where he was born, are different from those from Buraydah. These strong ties to the place and the different tribal affiliations and 'asabiyyas (group solidarity and blood bonds) make the cohesion of any movement less successful. This is probably one reason why the Buraydah incident did not spread beyond its local setting.

In addition to its general religiosity and conservatism, the poverty of Buraydah made it a fertile ground for the elaboration of a discourse of resistance colored in religion. Critics of the royal family and the Saudi regime in general fully exploited these openings. Buraydah's poverty and conservatism provide the local context for al-'Auda's sermons. Al-'Auda was born and raised in this area, and thus his worldview is very much linked to the region's social, economic, and political problems. Although his message is broader and includes the larger Islamic world, his sense of injustice gave his message a local appeal. Attendance at his sermons in the mosque increased when he began his political sermons. He himself describes this increase in an introduction to one sermon. He says, "I admire what is happening. Yesterday there were two lines of young men in midday prayers. Now there are more than five lines. Brothers, I was called by a few housewives, some of them are elderly. . . . One woman told me . . . that neither she nor her guests ate their food last night . . . because of the arrest of the 'ulama."[3] Five lines in a mosque, no matter how big that mosque, would not be more than 100 to 200 men. Thus we have to be cautious when assessing the ability of these leaders to mobilize others during these events. However, it is possible over time that these sermons and that particular religious discourse could gain roots and provide an ideology for a resistance movement. So far it has not. Nonetheless, it is important to discuss the ideas that saturate the cultural realm of Saudi society or in this specific case, the Qaseem region.

Like other preachers in Saudi Arabia, al-'Auda used the Gulf War and the focus of the world media on Saudi Arabia to popularize some of his criticisms of the government and the society at large. His eloquence, charisma, industriousness in producing tapes that address almost every topic that arises, and ways of engaging public debate made him a symbol and a leader for what later became the Saudi opposition both at home and abroad. His taped sermons informed the activities of other Saudi groups, especially the CDLR and Movement for Reform in Arabia, two movements that I will discuss in separate chapters later. Here I discuss 15 of Sheikh al-'Auda's most important taped sermons as a way of mapping the intellectual currents that have led to the nascent Saudi resistance.

Not only did he preach and record sermons, but al-'Auda participated in writing and signing petitions to the king asking for reform. He was among the signatories of the Khitab al-Matalib (Letter of Demands), a letter that was presented to the king in 1991 asking him to reform the Saudi system of governance, namely to have a Shura Council and to reform the economic, political, and defense systems. Al-'Auda also signed Muthakerat al-Nasiha (Memorandum of Advice) a year and a half later. From 1990 to 1994, al-'Auda's name became prominent in Saudi Arabia and in Western circles interested in Saudi opposition. Due to the increased demands by various forces in Saudi society and the tension associated with the war and its aftermath, the state became disturbed. Thus the Ministry of Interior warned all preachers, including al-'Auda, not to discuss political issues. On September 11, 1994, he was called into the governor's office in Qaseem and asked to sign a document saying that he would not deliver sermons. He refused and was arrested two days later.

The Saudi opposition abroad effectively used the events surrounding al-'Auda's arrest. The opposition propagated a videotape and cassette tapes that claimed to be an actual recording of the arrest of the sheikh and what was later called Intifadat Buraydah (Buraydah uprising) by the Saudi opposition abroad, although I did not hear this expression used there myself. In 1994, the farmers of Buraydah were agitated because the government did not deliver their subsidies on time. This so-called Buraydah uprising is important to describe as a way to provide a context for both al-'Auda's ideas and his influence. The CDLR praised the Buraydah uprising, describing it as a way of highlighting the power of the opposition in the Qaseem region. The videotape of the protest march was widely circulated. Like many researchers, I accepted the videotape at face value when I started collecting my data on the Saudi opposition. I later realized that the authenticity of the tape was in question. While some of the tape seems authentic, it may have been edited to imply events that did not in fact occur. Obviously the sheikh was arrested, but it is not clear that he was arrested in a mosque while delivering a sermon, as the tape alleges. In the videotape section that involved Sheikh Salman al-'Auda a group of thobed men (i.e., men in traditional Saudi garb, "thobe") are shown gathering around a police car as the commentator describes this as the arrest of the sheikh in a mosque. A prior picture showed the sheikh's face as he delivered a speech. However, the speech could have been recorded else-where. At any rate, by local accounts, the demonstration began with a small number of people. Others gathered in the area because they were curious about what was happening, not necessarily because they wished to join a demonstration against the government. Nevertheless, the gathering ended up being a small march, and the crowd gained a momentum of its own. In so-cial science terminology we refer to this sort of demonstration as an anomie demonstration. However, since political demonstrations of any kind are very rare in Saudi Arabia, if al-'Auda was behind all that happened in Buraydah, it is very important to know about the man, his ideas, and his organization, if he has one. This is particularly true since other opposition leaders, such as Sa'd al-Faqih, the head of MIRA, consider al-'Auda as "the most influential preacher in Saudi Arabia."[4]

When I went to Buraydah and 'Uniyzah (two towns in the Qaseem re-gion) to investigate the incident, very few people wanted to talk about it as an uprising, although they did discuss Sheikh al-'Auda, his speeches, and his followers. In an interview with Sheikh Mohammed bin Otheimeen, a mem-ber of the Council of Higher 'Ulama and the most respected alim in the Qaseem region, he said that the government had managed to eliminate the reasons behind the protest and that he and many other men of religion in the area were able to quiet the youth. However, he added that if the government returned to its old ways, they might demonstrate in the same way.[5] The sheikh was also careful in his assessment of al-'Auda as a sound Sunni man of religion. Although he did not accuse al-'Auda of being heretical, Otheimeen said that "like many others, he can easily go astray at times." These comments are revealing since Bin Otheimeen is not willing to condemn al-'Auda. Dur-ing my interview with Sheikh bin Otheimeen, it became apparent that this may be the general attitude among council members. It also appears that al-'Auda, no matter how extreme he might be, is part of the conservative trend that the establishment ulama use whenever they feel that their position in government has become weaker in relation to the secular trend. The govern-ment gave the conservatives more power after arresting al-'Auda and Hawali. In a group model politics, al-'Auda and his followers functioned to maximize the interests of the establishment 'ulama and the conservative trend vis-à-vis other groups competing for the attention of the government.

The history of these movements would be incomplete without an under-standing of their intellectual aspect. Al-'Auda's tapes address various topics, ranging from "Why Do States Disintegrate?" to "Freedom of Opinion."

These tapes reflect aspects of al-'Auda's political thought, his views about the Muslim world, and his concept of the nature of Islamic governance, including the government of Saudi Arabia. In these tapes al-'Auda articulates an elaborate critique of the dominant intellectual trends in Muslim societies in general and hints at the similarities between the general condition of the Muslim world and Saudi Arabia. Al-'Auda's tone varies over time and in relation to political events. Some tapes were recorded during the Gulf crisis, others were recorded during and after the war, and many others were recorded in prison and smuggled outside. The latter are propagated by MIRA in an edited format, and their authenticity cannot be verified absolutely. However, I have relied on my own recognition of al-'Auda's voice and his rhetorical style, both of which suggest to me that he is the speaker.

In al-'Auda's early tapes, his criticism was very general, with no mention of Saudi Arabia's ruling family. The only mention of the ruling family was an indirect reference to a drunken amir (prince). After he made this charge, he was confronted by the council and made to withdraw it. In an interview, Sheikh Salih al-Luhaidan, a member of the Council of Higher 'Ulama reported: "I confronted al-'Auda and asked him to weigh this unsubstantiated accusation against the Islamic teachings he claims to know better than we do [a reference to the Council of Higher 'Ulama]. According to Islamic jurisprudence, to make such an accusation, he has to provide proof. When I confronted him with this, al-'Auda retreated and withdrew his charge."[6]

In his later tapes, however, al-'Auda has become critical of the Saudi system, usually indirectly, but sometimes directly as well. This is obvious in one of his most important sermons, entitled "Asbab Soqout al-Dewal" (Why do states disintegrate?), which constitutes his most militant critique of Saudi Arabia. Al-'Auda presents his critique as part of general lecture on the reasons behind the disintegration of any political order, using the classical sociology of the fourteenth-century Arab historian and sociologist Ibn Khaldun as the model by which to judge societies. His other most important sermon is "Al-Shareet al-Islami Ma Lahu wa Ma 'Alih" (The Islamic tape: an assessment). "Why do States Disintegrate" provides a critique of Saudi society and government, although indirectly, and in "The Islamic Tape," he faces off with one of the major leaders of the liberal trend in Saudi Arabia, Ghazi al-Qusaibi, the current Saudi ambassador to Great Britain. This sermon is a reply to a book published by al-Qusaibi during the Gulf War entitled *Hata la Takoon Fitnah* (Lest it become a reason for sedition).

Al-'Auda's Critique of the Saudi Political System

Depending on his audience and the date of the sermon, al-'Auda's characterization of Saudi Arabia's sociopolitical ills varies. In one sermon delivered right before his arrest, he sees Saudi Arabia as ripe for the type of political violence seen in Egypt and/or Algeria. Other times al-'Auda sees Saudi Arabia as an oasis of peace as long as the state reclaims its religious basis. In one sermon he tells his audience that what has befallen Egypt and Algeria is a result of dictatorship and the muffling of counteropinion and voices of dissent, although he does not blame these governments alone for the violence but also the Islamists. "Of course not only governments are guilty, but the Islamists as well. Yes, there are faults from both sides, but any society that is not based on justice and Shari'a will reach the same situation." This is a very serious warning to the Saudi government. However, he urges it to speed its process for reform. "I'm afraid that this country's future will be similar to that of neighboring countries. God's grace will only come with the reform project and justice."[7] Al-'Auda emphasizes the immediate need for dialogue, using the Algerian example to bring about this sense of urgency:

After the Muslim leaders won the elections in Algeria, and the army's cancellation of the results, the country has become mired in violence. Now after three years of killing, they call for a dialogue between bil Haj and Madani and with the Islamic movement at large. We tell all the Muslim leaders that dialogue should have occurred before these losses. . . . Do you want to drag this country to a situation similar to neighboring countries where Muslims are slaughtering each other?[8]

After making such a veiled threat to both the state and the secular forces, al-'Auda comes back to appeal to the idea of the uniqueness of the Saudi situation. Nonetheless, he believes that dialogue is the only solution. In the same sermon he continues:

This country is different. It is united under the banner of Islam not because of this person or that person. . . . This state is an Islamic state and whenever this state moves away from Islam it negates its own foundations. Our people gathered around religion. I remind the Muslim leaders that the security measures will only complicate the problem. People will become bolder. It's a dangerous situation and we have to be frank with ourselves, our rulers, and our 'ulama. Only by frank debate we can be taken out of this darkness.

He urges not only for reform but for the return of the original contract and alliance between the state and the religious forces on which the foundation of the modern Saudi state was based. In "We Are Advocates of Peace and Unity," a sermon he taped in 1991, he says, "for the unity of this land to be preserved, we have to return to fundamentals and reform our society. . . . This country can be only united under the Shari'a with the Sunna and the Quran as our only reference." He criticizes the politics of expedience where loyalty is based on the distribution of largess and money and argues for the "affiliation of the hearts and the prevalence of justice." In spite of his criticism of Saudi system, al-'Auda does not place sole responsibility on the government. Instead he says, "the issue is not one individual, neither an alim nor an official, but the whole nation. Whatever the kind of ills in this society, we should all feel responsible for them." He calls for a dialogue about many issues of concern to him and the conservative trend in Saudi Arabia and asks for freedom to air these grievances, saying: "Instead of having a dialogue with the Israelis and others, we need a dialogue at home."

In "Why Do States Disintegrate?," al-'Auda outlines 12 points that need to be addressed by the Saudi government. These criticisms were central to the reformists' camp and formed the basis for the Letter of Demands and the Memorandum of Advice. It is important to analyze this sermon as al-'Auda's diagnosis of Saudi Arabia's problems. It has the potential of clarifying his political thought and also gives us a glimpse into his political program and his vision of the alternative society he advocates. Later in this chapter I compare some of his ideas with those of other Saudi preachers.

According to al-'Auda, states disintegrate when some of the following conditions are met: 1. The state is incompatible with time and place, 2. Tyranny prevails and Shura (the Muslim system of consultation) disappears, 3. The ruler fails to devise a merit-based system for the selection of those who support him in conducting the affairs of the state, 4. The state's justice system becomes corrupt and selective, 5. No system oversees both the private and the public conduct of state officials, 6. Corruption becomes endemic in the economic order, 7. The educational system becomes corrupt, 8. Moral corruption and extravagant spending spread, 9. The ruler fails to distinguish between his friends and foes, 10. The state loses its raison d'être, 11. Outside powers conspire against the state, 12. The state suffers from internal divisions.

Al-'Auda explains the issue of state incompatibility in state and time to his audience thus:

> For the state to be unnatural in space and time is to find, for instance, a Christian state in a Muslim cultural domain or a Shi'a state in a Sunni surrounding. For instance, the Egyptians did not accept the Fatamid state. The same goes for the states in the Levant after the Crusades. This is also true of Israel, in spite of its power and its democratic claims and its propaganda. . . . This is because all these states are built in a place where it is alien or at time when it is foreign.[9]

The second reason for the collapse of a political order, according to al-'Auda, is tyranny, the absence of Shura, or when one viewpoint prevails in the society. He tells his audience that people resent those who disrespect their minds. "The pharaoh," he tells his listeners, "used to give his subjects one hundred thousand Pharaonic dinar," but the subjects hated the pharaoh because he disrespected the people's minds, interfered with their religious and intellectual freedoms, and asked them to worship him. While this statement contains historical errors, this is not the place to argue them. What we are concerned with here is not historical accuracy as much as al-'Auda's strategies for mobilizing his audience into criticizing the government. The implied comparison between the current Saudi state and his imagined pharaonic state would not escape the audience.

He further explains that the Islamic state of the Prophet that used Shura as the basis for governance was very successful. It was followed by "other Shura, not democratic, states during the rule of the first four caliphs." The fact that a government is not democratic, according to al-'Auda, does not mean that it is authoritarian. The states that kept the spirit of the Shari'a, such as the Ummayad, the Abbasid, and the Ayubids, continued. However, the ones that broke away from Islam, such as the Ottoman Empire, were destroyed due to the absence of Shura and the absence of constitutional life. Here al-'Auda fuses the language of constitutionlism with that of Islam. He tells his audience that the collapse of the Soviet Union was a direct result of dictatorship. The same goes for the Iran of the Shah. However, al-'Auda does not have any good words for the Khomeini regime that followed in Iran. He says, "After the Shah's dictatorship, the authority went to another dictator, Khomeini, who ruled the people like a pharaoh." In this segment he praises the style of governance in Europe and the United States and describes it as more stable than both communist states and modern Arab and Muslim states. "However, we differ with these states in the frame of reference. They think that the nation is the source of all authority and legislation and we think that Shari'a is the source. Nonetheless, we share with them the respect for the individual. We differ with the pharaonic model and the communist model because of their contempt for the individual." He contrasts his government's handling of public opinion during the Gulf War with that of the United States. "If we are to contrast the modern Muslim states with the United States of America, for example, we realize that America gauged public opinion before going to war with Iraq, but in the Muslim countries there was no respect for public opinion."

The third reason for the collapse of a political order, according to al-'Auda, is that the ruler chooses incompetent advisors and subordinates. He argues for a system of selection of those in government based on merit. He tells his audience about a joke told about Nasser of Egypt. When Nasser asked a donkey in the zoo why he accepted being in a zoo rather than being free like other donkeys, the donkey answered, "I do not need freedom. Here

I eat well as long as I don't make a lot of noise or create disturbances." Nasser then declares that this donkey would make a good member of the People's Assembly. This joke was later repeated in Saudi Arabia about the Shura Council during its first term. Humor is central to al-'Auda's tapes; he uses it to break the somber mood of his sermons.

He also recites stories about the fate of Anwar Sadat. Sadat's assistants did not tell him what was actually happening in Egypt, and later he was surprised by the demonstrations against him. This was part of the problem that led to his being killed in a military parade. "When rulers bring hypocrites closer to them and marginalize those who are honest and qualified, the country is heading for trouble," al-'Auda says. By hypocrites, he apparently means the liberals and secular forces in Saudi society. He would rather have the state depend on religious people like him as advisors, instead of the U.S.-educated technocrats.

Another reason for the disintegration of the political system is when the justice system becomes selective and arbitrary. This point will be elaborated even further when we discuss al-'Auda's views of human rights in Islam. Al-'Auda starts this section by quoting the twelfth-century theologian ibn Taymiyyah as saying that God is behind a just state, even if it is an infidel state, and that God undermines a tyrannical state, even if it is a Muslim one. "Justice is the foundation of rule," al-'Auda says.

The fifth reason for the destabilization of a state is the absence of a system that oversees the behavior of government officials both in the private and public realms. Al-'Auda devotes part of this section to the second Muslim caliph, Omar ibn al-Khattab, who insisted on what we call today transparency in almost all the activities of his civil servants. Al-'Auda's major criticism of Saudi Arabia is that its information system does not reflect its Islamic nature. "If we want to be well intentioned we would say that there is an absence of a system that oversees this ministry." Al-'Auda gives a few figures about the programs on Saudi television. He says, "Twenty-five percent of the Saudi media programs are religious. The question then is what do they broadcast or publish the rest of the time. I hear music, songs, plays, and other things. This is all due to the absence of censorship system." Like the rest of the preachers of Saudi Arabia, al-'Auda is extremely ambivalent on the issue of freedom of speech. He wants the state to censor all voices that are different from his vision of the Saudi society. He wants cassette tapes to be uncensored, but he thinks the satellite dish brings cultural pollution. He urges the state to weed out the secularists from the Saudi media and information system, and yet he accuses al-Qusaibi of doing the same thing in urging the state to take action against the Islamist preachers. This area is very indicative of the situation of the Saudi opposition. Because the movement is very recent, it lacks clarity on politically and culturally contested values, such as freedom of expression and human rights. This ambivalence harms the movement's credibility both inside and outside Saudi Arabia. The leaders of this movement, including al-'Auda, appear to want freedom of expression for a comparatively narrow range of Islamic criticism of the government, but certainly not for all points of view, especially views they regard as secularist or heretical.

One of the most popular critiques of the Saudi state after the war is what al-'Auda mentions sixth: that the Saudi economy will suffer greatly unless the state takes on a serious program of restructuring and privatization. The focal point of this critique is that the Saudi economy is mired in corruption, bribes, and extravagant spending. Al-'Auda launches a serious attack on the monopoly of certain families in business, referring, by implication, to those families with connections to the royal family. While many Saudis feel that their living conditions and salaries are far better than those in neighboring countries, al-'Auda tells them that this is the wrong way to judge the quality of life. The quality of life should not be measured by salaries or how many Saudi riyal the average person makes, but by the purchasing power of that riyal. Beyond these points, al-'Auda's economic knowledge stops; he uses no specific evidence of inflation or other economic indicators to support any of his claims.

Al-'Auda sees the rise of secular education as the source of all ills in Saudi Arabia; this is his seventh point. In spite of the obvious religiosity and conservatism in Saudi Arabia, al-'Auda accuses the society of religious laxity due to the want of religious material in the school curricula. Clearly, he is discussing primary and high school, for there are three religious universities in Saudi Arabia. Indeed, many Saudi liberals consider graduates of these religious universities to be the source of the revivalist movement in Saudi Arabia. Saudi officials and liberals alike argue that lack of technical skills in a globally integrated economy will leave graduates of the religious universities unemployed, which will in turn lead to more criticism of the government colored in religious language.[10] Nonetheless, al-'Auda sees Saudi affluence as driving a culture of extravagance and moral corruption. He chastises the state for following liberals' advice. The state's inability to differentiate between friends and foes, he argues, is the heart of the problem. In his view, the religious people are the friends of the royal family, because the state was based on the intertwining of religious authority and royal power. Thus indirectly, like most men of religion in Saudi Arabia, he is asking the state to recruit more religious people into government at the expense of secular technocrats. Competition to win favors with the ruling family appears to be at heart of the conflict between the secular trend in Saudi Arabia and the religious one.

His ninth point focuses of the foundations of the state. If these foundations are eroding, then the state is likely to collapse. This is an indirect warning to the royal family that a gap is growing between the royal and the religious people in the society. Since the state was a marriage between the royal family and the religious people, those in power should think twice about undoing the foundations of the state. Al-'Auda sees Saudi Arabia as a religious state with a mission: to propagate Islam. Anything less is a violation of the contract between the religious elements of Saudi Arabia and the royal family. In his tenth point, al-'Auda indirectly criticizes the involvement of Americans in the affairs of Saudi Arabia, which he sees as another variable that might contribute to the collapse of the Saudi state. Finally, he warns of internal divisions within Saudi society. This warning is not as consistent in the rest of al-'Auda's sermons, in which he argues for a dialogue between the liberals and the conservatives.

Saudi Nationalism and al-'Auda's Religious Discourse

Although al-'Auda is considered to be one of the harshest critics of the regime, he is nonetheless a Saudi nationalist at heart. His conservative nationalism is very clear in two sermons, "Jazirat al-Islam" (The island of Islam) and "Qadar al-Allah fi Hathehi al-Jazerah" (This island and God's will). (Al-'Auda uses the word "island" to refer to the Arabian peninsula.) In the first sermon, al-'Auda emphasizes Saudi Arabia's unique identity, stating that when God chose it as the birthplace of Islam, it was no accident. The wisdom of this choice is based on the quality of its people; according to al-'Auda, Satan failed to win over the people of the peninsula, and thus it remained the land where only God is worshiped and will remain so forever. God also secured the future of the people of the area by placing the riches of the world (oil) beneath them. Al-'Auda further emphasizes that God wanted it this way as long as the land was kept for worship and remained free from infidels. Al-'Auda cites certain sayings by the Prophet that support a view of a kingdom free from non-Muslims. This view is part of general Saudi response to non-Muslim residents, namely Western experts and south Asian workers. Thus al-'Auda uses a political issue, foreigners and their social behavior, which many conservative forces in Saudi Arabia see as a form of cultural pollution, as part of a religious argument. In al-'Auda's imagination, Saudi Arabia and its two holy mosques represent the center of the universe. Every event that takes place in Saudi Arabia has cosmic ramifications. His view of Saudi Arabia is akin to the American Christian right's view of Israel, which assumes that all events relating to the end of the world will take place there.

Since the coming of Islam, al-'Auda argues, the age of Jahilia (ignorance) has gone forever from this land. This was further insured after the coming of the Mowahiddoon movement (a movement that aims at purifying Islam from any cultural practices unrelated to the purity of the faith). This movement was led by the eighteenth-century Muslim reformer Sheikh Mohammed bin Abdul Wahhab. The mission of the Saudi state is to ensure the continuity of this movement and its form of pure Islam. Tawheed (God's oneness) as a doctrine is the main pillar of Saudi society. In spite of its imperfections, Saudi Arabia is still a place where men enjoin doing good and forbid doing evil, which is incidentally the motto of the morality police, the mutawaeen. Al-'Auda is proud of the Islamic research coming out of Saudi Arabia to teach the rest of the Muslim world. Like the government and its officials, he emphasizes the image of Saudi Arabia as an oasis of peace. He alerts his audience to the difference between the reformist movement and what has become known as "Islamic extremism." "We should not confuse the growing of beards with extremism," he says in "The Island of Islam." "This land has been saved from extremism because of its pure tradition." With regard to cultural questions, al-'Auda's discourse is highly xenophobic. He argues that to protect Saudi Arabia from any form of cultural pollution that might infect the pure faith, Saudis should work hard and pressure the government to cleanse the place of non-Muslims (foreign experts, servants, and drivers, etc.). In "This Island and God's Will," he also wants the government to expel what he calls al-Rafida (the rejectionists), a reference to the Shi'a of the Eastern Province. In "The Island of Islam" he reemphasizes the same concepts: Saudi Arabia is central to this world, and its safety depends on the continuation of the Wahhabi revivalist movement. "Anyone who tries to do harm to what is between the two mosques will suffer the curse of God," he says. This is an indirect condemnation of the earlier movement led by Juhaiman al-'Utaibi and his takeover of the Grand Mosque. Al-'Auda emphasizes verses from the Quran that portray the mosque as a place of peace. In this regard al-'Auda is not different from any Saudi speaking about Saudi Arabia.

The desert for al-'Auda works as a natural barrier protecting Saudi Arabia from external invasions and from the cultural pollution of Byzantium and Persia. He reminds his audience that God made the Saudis the custodians of the world treasures. (Oil is but one example.) Al-'Auda also pushes a line of racial superiority, unprecedented in Saudi revivalist thought, claiming that the people of Saudi Arabia are strong in physique and mental abilities because of environmental conditions. Thus they are capable of invading the world, in al-'Auda's view. "The whole world cannot do without the peninsula, but the peninsula can do without the rest of the world," he says in "The Island of Islam." The Arabs are better because of their language, their minds, and their abilities to memorize, he adds. This racialist discourse is different from the discourse of almost all religious preachers, both inside and outside Saudi Arabia. It may be a response to the discourse of the expatriate community in Saudi Arabia who see Arabs as inferior. The power of this discourse comes from the fact that al-'Auda uses religion to sanctify a racial message that otherwise would have remained within the zones of local resentment. However, this ability to color local political issues and turn them into religious ones, a device that makes people feel moral and patriotic about their xenophobia, makes al-'Auda both appealing and dangerous.

Al-'Auda is certain that nothing will shake the stability of the kingdom. "The future of this place is known, because the Prophet has said that Mecca will never be invaded by external forces," he continues. Thus in al-'Auda's imagination, Saudi Arabia is a well-defined place. The Saudi state with its current borders and its Islamic doctrine that enjoins good and forbids evil is the place where he is most comfortable. His critique of the government focuses on its ability to do more; nonetheless, he sees Saudi Arabia as the place that will teach other Muslims the purity of Islam. Like most Arab nationalists, al-'Auda is still trapped in the modern concept of nationalism, even if his nationalist tendencies are articulated in the language of Islam and Islamic revivalism. In "We Are the Advocates of Peace and Unity," al-'Auda sees Saudi Arabia as a religious state with a mission: to propagate Islam.

Al-'Auda and the Saudi Secular and Modernist Trend

Some of al-'Auda's tapes are part of the larger debate in Saudi society between the modernist/secularist trend and the conservative/traditionalist trend. The debate started over a relatively safe issue, modernity and it implications for Muslim societies, particularly Saudi Arabia. The clash between the liberal and the conservative trend in Saudi Arabia began before the Gulf War. I would like to use the year 1987 as a starting point for this clash; although the divide between the liberals and conservative in Saudi society started earlier, the actual articulation of this clash in public did not begin until 1987. At that time actors in Saudi public discourse, namely intellectuals, started to take sides. Newspapers became known as either liberal or conservative. However, the story did not heat up until the publication of Awad al-Qarni's book *Al-Hadatha fi mizan al-Islam* (Modernity on the Islamic scale) and the taped speeches of Sa'eed al-Ghamedi, entitled "Al-Hadatha" (modernity) (see Chapter 1). Al-'Auda's "Islamic Tape: An Assessment" is a continuation of this conflict that is central to the rise of Saudi dissent.

Al-'Auda's "Islamic Tape" is devoted to an attack on one of Saudi Arabia's foremost secular icons, Ghazi al-Qusaibi, a poet, diplomat, and staunch ally of the royal family. This sermon is a response to a series of articles published by al-Qusaibi during the Gulf War in *Sawt al-Kuwait*, a now-defunct newspaper published from London during the Gulf War. The articles were col-

lected in a well-known book entitled *Hata la Takoon Fitnah* (Lest it becomes
a reason for sedition). In this book, al-Qusaibi accuses the religious right of
attempting to undermine the state, calling them small Khomeinis and Saddamists (supporters of Saddam Hussein). The basic motive for al-Qusaibi's
writings, al-'Auda sarcastically comments, was to "protect the religion and
prevent sedition and divisions within society." As for the modernists in this
society, they are described as "those who are for unity." Al-'Auda devotes
much of his sermon to ridiculing al-Qusaibi and his "pretentiousness." He
uses the tape to refute al-Qusaibi's ideas that the tapes are seditious and instead suggests that the modernists are interested in stifling freedom of opinion. He accuses al-Qusaibi of double standards: "If you are critical of the
Islamic tapes, why aren't you critical of those who embrace colonialism and
propagate Western ideas?" he says. He tells his audience that since the secular forces control the press, the Islamic forces have two things left: the tape
and the mosque.

As a response to al-Qusaibi's idea that the preachers should stay out of
politics, al-'Auda points out that Islam and politics have always been interrelated and that if the modernists want the clerics to concentrate solely on
matters of religious ritual, they will have to abandon centuries of Islamic tradition. Thus he uses this to accuse al-Qusaibi of deviation from religion.
"Don't you know that by saying this you have canceled the fatwas (religious
opinions) of many of the religious leaders that were issued in matters related
to life?" he says. He then points out that if the modernists wish the clerics
to speak only of religion and not social and political issues, they should do
the same and speak only on topics within their own area of expertise. He
points out that al-Qusaibi, who claims to be a poet and literary critic, has
written on economics, industrialism, health, and international relations. He
also claims that al-Qusaibi "wrote a poem supporting Saddam during his
war against Iran, ignoring Saddam's massacre of the Muslim Kurds and the
killing of Sunni 'ulama without any guilt or regret." He goes on to say that
al-Qusaibi "insinuates that the speakers of these tapes are a continuation of
the Baghdad broadcasting. . . . Why do you attack the Islamists and call
them fundamentalists and Saddamists, terms used by the Western enemies?
You call us people who want to rule. You claim that al-Turabi [of Sudan]
wanted power and called us similar to him. But we ourselves are against Saddam Hussein. Some of those connected to the Islamic movement are supportive of Saddam. But I talked about this and called them those who were
misled by the rhetoric of the Ba'th party."

Al-'Auda claims that in an interview with Okaz, al-Qusaibi advocated
"women's driving and exposing their bodies." He then attacks al-Qusaibi's
poetry as immoral. He quotes some explicit poetry (selecting passages sure
to outrage a conservative audience) and, after quoting them, asks God's

forgiveness. "I quote to you these rotten words in these sacred places just to show to you who is speaking and who is dangerous." He then turns the argument around to claim that it is al-Qusaibi who is dangerous and seditious. "Why are not you against the poets like Nizar Qabani who makes fun of God and who is a self-declared atheist? He is against this nation. How can you support Taha Hussein who doubts the historical existence of Ismael and Ibraheem?"

Although some of al-'Auda's arguments do have larger implications for Muslims in general, most focus on the specific charges that al-Qusaibi has leveled against him, turning them around to criticize al-Qusaibi for the same failings. In essence, the tapes sound like one side of a personal quarrel between two men with different political opinions, the sort of dispute that in the West would have led to an angry exchange of letters to the editor. The main difference is that in Saudi Arabia these conflicting opinions cannot be presented to the same audience because of the restrictions on the press.

Al-'Auda continues, in "We Are Advocates of Peace and Unity," using other Muslim countries as examples to show the danger of the secular trend and effect of adopting Western values in social, religious, and political spheres. Three Muslim countries where Western liberal thought and values have taken root are Egypt, Algeria, and Tunisia. The result of this is dangerous for the Islamic faith. Al-'Auda cites the Cairo Conference as but one outcome of this trend of secularization. "Dear brothers, the issue is that our religion, our values, and our teachings are under attack. Some 17 billion dollars were devoted for this conference to subvert our religion and limit the Muslim population to weaken the umma. This is all done publicly in Cairo in a conference that includes Jews, Christians, and unbelievers to sign a document that supports abortion and premarital sexual relations." Al-'Auda portrays these activities as the source of all evil in the Muslim world. It is not religious extremists who are responsible for social decay and the collapse of political orders, but leaders and elites who denounce their Islamic values in favor of Westernization and secularization. Thus he denounces the leaders of these countries who champion Westernization, which is nothing but "a code word for the destruction of Islam and the Islamic movement." He warns Saudis that the outcome could be the same if they allow the secular forces to flourish there. He asserts that in Tunisia and Algeria, "the government takes every religious element out of the school books and propagates vice instead of a virtue." On the tape, the audience's outrage is audible. He further reports that in these countries government money is devoted to killing preachers and to suppressing Islam. "Women who walk around veiled are exposed in the street. . . . In Tunisia women are fired from their jobs because they are Muslims and veiled."

To al-'Auda, the consequences of modernity and secularization are the imprisonment and torture of those who believe in Islam. Indeed, one of his main points is that throughout the Muslim world, Muslim conservatives like himself are being silenced by secular governments. According to al-'Auda, this practice is beginning in Saudi Arabia. It all begins with information, he reports; the Saudi press "practices the destruction of our young minds." This destruction begins with replacing God's teachings with man's teachings. In a conservative and religious society like Saudi Arabia, the consequences of modernity are indeed frightening and fuel the anger of the traditional forces against secularists such as al-Qusaibi. The main surprise about the Saudi response is that al-Qusaibi has not yet been declared an apostate who, like Salman Rushdie, "deserves to be killed for his ideas" according to al-'Auda. The angry responses of al-'Auda's audience seem to indicate that he has convinced them of the danger of secularization and Westernization and enraged them about "the dirty tactics of the secularists whose sole purpose is to destroy Islam from within."

Al-'Auda and the Question of Islam and the West

To begin with, al-'Auda is very suspicious of anything remotely relating to the West. He accuses the West of ignorance of Islam and Arab culture and of conspiring against the region. Sometimes, however, he praises Western style of governance, whenever it serves his own purpose and provides a point of contrast to Saudi rule. He admires democracy but not for Saudi Arabia; for Saudi Arabia he wants a theocracy. Indeed, from his taped sermons a love-hate relationship between al-'Auda and the West can be discerned. He certainly condemns Western culture as morally corrupt and backward, but Western style of governance is, in his eyes, closer to Islam than the current autocratic governments of the Arab world. He is also very critical of researchers in the West who study the Muslim world and Islamic revival. In "The Islamic Tape," he says: "The Western discussion of the taped sermons has focused on comparing Saudi Arabia with Iran and suggested that these tapes might lead to an overthrow of the Saudi government, just as the tapes of Khomeini helped to undermine the Shah's regime." Al-'Auda dismisses this suggestion with an appeal to Saudi nationalism: "In the West . . . they do not know the difference between good places such as Saudi Arabia and a Shi'i country such as Iran. Here the Sunni school dominates. There are historical differences between the two countries. Iran is a country full of problems, whereas this country is the land of the Holy Mosque. It is the land of peace. Comparing Iran to Saudi Arabia is like comparing wine with milk." He criticizes Western governments for various reasons; some concern U.S.

policy vis-à-vis the Israeli occupation of Palestinian land; others relate to the West's selective use of human rights to advance political interests.

Unlike Hawali, al-'Auda did not devote a book to the question of Palestine; rather he addresses the issue as part of the larger issue of the West's violent campaign against Muslims. In answer to a question from his audience, al-'Auda replied: "The issue of Palestine is with us every day. Suppose that the massacre at the Mosques happened against Americans or any other group. We would have seen warships cruising the area. We Muslims are forced to suffer pain without complaints because our complaints are annoying to those who are torturing us. Our blood in Palestine is seen as the cheapest blood. But the nation is becoming more aware. This is obvious in Muslim support for the Bosnians. The world will gradually become aware of Muslim pressure."

He also suggests that the West's supposed concern for human rights is part of a double standard, stating in "The Islamic Tape":

> The West does not care about the life of Muslims. Even when they talk about human rights, they are talking about the rights of White people, about American and European Christians. As for Muslims, the West does not care. It would be disturbing to the West to know that the Muslims represent one-fifth of the world population. But the West would like to see us as numbers only, not as human beings. The West has succeeded in creating divisions among Muslims. This is why we don't sympathize with other Muslims. Muslims are called Gulfis, Levantines, Egyptians, Kurds, etc. This fanaticism about race is very dangerous. Take the Kurds for instance. They are a group of Muslims who contributed a great deal to Islam. It is enough to mention Salah al-Deen al-Ayubi and the Ayubid state. Now we see the Kurds as enemies because the colonial powers wanted us to believe so.

Al-'Auda admires the West and its style of governance whenever he speaks of freedom of expression. "You all know the kind of freedom of opinion in France, Britain, Germany and the United States of America. Unfortunately, in Israel there is more freedom than we find in many Arab states," he states in "Freedom of Opinion." He reminds his audience that in these countries, freedom of opinion is not a source of discord but rather a source of unity and strength. He would like Saudi Arabia to have a similar system, but within the confines of the Shari'a (Islamic jurisprudence). He disapproves of freedom of religion or any freedom of opinion that contradicts his opinion. "We don't want freedom of expression that allows one to openly embrace heresy, but freedom of opinion that encourages the reform of our society and the promotion of public good." Again the notion of public good is defined as what is good for Muslims. Of course Saudi Arabia does not have non-Muslim minority, except for the foreign workers. Al-'Auda also uses examples from Islamic history that support his point, namely his right to criticize the regime. The example of Omar ibn al-Khattab, the second Muslim caliph, is frequently cited by Islamic activists in the region to maximize their zone of freedom vis-à-vis the ruler. Indeed, Omar allowed ordinary Muslims, including women, to criticize him to his face. "The main point is that throughout Islamic history, criticism of the ruler has been an honored tradition as long as it falls within the confines of the teachings of the religion," al-ʿAuda argues. Many examples in Muslim history support both a liberal view of governance and a totalitarian one.

Human Rights and Islam

Instead of addressing the issue of human rights directly, al-ʿAuda's discourse is entangled in the politics of the region. In "Al-Tanseer fil Khaleej wa Shibh al-Jazeerah" (proselytizing in the Gulf and the Arabian Peninsula), taped in 1992, he addresses far-ranging issues, from the Western powers and their policies and their double standard regarding Arabs and Muslims, to Christian missionaries and their history of proselytizing attempts in the Gulf, to a possible conspiracy by the United Nations to undermine Muslims and Islam. Thus al-ʿAuda's views on human rights cannot be considered without addressing how he presents these issues to his audience. It is very important to note that al-ʿAuda is different from other Saudi preachers in this regard. Other Muslim preachers and activists outside Saudi Arabia have argued the compatibility of Islamic ideas of human rights and the Universal Declaration of Human Rights. Thus, what matters here is how al-ʿAuda presents the issue of human rights to his Saudi audience and to what degree the discourse of human rights, local or universal, serves the purpose of a political movement. As we will see, al-ʿAuda confuses the political practices of some Western states with the philosophical and legal documents concerning human rights. Apparently he is unaware of the distinction and cites the political abuses of some Westernized Third World countries as if they were part of the intellectual and moral concept of human rights. In "Islam and Human Rights," he says: "The issue of human rights is an old one and came with almost all [our] revelations. Those who are championing it [in the West] did not know about human rights until the French revolution, which freed them from their medieval ideas." He goes on to say that after World War II, the human rights declaration was signed by all states, including the United States, whose population was then racially segregated, with many basic human rights denied on the basis of skin color. "Our problem with human rights as it stands now is that it is a tool used by powerful states to attack weaker ones." Furthermore, according to al-ʿAuda, it is difficult to discuss Islam now given that the West knows only stereotypes and its media propagate an image of Islam as the religion of "polygamy and jihad, which they translate as violence." The West portrays Islam as a religion that does injustice to women and a religion in violent confrontation with others. He observes, "We cannot learn human rights from an infidel world [the West] that buried more than 80,000 people alive and burned many more." This is a reference to Nazi Germany and its practices.

Al-'Auda is highly critical of the notion of rights when it comes to the freedom of expression by religious forces, which he believes are abridged by most human rights groups. He continues: "Human rights have become the exclusive domain of secular forces. . . . We as preachers are excluded from the human rights debate." He argues that there are many Muslims who suffer from human rights abuses all over the world. Many Muslims, according to al-'Auda, are robbed of their humanity daily. He cites Bosnia and Palestine as prime examples.

In Islam "God elevated humans. . . . If we look at Islam's legacy, we will realize that it was kind to the weak: the slaves, women, orphans, and the feeble-minded. All these issues are addressed by the Prophet in his farewell speech [Khotabat al-Wada'], long before the West knew of the concept of human rights." Al-'Auda further argues that the ruler must protect the rights of the citizens to have food, to travel, to study, and to work. "If the ruler does not facilitate these things and provides obstacles instead, then he is abusing his people's rights." For al-'Auda, this idea is enough to silence any Western criticism of the way Islam is interpreted in different parts of the Muslim world and its relationship to the Universal Declaration on Human Rights.

Al-'Auda continues, outlining what he considers some basic differences between human rights in Islam and those signed by the international community. First, there is the moral difference between rights and freedom. Islam came from God and thus takes into account God's order, which is not something that one has a choice in. Women's modesty should not be infringed upon in the name of freedom. "Even in the West you have these examples. In France, for example, they took a film company to court because it offended public morals and the sensibility of the French [He does not give the specifics of the case]. Here we have the Islamic laws that we must not offend, not merely habits, customs or sensibilities."

Another difference is the freedom to change one's religion. In Islam changing religion is not permitted. "In the issue of religion we should take power relations into account before we discuss this issue. The Christian West can exploit the hunger and poverty of Muslims in different places in the world and convert them to Christianity. So it is not a simple issue of freedom of religion." Again, he does not provide any specific examples of Muslims being pressured into renouncing their religion, nor does he explain how this is comparable to Islam's not permitting people to change their religion.

Al-'Auda continues: "We differ from the West on the issue of woman's rights. We see that both men and women have rights that are different from each other. There are rights for men that women do not enjoy and there are rights for women that men do not enjoy. They are separate sexes. Women are equal to each other and men are equal to their counterparts. We talk a lot about what women should do toward their husbands, but we do not talk what husbands should do toward their wives." It is interesting that he does not specify which rights each sex enjoys and seems to sidestep the question of whether men and women are equal, and yet does suggest that the Islamic discussion of women's rights has not focused enough on women's rights as opposed to their duties.

In another sermon, al-'Auda is critical of the Cairo Population Conference and sees it as a conspiracy used by the West to undermine Muslim values in the name of human rights. He says: "Dear brothers: the conspiracy now is after the eradication of Islam. It is not attacking the extremists. It is not an issue sponsored by few governments but by the United Nations. All Muslim states are part of this organization. They abide by its rules and regulations and its decisions. The UN sponsored the Population Conference in one of the most populous Muslim countries: Egypt."[11] The aims behind this conference, al-'Auda believes, are to propagate vices such as premarital sex and make it a right for everyone. His views of the UN and its impact on Muslim societies are:

> The U.N.-propagated law will be binding for everyone. Thus a woman could complain to the U.N. if her son prevented her lover from living with her. All human rights organizations would be on her side. The conference would also make abortion legal as a way of covering up immoral sexual relation and of killing babies. This conference also equates men and women in matters concerning inheritance, which violates our belief system. This will be part of human rights and the countries that sign this document will be obliged to follow these laws. This is all theoretical, brothers. Let me also tell that the media is practicing the same role without telling us publicly that they do the same thing: propagating values against our religion. Yes, the ministers of information didn't meet and permit premarital sex, but their media agreed to show forbidden relations and pictures that reveal women's legs, thighs and breasts. And I say very clearly it shows even vaginas. It is to be shown here in this country near the house of God in Mecca. And this happens at a time where those who advocate religion are being harassed.

It is not clear here if al-'Auda is offering his interpretation of an actual event, or if he is simply repeating a rumor. At any rate, it seems highly unlikely that such a film would be shown in Saudi Arabia, unless he is speaking of privately circulated (and illegal) pornography.

The same issues are raised in "Islam and Human Rights," the sermon he delivered especially to address the issue of human rights. In one section al-'Auda confuses the issue of human rights with the policies of certain Western states in the Arab and Muslim world. He chastises the West for "denouncing religion as a reason for discrimination, and then insisting that the president of Lebanon should be a Christian." He also argues that the theory of human rights as articulated in the West and the practice of human rights are two different things and that listeners should not be mislead by ideals. He criticizes Western states as hypocritical: "At the same time we listen to them talking about turning the other cheek and the tolerance of Jesus, we see them discriminate against immigrants in France and Germany." This is not the place to argue whether al-'Auda's understanding of Christianity is right or wrong; what matters is what he preaches and who is listening to the message. Throughout his discourse, al-'Auda sees Islam as a superior tradition; if the West has anything to teach Muslims, he believes, it should rectify its own internal problems before preaching to outsiders.

The issue of double standards is also central to al-'Auda's strategy of discrediting the Western concept of human rights. He tells his audience: "The same U.S. that interferes to protect the Shi'a in southern Iraq does not interfere when Muslim rights are abused in Bosnia and Palestine." He tells his listeners that they suffer from human rights abuses by the West directly and indirectly under a government that allies itself with the West.

He urges his audience to have their own organization to advocate for the human rights of Muslims. "As preachers," he says, "we should be advocates of the rights of those who have been wronged. We should also have freedom of expression and information to expose these violations."

How to protect Muslim rights both at home and abroad? Al-'Auda suggests the independence of the judiciary and separation of power as a first step. In this, interestingly, he would like Saudi Arabia to emulate Western models. He says: "In the West the parliament checks the power of the executive." He also suggests that the Saudi press could work as watchdogs. Good reporting can provide protection to human rights. There also has to be an ombudsman, something that has a long tradition in Islam. He also refers to al-Hisba—that is, the concept that everyone in the community has the right to bring suit against the government and guide it toward the Islamic way:

> We have to teach people their rights and their duties. . . . We need also a critical press. We have to build an organization to defend the rights of Muslims. The current organizations for human rights are controlled by the West. We should have Muslim organizations and we should have studies about human rights in Islam. The 'ulama also should show people what their rights are and guide this process.

Without these changes in the state and society, al-'Auda believes that the future of the Muslim world is bleak.

Islam and Normalization with Israel

Israel and the peace process between the Arabs and Israelis are central themes in al-'Auda's discourse. Unlike Hawali, he uses taped sermons rather than books to discuss the relations between Arabs/Muslims and Israel. Al-'Auda is very suspicious of any Jewish diplomatic move. He sees it as part of a larger strategy of subjugating the Arabs and Muslims and redrawing the maps of the region. One issue that concerns him is the discourse of normalization of relations between Arab states and Israel that dominates liberal circles in the Arab world. In a 1992 sermon entitled, "Normalization," he defines "normalization" as "reorienting the Arab and Islamic mind toward the Jews and the relations with them."[12] That is, he sees those who are calling for normalization of relations as people who want to brainwash the Arab public and make them forget Israel's atrocities. He accuses them of being agents who work against Islam. In the past they were the servants of the Soviets; now they are the servants of Israel. He plays on his audience's fear when he tells them that normalization would mean the "the removal of verses from the Quran that are hostile to Israel." Nothing outrages Muslims more than any change in the word of God. Al-'Auda portrays the attempts to remove statements hostile to Israel from school curricula as a step toward changing Islamic texts. He also tells his audience that nothing frightens the West more than Islam and what it instills in the people. This is the main reason for the rise of studies in the West and Israel of the "Islamic revival." He says: "There are books in Israel that study the effect of Islam on various political issues" and lists many studies published at Tel Aviv University and the Truman Institute.

Normalization of relations, according to al-'Auda, means that the "Jews are not fighting from outside. They are asking for normalization to change our minds." He mentions the diplomatic exchanges between Arabs and Israelis and conferences where Arabs and Jews met to discuss peace, from Camp David to Jordan, and portrays these meetings as part of the larger plan to undermine Islam and the Muslims. "This is no longer at the level of ideas. These people are now moving to implement this plan," he says.

Al-'Auda is also suspicious of any interfaith dialogue and sees it as a way of diluting Islam and its message. He reminds his audience that the plan started with the Egyptian president Anwar Sadat, who had to build a place of worship that includes the three religions in Sinai: "This is not about our common humanity, but about the distortion of the beliefs of Muslims."

Al-'Auda outlines the aims and objectives of Israel with regard to peace with the Arabs. He says that the main goal of Israel in peace and war is to dominate Muslims. It is an attempt to control Arab oil and convince the world to remove the economic boycott that costs Israel 10 percent of its gross domestic product. It also is an attempt to control the water of Lebanon and Jordan and perhaps the Nile. He then shows that the outcome of this process is to humiliate Muslims. Of course many of the Israeli policies, especially after the coming of Prime Minister Benjamin Netanyahu, lend credence to al-'Auda's conspiracy theory and his xenophobic discourse. The Arab press, especially newspapers associated with the left, and Arab nationalists talk about normalization in the same way. They see Western discourse regarding the protection of non-Muslim and non-Arab minorities in the Arab world as part of the Israeli plot to undermine these states from within by using indigenous populations to fight a proxy war for Israel and its strategic aims.

Conclusion

Al-'Auda's taped sermons are part of a trend that criticizes the Saudi state while praising an Islamic state that applies the Shari'a. At one extreme, al-'Auda sees the future of Saudi Arabia similar to that of Algeria and Egypt (two countries plagued by violence), while at other times he presents the kingdom as an oasis of peace that God willed to be unshakable. Between the two extremes, al-'Auda presents Saudi Arabia as an Islamic state that needs some reform. The review of his taped sermons shows that al-'Auda is a powerful preacher, although not of the same caliber as Safar al-Hawali or Sheikh Hassan al-Saffar. However, the discourse of the three men intertwines and weaves in and out of one another to form what can be termed a new culture of dissent in Saudi Arabia or a new interpretation of Islam on a global scale. The sermons show al-'Auda not only as a theologian but also as a political activist who uses his material selectively to enrage his audience against both the internal order of Saudi Arabia and the world order at large. Whenever he is pressed to answer to issues such as human rights or the rights of women, he usually lapses into a defensive discourse concerning Muslim suffering. Al-'Auda's discourse has gained him some support, and his sermons also have been used by other opponents of the state. However, he vies for this audience with many other preachers, with the discourse of the state, and with the discourse of the liberal orientation inside Saudi society. Even in Buraydah, his birthplace and where he has the largest following, he had to share his audience with influential Sheikh Mohammed bin Otheimeen, a member of the state-sponsored religious establishment.

Nonetheless, al-'Auda sees himself as an activist with concerns that go beyond Saudi Arabia. In "We Are Advocates of Peace and Unity," he speaks to the Islamic nation at large and urges his fellow 'ulama and preachers to follow suit. "We live with our Muslim brothers in Bosnia, Palestine, Egypt, Afghanistan and other places. It is a treason to the religion to ignore them. . . . Our issue is not local or specific, it is about the whole Islamic umma. We worry about Muslims all over the globe." This global component of the message is part of a dominant view among the Saudi preachers who think of themselves as the guardians of the faith. Al-'Auda's tapes were popular in Saudi Arabia between 1990 and 1994, until a new phenomenon that captured the imagination of the Saudis emerged: the faxes coming from London criticizing the royal family and signed by the first formal Saudi opposition group abroad, the Committee for the Defence of Legitimate Rights. In fact, some of the faxed messages contained many excerpts of al-'Auda's sermons. The use of fax machines and the Internet as new tools to criticize the government is both exhilarating and thrilling to Saudis whose history of dissent has been very short. I turn to this new opposition in the following chapter.

CHAPTER FOUR

Muhammed al-Mas'ari and the Committee for the Defence of Legitimate Rights

[E]very mass political activity requires group feeling. This is indicated in Muhammed's saying: "God sent no prophet who did not enjoy the protection of his people." If this was the case with prophets, who are among human beings those most likely to perform wonders, one would [expect it to apply] all the more so to others. One cannot expect them to work the wonders of achieving superiority without group feeling. Many deluded individuals took it upon themselves to establish the truth. They did not know that they would need group feeling for that. They did not realize how their enterprise must necessarily end and what they would come to.

—Ibn Khaldun, *The Muqaddimah*

Initially, the Committee for the Defence of Legitimate Rights (CDLR) generated a great deal of interest both inside and outside the Kingdom of Saudi Arabia. For one thing, Muhammed al-Mas'ari represents a different kind of opposition, made possible only by postmodern means of communication. Mas'ari's group is neither a mass-supported violent challenge to the government nor a nonviolent movement with mass support. It is uniquely Saudi and uniquely postmodern at the same time. In the past, dissidents like Mas'ari, men who criticized the regime intellectually but took no action, violent or nonviolent, attracted few followers and offered little threat to regimes. All a government had to do was exile them and ban their books. Gradually they would lose touch with events within their country and lose whatever following they had as their ideas came to seem more irrelevant to current problems. With postmodern means of communication, however, dissidents like Mas'ari can stay in touch with followers and recruit new ones even from exile; not only could his message not be stifled but it could change in response to new conditions within the country. However, it would seem that the nature of postmodern media in itself has the power to alter the original message. This chapter examines the extent to which postmodern dissidents represent a real threat to the status quo of current regimes such as Saudi Arabia. To what degree has Mas'ari succeeded? To what extent has he failed? And more important, assuming that the message itself has widespread appeal, how much of this success or failure is caused by the media and how much by the personal traits of the messenger? To answer this, we need to look at the details of the lives of Mas'ari, the man, and the CDLR, the organization.

Although the CDLR succeeded in exploiting all the contradictions and distortions of the postmodern media, it was also a victim of that process. In its quest to market itself to the broadest global constituency possible, the CDLR seems to have lost its main base of support at home. The local constituency watched as Lajnat al-Difa' 'An al-Huquq al-Shar'iyya became the Committee for the Defence of Legitimate Rights (CDLR). Of course, the Arabic meaning of the term does not fully correspond to the translated name. The definition of the word "al-Shar'iyya," translated as "legitimate" is central to how this group is perceived. While "legitimate rights" connotes legal rights in English, the term "Shar'iyya rights" refers only to the rights of individuals as specified in the Islamic tradition or Shari'a, which includes the Quran, the sunna, and the various schools of Islamic jurisprudence. Thus, from its inception, the CDLR was not the human rights group that some journalists and scholars hoped it was, nor was it the revolutionary Islamist group others feared it could be. However, it did present itself as a human rights organizations to Western liberals and as an Islamic organization to Saudi Islamists, as part of its own process of multiple identity construction. The CDLR emerged as an Islamic opposition group bent on reforming the Saudi government by exposing what its leaders interpreted as corruption and mismanagement. This overarching objective aside, the committee's specific purpose and focus have changed with time and place. Historically, the CDLR has gone through three important stages that have shaped its discourse and political program: (1) the inception of the organization and its work inside Saudi Arabia; (2) the relocation of the organization to London;

and (3) the split within the organization and consequent rise of a rival movement, the Movement for Islamic Reform in Arabia (MIRA).

The CDLR was the first Saudi opposition group that, unlike earlier
Shi'a groups, appealed to the mainstream Saudi culture. Moreover, the
Saudi government's efforts to counter CDLR initiatives inadvertently bolstered the group's domestic notoriety and international support. Despite
the widespread interest in these new developments, scholars generally ignored the factors behind the CDLR's creation. As a result, they could provide only limited insight into the committee's objectives and actions. A
more thorough analysis of the CDLR's claims, demands, and societal role
requires greater attention to the movement's political context and historical
evolution.

However, before discussing the CDLR's central message and changing
role, I offer a brief overview of the events that preceded its creation and contributed to its later development. The narrative of Saudi opposition predates
the CDLR and, just prior to the committee's creation, included the rise of
new critical voices. Voices of powerful preachers such as Hawali and 'Auda
captured the attention of the Saudi audience via taped sermons. Appearing
in the wake of the Gulf War, the tapes echoed widespread discontent with
foreign influences and cultural penetration. The physical presence of American troops on Saudi soil served as a poignant symbol of Saudi dependence
on the West and lent credence to the sermons' warnings and denunciations.
In addition to shaping the context from which the CDLR later arose, these
early critical voices left a lasting mark on the group's direction and vision. A
later section of this chapter discusses the core program of the CDLR as it operated from London. The CDLR's encounter with the various Islamic
groups there and its interaction in this new global arena, I argue, is a turning point in the history of the movement. The CDLR's use of technology to
reach a wider audience and the problems associated with it are also central
to my discussion. Although I discuss the CDLR's initial success in shaming
the regime into taking some steps toward reform, I also examine several factors contributing to the decline of the CDLR's influence on Saudi politics
in recent years.

Like all media phenomena, images and the politics of identity construction of both the self and the other were central to the CDLR. The group
has selectively engaged in centralizing an image of the self as a powerful
movement facing a crumbling regime. It has also been fairly adept at mar-
ginalizing any discourse that attempted to identify its actual power base and
determine whether it presented a credible challenge to the ruling elite.
Confusing this politics of identity construction with actual reporting on
the CDLR is dangerous. In this chapter I present various elements of the
CDLR's constructed image, not to assess the accuracy of reporting but to

understand the phenomenology of a cyberresistance movement and a hyperreal state. As the French philosopher Jean Boudlarared would have it, the sign for the real should not be confused with the real itself, or, as a desert proverb would have it, a mirage should not be mistaken for reality. As a prelude to this examination of identity construction, I consider how Mas'ari himself selectively narrates his life and that of his family in order to present himself as an alternative to the royal family and establishment 'ulama. On the level of both the overall organization and its individual leaders, the construction and projection of a legitimizing narrative is a source of power and direction.

The Rise of the CDLR and Saudi Popular Discontent during the Gulf War

During the Gulf War and after, Saudi political language underwent a transformation that was reflected and shaped by the cassette tapes of Safar al-Hawali and Salman al-'Auda. These preachers galvanized the public by harnessing Saudi anger over the war and disillusionment over Saudi Arabia's dependence on foreign protection. They used these issues to draw attention to government weakness, specifically those concerning defense, government spending, political participation, and women's rights. As a result, Saudis have become more involved in public life and have engaged the government on these and other issues. Regardless of the identity of those criticizing the Saudi government and the nature of issues on the table, the idea of criticism seems to have gained momentum in Saudi Arabia. Although criticism of the ruler had not been a Saudi political tradition, the form and language of this new criticism was uniquely Saudi; it began with petitions and letters of advice to the king rather than overt opposition. Political activities then shifted from offstage grumbling to onstage discourse involving open criticism. Organized opposition culminated in the creation of the CDLR.

As a formal organization, the CDLR was launched on May 3, 1993. The steps leading up to its creation reveal the context from which it emerged as well as the unique role it assumed within the opposition movement. Sa'd al-Faqih, a founding member who initially directed day-to-day operations, described the opening scene: "Everything appeared to be in place: charismatic preachers, thousands of enthusiastic followers, and a religious public. What was missing was an effective organization to channel this energy and pose a serious challenge to the regime."[1] Five prominent Saudis signed the first communiqué: Hammed al-Suleifeih, an educator; Abdullah bin Suleiman al-Mas'ari; a retired judge and the former head of the Saudi diwan of ombudsmen, Abdullah bin Abdul Rahman al-Jibreen, a member of the fatwa committee; Abdullah al-Hamid, a professor at King

Saud University; and Abdullah al-Tuwaijri, a professor at Imam University.[2] The efforts of these men were crucial, and perhaps indispensable, in the rise of the CDLR; they gave the organization legitimacy in the eyes of the Saudi public. It was essential that the group's foundation be based on the Shari'a and consolidated by credible scholars in order to appeal to the wider Saudi audience. The real activists who were behind the movement, however, were five young Saudi professionals with a very strong Islamist orientation, including Mohsen al-'Awaji, Khalid al-Hmeidh, 'Abd al-'Aziz al-Qasim, 'Abd al-Wahhab al-Trairi, and Sa'd al-Faqih. Al-Mas'ari described the group and its activities, "We had to be very secretive about everything, the letter of demands, the cassette tapes, the Memorandum of Advice, and all that, even until the launching of CDLR. People knew about us only when we left for London."[3]

In May of 1991, after 30 meetings, the group drafted a letter of demands to be sent to the king in the name of the Islamic leaders. It was signed by many Saudi Islamists and intellectuals. Although liberals previously had submitted their own letter to the king demanding codification of Saudi Arabian laws, the Islamists' letter appeared independently and not as a response to the liberal forces. It addressed various issues ranging from bureaucratic corruption, to legal codification, to Islamic human rights. The CDLR's view of Islamic rights focused primarily on the right of the clergy to criticize and advise the monarchy.

At this stage, the Islamists did not adopt an overtly confrontational stance vis-à-vis the state. In fact, their initial demands were addressed to both Sheikh Abdul Aziz bin Baz (Saudi Arabia's grand mufti) and the king. Before the letter of demands became public, the group met with the sheikh and asked him to endorse their demands. Despite his position at the forefront of the official religious establishment, bin Baz approved the initial draft of the letter.[4] The group circulated the letter among themselves; gathered more signatures from Saudi notables, university professors, and judges; and then three sheikhs went to Jeddah, the Saudi summer capital, to deliver the letter to the king: Abdul Mohsin al-'Ubaikan, Abdullah al-Tuwaijri, and Sa'eed bin Za'er.

The group later circulated a cassette tape known as the "Supergun," explaining their demands in popular terms and elaborating on the religious justification for those demands in an effort to mobilize wider support. It is significant that the most famous religious leaders, such as Hawali and al-'Auda, were not asked to deliver this speech themselves. The group looked for an unknown voice, since neither Hawali nor al-'Auda was willing to risk arrest at this stage. Both Hawali and al-'Auda's argument remained an indirect criticism of the state and society, without the rhetoric of explicit demands and mobilization.

The Saudi authorities asked the Council of Higher 'Ulama to respond to this new criticism. This gave the government two advantages: it managed to put the request in the hands of the 'ulama and thus make them at that moment the guardians of the state; and it took the royal family out of the confrontation, making it seem a dispute between the young and old Islamists of Saudi Arabia. The older and more established council and the Grand Mufti of Saudi Arabia criticized the letter on the basis that advice should be private were it meant for the sake of God. If advice became a popular issue, then the aim behind it would be politicized and used to bolster the group's stature. Thus the 'ulama objected to both the style and the substance of the group's advice.[5] To counter this criticism, the group worked on another document, which became known as the Memorandum of Advice. This document was a comprehensive program in the form of advice to the king. Later it provided the basis and frame of reference for most Saudi Islamist groups, including the Committee for Advice and Reform (CAR), headed by the most radical Saudi Islamist, Usama bin Laden.

The launching of the CDLR as a formal organization was the third step after the Letter of Demands and Memorandum of Advice (see Chapter 1). Although the group later developed into a formal opposition group, originally it wished to avoid being seen as a political party; instead it presented itself as a human rights organization working within the confines of Islamic law. According to the first communiqué, the committee's work was in keeping with the teachings of the Quran, the Prophet's sayings, and Islamic consensus. The first communiqué depended very heavily on the writings of the fourteenth-century scholar Ibn Taymiyyah, especially his famous collection of legal opinions entitled al-Fatawa. This book has acted as a reference for almost all Arab Islamists from Egypt, to Algeria, to Saudi Arabia. Nonetheless, the group claimed that it was "not a political party as alleged by the press and does not seek political aims."[6]

As soon as the organization announced its formation, the religious establishment cast doubts on its purpose. On May 12, 1993, the Council of Higher 'Ulama issued a communiqué in which it denounced the committee and portrayed it as incompatible with Islamic rule. "The council finds the behavior of those who signed the document [of the CDLR] strange. The council unanimously denounces this organization as illegitimate because Saudi Arabia is a country that rules according to Islam. Islamic courts are all over the country and no one has been prevented from complaining about any injustice to the specified agencies or to the Ombudsman."[7] Confronted with this criticism, the group responded with another communiqué dated May 26, 1993. This communiqué is important for two reasons: It clarifies ambiguities that led to the denunciation by the religious authorities and contains what may be considered the group's ideological apparatus, and also states the group's purpose and motives.

Inside the Kingdom: Construction of Identity

The CDLR took advantage of the media focus, especially that of the Western media, on Saudi Arabia in the aftermath of the Gulf War. In fact, the CDLR was probably more effective at exploiting the media than in advancing any of its other objectives. From the first day it was launched, the CDLR became a media phenomenon. The group was first announced on BBC radio, the Voice of America, and Radio Monte Carlo, three stations that have a wide audience in the Arab world, particularly Saudi Arabia. Not only did radio stations and newspapers take an interest in the CDLR, but some Western governments also approached the organization. On March 11, 1993, Mas'ari met with Robert Frazier and Henry Bisharat, political officers attached to the U.S. embassy in Riyadh. After the meeting, Mas'ari was convinced that the United States would support him in his campaign for human rights in Saudi Arabia.[8] The Saudi government protested this meeting through its ambassador in Washington, suggesting that it did not take the possibility of U.S.-CDLR cooperation lightly.

Until this point, Muhammed al-Mas'ari was unknown to the public. In fact, some Saudis claim (and he has not contested their view) that Mas'ari's leadership of the CDLR was an accident, and that Mas'ari seized the opportunity when the English BBC wanted to interview his father, Abdullah, the formal head of the committee, by telephone. The father suggested that since he did not speak English, it would be better for them to speak to his son Muhammed. Muhammed answered on behalf of his father and thus began speaking on the group's behalf to the media. His voice and delivery captured the imagination of the audience. As his name became synonymous with the CDLR, the group appointed him its formal spokesman. Thus Mas'ari's rise to leadership of the CDLR was a direct product of the media attention the group—and thus its spokesman—came to enjoy.

Muhammed al-Mas'ari and the Politics of Identity Construction

The CDLR's use of the media to construct and project its organizational narrative was an extension of wider efforts to selectively forge a group identity. This active engagement in the politics of identity and identity construction not only shapes collective discourse but is also embodied by Mas'ari himself. Personally, Muhammed al-Mas'ari is an impressive man, physically imposing, eloquent, and personable. All things being equal, he would seem to possess all the requirements of a charismatic leader. However, all things are not equal, and despite Masʿari's intelligence and charm, he lacks the tribal qualification to challenge to Saud family and therefore has found it necessary to recast his identity. Given Masʿari's symbolic significance as a leader, his individual narrative has a direct bearing on understanding the CDLR.

Because he lacks important tribal connections and has not demonstrated notable prowess as a religious scholar, Masʿari relies on a self-constructed narrative in order to define his position vis-à-vis state and society. In constructing this narrative, he seeks not only to reshape his own identity but also those of his father, other elite scholars, and the Saudi royal family. His efforts to establish his credentials as a defender of Islam and position himself as a guard against religious deviation on the part of the state have led him to cast aside certain aspects of his identity and embellish others. The narrative that emerges, while not entirely convincing, is central to Masʿari's understanding of Saudi Arabian life, rule, and resistance. It reflects his attempt to draw selectively on the past and present in order to position himself between religious scholarship and secular governance. From this position he presents himself as an advocate of society and Islam seeking to redirect a misguided state.

In his efforts to construct a narrative of religious scholarship and resistance, Masʿari must distance himself from certain aspects of his personal history and identity. Apparently his family is not tribal. Although Masʿari says his family comes from the al-Dawasir, an important Najdi tribe related to the Sauds by marriage, the fact that his grandmother was an Ethiopian woman makes his own branch of the family khadiri, or nontribal. In Saudi Arabia, khadiris are excluded from political power, since the men could not marry women from tribal families and thus were unable to form the kind of political alliances through marriage that were at the very basis of the Saudi state. The nontribal families also have a lower social status.[9] Masʿari hesitated to acknowledge that he is not a tribal Saudi, claiming at first that it was a slur spread by the Saudi royal family. However, in an interview he later said, "We intermarry with the khadiris,"[10] something a tribal Saudi would be unlikely to admit. Masʿari, however, attributes his family's intermarriages with nontribal people to religious beliefs that compel him to ignore issues of tribalism and lineage. Indeed, Islam emphasizes equality among believers, distinguishing between them only on the basis of their piety.

Two other factors also make him an outsider, although to a lesser degree. First, since his mother is Egyptian, some critics deny that he is a true Saudi. Second, he did his graduate work in Germany during the 1960s, lived in the United States during the 1980s, and was at one time married to an American woman, all of which leave him open to the charge of being influenced by the West and thus not a true Islamic reformer. Moreover, Mas'ari has to counter opponents' portrayal of him as an ungrateful and dissatisfied lower-class man who has been influenced by Western ideas to turn against his royal Saudi benefactors. Furthermore, he has to establish that his criticism is not made merely to draw attention to himself but to improve the government of his country, a difficult task since he is forced to voice his message from outside Saudi Arabia.

Despite his efforts to establish his individual credentials, Mas'ari also lives in the shadow of his father, Abdullah al-Mas'ari. By building on his father's identity, he enhances his own personal narrative. Abdullah al-Mas'ari, not Muhammed, signed the initial letter announcing the CDLR. Abdullah was the formal head of the CDLR. Furthermore, Abdullah had strong contacts; he was a younger contemporary of the founder of Saudi Arabia, Abdul Aziz ibn Saud, and had been a classmate of the current Grand Mufti, Abdul Aziz bin Baz.

Sheikh Abdullah al-Mas'ari, born in 1918 in Farqat bani Tameem outside Riyadh, moved to the Saudi capital in 1930s to study religion. According to Mas'ari, his father soon became the favorite student of Muhammed bin Ibraheem Al al-Sheikh, the chief imam and educator in the Najd and a grandson of Muhammed bin Abdul Wahhab. Muhammed presents his father as the most important figure next to the chief imam. Among the students who were studying under al-Sheikh along with Abdullah was the current Grand Mufti and the head of the Council of Higher 'Ulama, Sheikh Abdul Aziz bin Baz. Muhammed presents his father as a colleague and friend of both the current Mufti and the founder of the kingdom, King Abdul Aziz Al Saud (generally referred to as Ibn Saud in western writings).

Mas'ari highlights his father's role as part of a group of learned men who were devoted to Islam rather than to the royal family. Because Saudis admire those who stand up for Islam against all powers, including those of the king, men who have demonstrated this religious devotion earn popular respect. For this reason, Mas'ari emphasizes that his father was part of a circle of elite scholars. He goes even further to suggest that Sheikh Abdullah was the most knowledgeable and intelligent student, and implies that his father, rather than bin Baz, merited the title of Grand Mufti.

Mas'ari constructs others' histories as well. He denies that bin Baz has any superior knowledge in religion and attributes bin Baz's current standing among the Saudi 'ulama to his oppositional stance. "Although bin Baz is not as well versed in Islamic jurisprudence as people like bin Otheimeen [a member of the Council of Higher 'Ulama], his history as a figure who stood up to King Abdul Aziz and King Saud gave him credibility. Until this day, this political legacy is more important than the religious credentials."[11]

Mas'ari recounts a story in which King Abdul Aziz wanted the zakat (Islamically-prescribed charity money) to go to the state treasury, while bin Baz insisted that the money should go to the poor. To appease bin Baz, the king told him that he was like bin Baz's father because he was older. According to Mas'ari, bin Baz replied that although he respected the king as his senior in age, he had to speak according to the teachings of Islam. "Standing for one's religion is well-respected in Saudi Arabia," Mas'ari says. Mas'ari further recounts that bin Baz also defied King Saud, who exiled him to Medina to avoid dealing with him. By recounting these anecdotes, Mas'ari hopes to create a split between the Islamists and the royal family. Moreover, he draws an implicit contrast between the past and present role of the religious establishment. While acknowledging that religious officials once had the power to resist royal authority, Mas'ari implies that bin Baz and other establishment muftis are no longer faithful to this legacy.

According to Mas'ari, his father, Sheikh Abdullah, had similar confrontations with powerful Saudi kings. Unlike bin Baz, however, he remained faithful to his principles. This is why he founded and assumed leadership of the CDLR. Mas'ari recounts two confrontations his father had with King Saud and then with King Faysal. One was a case in which his father defended the rights of the working classes, although very few Saudis fit this characterization, since in Saudi Arabia the working class is largely comprised of foreign workers. The ruling king, by contrast, was on the side of the employer. In the words of Mas'ari: "It was a case in which a man was dismissed from his job for no apparent reason. The court established that his employer was at fault, and therefore required that he pay a fine of seventy thousand riyals as compensation. King Saud was extremely upset at the decision and commented that the court was created to provide just decisions to people rather than confirm an unfair one." The way Mas'ari narrates the incident is revealing; he positions the king on the side of injustice and his father on the side of justice. Sheikh Abdullah, according to Mas'ari, was extremely disturbed by the king's statement, which he saw as "an infringement on the very core of the court's authority and sanctity." Thus, he consulted with other judges who decided to present their collective resignation. They asserted that their resignation was necessary, stating "the court clearly lacks the king's valuable trust and high judgment. We, therefore, recommend that our place be filled with more qualified individuals." They submitted their proposed resignation along with their ruling, contending that "our decision in the case is Allah's decision/judgment for which you will be responsible on the day of judgment."[12] The court's decision was returned to them approved, the sentence was executed, and their resignation was rejected.

The second confrontation was with King Faysal, whom Mas'ari describes as "ruthless." Here again he portrays his father as a defender of justice, this time against an intrusive police officer. A case was presented to the court in which a person was arrested for smuggling cigarettes and selling them in the black market. The suspect denied the accusations and claimed that cigarette boxes found in his apartment were empty, yet he was still fined by the police. After reviewing the case, Abdullah al-Mas'ari wrote a severely critical decision and declared that the police actions were indeed illegal, since the police were neither a financial nor a judicial authority. He ordered the police to return the money to the suspect, a ruling that outraged the king. According to Mas'ari, "My father stood firm and when he knew of the king's anger at the decision, he sent his resignation to the king. The king rejected the resignation and the court's decision was upheld."[13]

This court, incidentally, was the newly established Diwan al-Madhalim (Ombudsman), which Mas'ari describes as an administrative constitutional court, much like the supreme court. It studies cases and, after reaching a decision, consults the prime minister, who in turn enacts the decision. Mas'ari believes the court was more independent at that time than it is today, since now the prime minister and the king are the same person. During his father's tenure, however, the prime minister was the king's uncle, who, according to Mas'ari, had great respect for scholars such as Abdullah al-Mas'ari. Muhammed emphasizes his family's close ties to the former prime minister and suggests that his father did the actual work of the court, while the prime minister acted as a figurehead out of "respect for Saudi customs."

According to Mas'ari, King Faysal respected his father for his adherence to his religious principles, but his father refused to exploit this respect to serve his own needs. Mas'ari says that when some friends advised Sheikh Abdullah to take advantage of this relationship and "request a piece of land, he continuously refused, stating that if the king wanted to give him a piece of land, he would do so without a request." He also recalled that when his father received a letter from the Saudi Commercial Bank with a fifty-thousand-riyal check from the king, the sheikh returned the check "assuming it was sent to him by mistake." "I was deeply influenced by this," Mas'ari says. Mas'ari's entire narrative, whether factual or embellished, suggests that far from being under the patronage and protection of the royal family, Abdullah al-Mas'ari acted as a religious counterbalance to the Saud family's rule, and the founding of the CDLR was merely a continuation of this role of loyal opposition[14] by a man who possessed greater ability and religious knowledge than the ruler. Mas'ari presents his own life as a natural extension of this narrative, hoping to convince others that he has faithfully continued his father's legacy.

In describing his education in Riyadh and the Hijaz (western Saudi Arabia), Mas'ari offers a comparison between himself and the princes. In both places he attended private schools with sons of the royal family, most of whom Mas'ari says he hated. He emphasized that the best of the students were black Saudis (like himself) and the sons of foreign officials. "The sons of the amirs were always very delinquent, and it was known that they never took their studies seriously." He did praise a few of the sons of the royal family, including Prince Ahmed bin Abdul Aziz, the current minister of interior, and Prince Faysal Ben Abdul Aziz al-Faysal. "Except for the these two, I really can't say that I've been honored with the company of any of the Saud students in school; their servants and drivers were smarter and more sophisticated than they were."[15] As in the narrative he presents about his father, Mas'ari again draws a sharp contrast between true religious scholarship and devotion and that of the official religious establishment and royal family.

By selectively fashioning his own narrative, Mas'ari mirrors the wider process of identity construction within the CDLR. Just as he highlights certain facets of his identity in order to establish his personal credentials as an Islamic scholar and opposition leader, the CDLR tailors its collective image in order to position itself vis-à-vis state and society. This process of "positioning" is neither static nor unambiguous, as was immediately evident upon the group's relocation to London.

Relocating to London and the Rise of Cyberresistence

The group's relocation to London is a landmark in its evolution. At this global moment, London is no longer just a Western city; it is also a center of Islamic and Arab activities. It is a cultural city where cultural production on a global scale is the norm. Muslim communities, natives and immigrants alike, interact among themselves and with other communities. London is also the center of Arab media. Major broadcasting corporations and newspapers such as Middle East Broadcasting Corporation (MBC) and *al-Hayat* are located there. The language of the London-based Arab media is certainly different from that of the media back home. Some newspapers and magazines that belong to Saudi owners allow diverse voices of Islamists and liberals. For instance, in *al-Majalla,* a Saudi weekly, Fahmi Howeidy, a moderate Muslim brother from Egypt, is given a two-page column in which he preaches moderate Islam and attempts to reconcile Islam and democracy and many other concepts. These essays influenced the discourse of Sheikh Hasan al-Saffar, leader of another Saudi opposition group that I will discuss in chapter 7.[16] In addition, London is also the host of more radical groups, such as al-Muhajiroon, a pan-Islamist movement led by the Syrian Omar Bakri. This group attacks U.S. policy toward Muslims, especially the unequivocal support the United States offers to Israel. Even Usama bin Laden has an office in London. The CDLR came to this capital and had to interact with the existing cultural debate on Islam and Islamic politics. This atmosphere has greatly influenced the course of the organization.

For nearly a year after the publication of the CDLR's second communiqué from Riyadh on May 26, 1993, and its third communiqué from London on April 20, 1994, the group's activities and its fate were the subject of speculation and rumors. The London communiqué indicated that the group was moving toward becoming a political opposition group rather than an apolitical human rights organization.[17] In contrast to the CDLR's initial declaration issue, this communiqué unambiguously confirmed the suspicions of the establishment 'ulama and government. The CDLR was not merely a nongovernmental association interested in human rights, rather, it was an opposition group that posed a political challenge to the Saudi regime.

If the CDLR was a media celebrity while inside the kingdom, its relocation to London gave it more access to both the traditional and new alternative media, which facilitated both its popularity and its contacts with its multiple audiences. Mas'ari himself took center stage in London and spoke in the House of Commons in June 1995, a picture of him addressing the house served as the cover photo of the group's monthly magazine.[18] As part of this continuous process of identity construction, the group stages news events to produce an image that magnifies its status in global spaces; in this way its local image and importance are exaggerated as well. Mas'ari's statements usually elicited a response from either the Saudi government or the Saudi media, and as the war of words intensified, the CDLR was given greater television time. Because Mas'ari's stay in London irritated the Saudi authorities, they pressured the British government directly and through companies with interests in Saudi Arabia to have him deported. Indeed, the British government decided to deport him to Dominica in the Caribbean, but Mas'ari successfully appealed this decision, and the court granted him political asylum in Britain. Ultimately, Saudi pressure on the British government bolstered Mas'ari's public image while creating a public relations nightmare for the Saudi government.[19] Mas'ari's asylum case became a cause célèbre and an international issue, as both he and the CDLR gained more media exposure in the West and Arab world. Mas'ari was interviewed by the Arabic BBC, the Voice of America, and others, enabling him to broadcast his personal plight and his group's message to a wide audience. Mas'ari was thus able to cast himself as a Saudi Sir Thomas More to King Fahd's Henry the VIII, an image guaranteed to resonate with Western audiences and win him the support of broadminded human rights activists.

Group leaders capitalized on this fame and began to use the media more effectively by faxing information to their supporters both within the kingdom and without. Then they branched out, using electronic mail and the Internet to enhance their image and recruit more supporters. The group soon established a CDLR Web site and launched an unprecedented wave of cyberresistance. The group's awareness of the importance of alternative in its fight against the regime and recruitment of followers predated its relocation to London. Even in the first issue of its newsletter, *al-Huquq* (Rights), in 1994, the CDLR demonstrated an acute awareness of the media's pivotal role in its struggle.

As the group evolved, the media remained a cornerstone in the campaign against the Saudi government. In another issue of al-Huquq, Mas'ari made it clear that he believed that Western media pressure on the royal family was likely to bring results and further his campaign of reform. [I]f anyone wants to influence the decision inside the Kingdom, all they needed to do was to publish an article in a Western newspaper. . . . the King showed absolutely no hesitation in talking to the Shiite opposition and released all their prisoners in order to curtail their activities abroad and win their silence."[20] By this time, the CDLR's belief in the influence of Western media on Saudi policymaking had been reinforced.

The CDLR and the New Media

The CDLR uses the new media not only to convey its own message but for information. The relationship between the CDLR and journalism will be discussed later, but an interesting section in most CDLR publications describes how to contact the group, receive its publications, or provide it with information. This is aimed specifically at those who support the group inside Saudi Arabia. The CDLR instructs its supporters to contact its London office through MCI, AT&T, or Sprint using an 800 number or by calling collect either from the kingdom or outside it. Inside the kingdom, for instance, supporters are to call MCI by dialing 1–800–11 and then entering the organization's credit card number. CDLR supporters can also make collect calls in times of emergency. These numbers change every two or three months for security reasons.[21]

Although it exploits almost all available means of communication, the CDLR is limited by the existing communication structure. For instance, most of its information is distributed either through the United States or Britain, because Internet facilities in the Gulf area are still very limited. The only existing nodes in the Gulf area are Gulfnet and Emirates net. Although these nets are government controlled, most universities in the Gulf have e-mail, so one person with access to the Internet can relay information to other e-mail users.

From London, the leaders of the CDLR have sent a steady stream of information critical of the Riyadh government. "Every week, via CompuServe, the CDLR faxes its newsletter to 600 distribution points in Saudi Arabia."[22]

It also transmits the same information through e-mail and its World Wide Web home page (http://www.ummah.org.uk/cdlr). The group uses similar means to gather news about the kingdom. According to CDLR leaders, informants include "disaffected Saudi businessmen, clerics, military officers, and intelligence officials."[23]

The Structure and the Content of the Home Page

In addition to the use of fax machines, the CDLR, at least before the split within the organization, was very successful in using the Internet to project its message in more than one language and in multiple formats. In fact, the birth of the CDLR was concomitant with the newly popularized use of the World Wide Web. Thus, the group grew with the phenomenon. It gradually evolved from having just an electronic mail list and relying on newsgroups to having its own home page with its own Web domain. As a cutting-edge resistance movement on the Internet, it engaged in cyberwars and cyberresistance. Other groups learned from the CDLR's example, just as it learned strategies and tactics from other groups.

Looking at the group's Web site reveals how the CDLR utilized this new medium to dispatch its message to the largest possible audience. The home page is divided into two sections according to language, English publications and Arabic publications. Of course, Arabic on the Internet is not very popular, since the Arabic Internet is currently an image-based construction. English, as a text-based language, is more accessible. This centrality influences the audience both in negative and positive ways. The audience can receive messages in Arabic, but it is difficult for them to send messages in that language. They thus usually use English to communicate with the group, which limits users to English-speakers.

The English publications include a weekly newsletter, The Monitor, CDLR's yearbook, and press releases directed to Western governments and media. The discourse is distinctly liberal, focusing on issues of democratization and human rights. The Arabic publications include a weekly newsletter, al-Huquq, and a monthly magazine, Ash-Shar'iyya. These publications, unlike the English ones, are directed to the Saudi public and Arabs living abroad. The discourse is conservative with a distinctly religious tone. Based on my interviews with CDLR leaders, it appears that the Arabic publications are more representative of the organization's beliefs.

In order to determine how these Internet publications reflect and shape the CDLR's identity and agenda, the following analysis surveys their contents, identifies their major themes, discerns the ideology of the group, and identifies whether there are differences between the Arabic and the English publications and to what degree these differences reflect variations in the intended audience. In this global moment, I expect to find a multiplicity of discourses based on the audience and language and a degree of interaction between the discourses where the global and the local shape each other.

Message Directed to the Arab Audience

I begin by describing the basic layout of the Arabic monthly *Ash-Shar'iyya,* first published in December 1995, and then provide a content analysis of one issue. *Ash-Shar'iyya* is an Arabic magazine aimed at the audience living inside the kingdom, in the Arab world, and in the Arab diaspora communities throughout Europe and North America. The issue published in August 1995 revealed a clear shift in the CDLR's communications strategy. The 50-page magazine is divided into about 8 to 10 separate sections. It opens with a two-page editorial followed by two pages of news relating mainly to the question of stability in the kingdom. This news section sets the agenda, emphasizing negative developments in Saudi Arabia. Another two-page section is dedicated to a discussion of the royal family with a special focus on its "internal divisions." The middle section of the magazine usually carries an opinion article, four pages documenting the history of dissent in Saudi Arabia, two pages of alleged governmental documents, and six pages dedicated to "Qadaya siasiyya" (political issues). The final section of *Ash-Shar'iyya* is divided into eight subheadings: "Diwan al Mazalim" (ombudsman); one page of letters to the editor complaining about perceived injustices; six pages for "Bohooth Islamiyya" (Islamic research); four pages of economic issues; two pages of translation from the Western media; two pages for literature; four pages for general letters to the editor; and finally a concluding editorial.

The contents of *Ash-Shar'iyya* reflect the organization's obsession with four main issues: divisions within the royal family over the issue of succession to the throne, corruption, the various forms of dissent within and the instability of the political order, and the disjunction between the practices of the government and the "real" teachings of Islam. A summary of a sample issue from December 1995 demonstrates how these central issues are presented in various forms.

First, the magazine editorial focused on the Riyadh bombing that killed five Americans. The main message was that the government was responsible for the violence due to its policy of arresting Islamic preachers and activists. Designed to cast doubt on the stability of the regime, the editorial stated: "The regime is not as stable as the media and Saudi Arabia's American friends would like to portray it to be."[24]

Ash-Shar'iyya analysts attribute the recent rise of violent activities to "the royal family's policies that aim at undermining the role of religion and consequently upsetting the delicate balance of the society." By arresting religious activists, the CDLR argues, the government left the Islamists with only one option: violence. "The solution to this violence is to rectify this imbalance between religion and politics in the Saudi society. The first steps toward this goal should include releasing the Islamists from prisons, allowing freedom of expression and association, and granting the people the right to question their leaders." The group further accuses the government of manipulating the official 'ulama. One example given is that of Sheikh bin Baz's recent fatwa against the CDLR. The group argues that bin Baz issued the fatwa in response to Prince Nayef's pressure and promises for the release of some political prisoners. Prince Nayef, according to the CDLR, deceived Sheikh bin Baz by obtaining the fatwa but arresting more Islamists.

In the same issue of *Ash-Shar'iyya,* four news items portray members of the royal family as the main source of social ills in Saudi society, including rising crime, drug use, and violence. According to the CDLR, all of these crimes are committed with the knowledge of the royal family or under the protection of some of the younger princes. Moreover, additional news items focus on the economic dimension of the monarchy's unjust and immoral policies. They paint Saudi Arabia as a very poor country, indeed. One news item claims that in the Hasa region, the Eastern Province, 1,500 homes are without electricity. While independent reporting has not substantiated this figure, it serves to highlight the government's inequitable policies. The monarchy's neglect of the "poor Saudis" stands in sharp contrast to the "extravagant" behavior of the royal princes.

Message Directed to the English-speaking Audience

The CDLR addresses its English-speaking audience through a weekly publication, *The Monitor,* with the stated purpose of making "the umma aware of the truth and what is happening around it and it is because we believe that the umma has a right to hear the other views that we have launched this weekly newsletter." Another purpose of *The Monitor* is to build an image of the organization and its leadership to counter what the CDLR labels "Saudi propaganda." As I show, the publication initially lacked journalistic professionalism, although it has improved in terms of both substance and format.

The first issue dated May 30, 1994, was divided into two sections, "Your Right to Know" and "News." The former identified the importance of government-media manipulation and its impact on the Islamic movement and explained why the group decided to publish this weekly. The "News" section contained ten news items, two of which were related to alleged arrests of activists inside Saudi Arabia. The remaining eight focused on the CDLR and its members, mainly Dr. Muhammed al-Mas'ari and Sa'd al-Faqih, and the government's response to the group's relocation to London. Initially the CDLR seemed to exaggerate the government's response to its activities. For example, it attributed the king's unprecedented two speeches and government arrests on the Qatari-Saudi border to the group's connection with each case. *The Monitor* of July 4, 1994 (no. 6), was dedicated solely to an attack on two members of the royal family, Prince Salman, the governor of Riyadh, and Prince Bandar, the Saudi ambassador to Washington. The section titled "Your Right to Know" was omitted. *The Monitor* of August 25, 1995 (no. 13), was similar to issue no. 6 in focusing on news items. It is worth noting, however, that this "news" was mixed with interpretation and opinion. During the first year of publication, the CDLR mixed serious news with trivial gossip. For instance, the third item of news reports "Fifty Yemeni Socialist Party women members have been moved to Jeddah. . . . [they are] hair dressing specialists [who] will practice the profession publicly." No one knows why this news item takes precedence, let us say, over an item reporting on Qasimi tribesmen angered by the government detention of one of its men, Muhammad al-Marshud.

This continues throughout 1994 until 1995. For example, *The Monitor* of November 18, 1994 (no. 22), begins with a lengthy letter addressed to Sheikh Abdul Aziz bin Baz. The first of two sections of the open letter praise the sheikh for his impeccable record and his experience as the religious leader of the state. However, the following section expresses the CDLR's disappointment regarding his fatwas against them. Interestingly, it attributes the fatwas not directly to him but to the royal family's success in exploiting weaknesses of the established clergy. Indeed, the exchange between Sheikh bin Baz and the leaders of the CDLR is very significant. Nonetheless, the English translation is very confusing to a non-Saudi reader. Apparently, some of the items in *The Monitor* are a direct and sometimes literal translation of an Arabic issue of *al-Huquq* and sound peculiar in English.

From the opposite angle, presenting the local audience with translated items from the Western media takes the global discourse into the local setting and thus socializes the local into the global. However, the news items that followed the preceding letter reflected a greater degree of journalistic professionalism and sophistication. The news items discussed reveal that both the Saudi government and the CDLR have recognized the paramount importance of the media both in promoting their agendas and in tarnishing the image of their adversaries.

The first newsletter of 1995 reveals that *The Monitor* of the previous years were merely experimenting with form and issues, suggesting that the group was still searching for the proper format. It is probably for this reason that the section "Your Right to Know" appears, followed by the news. However, there was a change in substance as well as in the quality of reporting. For example, a full page was devoted to the issue of budget deficit in Saudi Arabia. Also, for the first time, foreign policy items appeared as part of the issue, as did reports on sectors of Saudi society such as universities, electricity companies, and news from the various provinces. This section was a regular feature throughout the year. In an issue dated January 13, 1995, we are treated to an item that portrays Saudi Arabia as a country mired in sex and violence. Contrary to the first reports that portray Yemeni hairdressers as an offense to public morality in Jeddah, this report depicts a Saudi society in which guns, sex, and drugs are easily available. According to this issue, "a house was used as a discotheque with a large floor for exotic dancing—in other words a very sleazy night club. A huge supply of drugs and pornography was found together with photographs of the patrons of the club in compromising positions. Photographic equipment for producing pornographic films was also discovered."

The Monitor dated January 20, 1995 (no. 31), showed some improvement over the previous ones. "Your Right to Know" changed slightly; it now functioned as an editorial section. The topic for this particular week was whether to advocate reform or argue for the overthrow of the regime. The CDLR's position seemed to have shifted toward the inevitability of the overthrow of the regime, although it did not explicitly support this course of action. The editorial states that "economic, political and social . . . history records that the destruction of the Second Saudi State was brought about by the violent and bloody feuds which plunged the nation into disaster. We need at this very moment to be grooming alternative leaders."

Although the editorial section improved somewhat, the news section remained mired in sensational and unsubstantiated reporting. One example of these items focused on Maha al-Sudairi, the wife of the minister of interior who was supposedly shot by members of the royal family because of her shameful behavior. No credible source has verified this claim. Indeed, ordinary Saudis laughed at the idea when I interviewed them. Nonetheless, the news section did contain some substantive news. This particular issue contained two news items on Sheikh bin Baz and one foreign policy item on the question of the Yemeni border.

By February 24, 1995, the group decided to add another item to *The Monitor* entitled "Know Your Leaders," in which the group would be "investigating the four major political figures in the kingdom and the ones responsible for most of the corruption and disasters suffered by the nation and the whole Islamic world: Fahd, Sultan, Salman and Nayef." By enumerating the political figures the CDLR intended to criticize, the group implied support for Crown Prince Abdullah. This default category of royal princes represents the faction within the royal family that vies for power against the dominance of the Sudairi branch. In my interviews with CDLR leaders, they clearly stated that they would side with the government should Prince Abdullah take power in Saudi Arabia.

From the May 26 issue until the July 26, 1995, issue, a new series of long editorials (apparently taken from an ongoing research paper) focused on the legitimacy of the regime. Again, these editorials seem to be literal translations of works initially intended for an Arabic-speaking audience. A few years later the main issues appeared in a book authored by Sa'd al-Faqih on the legitimacy of the regime.

Reviewing the group's work during the first year, it seems that it was more interested in media confrontation than actual confrontation with the Saudi government. At the top of the group's achievements was the success of the CDLR's leaders in escaping from Saudi Arabia to resume their activities from London. Also listed was the group's ability to use the Western media to highlight the case of asylum for its leader, Muhammed al-Mas'ari. Indeed, this was rated as one of its main feats. The group considered the government's mishandling of the Mas'ari case in London another success. By mishandling the asylum case, the government inadvertently proved that the CDLR was much more media savvy than the Saudi Ministry of Information. Nonetheless, the government's failure to deal effectively with the British media is not necessarily permanent. The Saudi government may have learned from that particular media fiasco, a point I discuss in the final chapter on the government's responses to the various opposition groups. In its efforts to highlight its achievements, the group has deliberately chosen to put media resistance above actual resistance. In this *Monitor* (April 19, 1995), the CDLR seems to consider any degree of media coverage of its activities a victory over the government.

In spite of the CDLR's limited media sophistication, the group certainly got the attention of both the Saudi government and the outside powers. The issues that captured outsiders' attention include succession to the throne, economic problems, and internal dissent within Saudi society. These issues may lack merit or may not be of equal importance, yet the CDLR succeeded in advancing them to the top of the agenda of Western news agencies and Western media. As time passed and the monarchy retained its firm hold on power, however, questions regarding its stability gradually became subsumed by more pressing global events. Consequently, coverage of the CDLR and its message also faded, and the international media's focus shifted to other issues. The initial excitement surrounding the CDLR arose because it was the first organization in Saudi Arabia to criticize the government at a critical time. Now that criticism of Saudi Arabia has become more widespread in the West, the CDLR is less of a novelty. Moreover, the CDLR's propensity for exaggerated reporting damaged its credibility. This credibility was diminished further due to Mas'ari's new alliance with a radical diaspora group known as al-Muhajiroon, led by the Syrian Sheikh Omar Bakri.

The CDLR's Main Message

In spite of the shifts in the format and quality of CDLR publications, certain themes have remained central to the group's message. It attacks the regime on three fronts: domestic, regional Arab and Muslim, and international. On the domestic front, the group highlights government mismanagement of the economy, government deviation from the Islamic path, and problems within the royal family. These issues are neither the exclusive critique of the CDLR nor its inventions. In fact, earlier Shi'a opposition groups highlighted these same issues. The CDLR's criticism is similar to the Shi'a critique except that the former's perspective is Sunni/Wahhabi. Furthermore, the group targets various social groups and segments of Saudi society and clearly defines the differences among them along regional, tribal, and sectarian lines, emphasizing the conflicting interests between these groups and the Saudi royal family. On the Arab and Islamic front, the CDLR attacks Saudi Arabia's special relations with the United States, portraying Saudi Arabia as a state that does not support the rights of the Arab people in Palestine and supports Muslim fighters only if instructed to do so by the Americans, as was the case during the Afghan war. Internationally, the group attempts to tarnish the image of Saudi Arabia as a stable country, especially in the eyes of Western governments. By also highlighting Saudi Arabia's problematic human rights record, the group hopes to win the sympathy of civil society activists worldwide.

The CDLR's Critique of the Saudi State and Its Policies

Mas'ari's critique of the Saudi state focuses on two issues: the legitimacy of state inside and the its "external actions." The criterion for judging both is Islam, or the CDLR's interpretation of Islam. In both his books and his speeches, Mas'ari delivers a devastating indictment of the foundation of the Saudi state. In *al-Adellah al-Qat'iyya 'Ala 'Adam Shar'iyyat al-Dawlah al-Sa'udiyya* (Evidence of the un-Islamic nature of the Saudi state) published in 1995, two years after the establishment of the CDLR, he criticizes the basic foundations of the original eighteenth-century contract between al-Sheikh and al-Saud. Mas'ari states: "By accepting these conditions [that the Saudis are the leaders of the Muslims], the sheikh reduced the general Islamic mission [Da'wa] to a narrow provincial and racist ideology designed to serve the interests of the Sauds. It has served them ever since. Thus it lost its main purpose to lift the Muslims from their backward state."[25] This direct attack on

Sheikh Muhammed bin Abdul Wahhab is not likely to win Mas'ari many supporters among the mainstream Saudis. In fact, it could undermine his earlier, more popular criticism of corruption and the lack of power sharing. Nonetheless, Mas'ari's critique of the domestic politics of Saudi Arabia is less radical than his attack on Saudi foreign policy.

Mas'ari's critique of Saudi Foreign Policy

The leaders of the CDLR are critical of Saudi Arabia's conduct of foreign policy on numerous fronts. They criticize the kingdom's membership in the United Nations, an organization that they consider an advocate of anti-Islamic principles and an instrument used to dominate Muslims. In certain respects, the CDLR is not very different from members of the American ultra right-wing-militia, who think that the United Nations is part of a larger conspiracy to take over the United States. In addition to attacking. The group also is critical of the Saudi alliance with other Gulf countries and its participation in the Gulf Cooperation Council (GCC). This is because, according to the CDLR, the GCC charter also promotes anti-Islamic principles. Another component of the CDLR's attack on Saudi foreign policy is the dependence of Saudi Arabia on the United States for protection. Similar sentiments were first voiced in the fatwas of other preachers who saw the presence of U.S. troops in Saudi Arabia as anti-Islamic. Furthermore, the CDLR accentuates the differences between the United States and Saudi Arabia as a way of persuading its audience that America's commitment to the protection of the royal family is wavering, thereby creating a situation conducive to revolutionary action. The CDLR also has published a series of articles about the kingdom's secret relationship with Israel. I start by looking at the last one first, since it constitutes the ultimate critique of the regime's international conduct.

Saudi Arabia and Israel: "Secret Relations?"

Nothing is more sensitive within the Islamic and Arab circles than to be accused of having special relations with Israel, especially in the current tense atmosphere where the Arabs are involved in a peace process that promises them very little. The CDLR has taken advantage of this atmosphere by showing Saudi Arabia as more favorably disposed toward Israel than it actually is. In both its Arabic magazine and Arabic newsletter, the group gives front-page coverage to the visit of Jewish leaders from Britain to the kingdom. One report regarding these visits, translated from the British newspaper the *Jewish Chronicle*, insinuates that the kingdom has a special relationship with Israel and the Jewish lobby in Western countries. This news item is not presented in isolation, but in conjunction with an essay providing a historical context for this relationship. The essay traces Saudi-Jewish relations back to the founder of the kingdom, King Abdul Aziz, implying that the Sauds pay lip service to the Arab cause while, in fact, they are committed to peace with Israel. The conservative Saudi public is likely to be revolted by this news, given Israel's occupation of Jerusalem, the third holiest shrine of Islam, and the humiliation of the Arab and Muslim people of Palestine. Such rumors and innuendoes are likely to undermine the confidence of the ultra-right wing of the Saudi population. However, the sophisticated Saudi elite who represent the core support of the regime are not likely to be swayed by these arguments, given the scanty evidence that the group provides.

Another article focuses on "exposing the special relationship between Israel and Saudi Arabia." The CDLR claims that Israel is the main guarantor of the survival of the Saudi government. In an article in the Arabic weekly *al-Huquq* entitled "The Dirty Handshake," the group discusses the handshake between then Prime Minster of Israel Shimon Peres and Prince Saud al-Faysal, Saudi Arabia's minister of foreign affairs at the Peacemakers Conference in the Egyptian seaport of Sharm al-Sheikh. The group uses this handshake, coupled with some excerpts from the minister's speech in which "he condemned terrorism," to show to the Saudi public that the government is not only normalizing its relations with Israel but also "calling jihad terrorism." We need only to remember the discourse of Hawali and al-'Auda, their insistence on jihad as the only means to liberate Palestine, and their total antipathy to any kind of normalization of relations between Israel and Saudi Arabia to appreciate the potential danger of these statements. Between March and May of 1996, *al-Huquq* ran eight front-page articles under the heading of "Saudi-Israeli Relations: The Hidden Conspiracy."[26] In this series, the authors did not deal directly with the proclaimed conspiracy but focused on how Saudi Arabia is violating Islamic teachings by even contemplating the issue of peace with Israel. The group's position on the peace negotiations between the Arabs and Israel is very clear. Palestine can be liberated only through an Islamic jihad, not through negotiation. The article lists numerous fatwas issued by 'ulama from places as far away as India and Egypt to support the group's position. Again, the main purpose is to portray the Saudi government as betraying both Islam and Arabism.

Saudi Arabia and the United Nations

In another series of five articles in the weekly *al-Huquq,* Mas'ari blasts Saudi Arabia for being a member of the United Nations.[27] This series is a serialized form of a chapter in his book *al-Adellah al-Qat'iyya 'Ala 'Adam Shar'iyyat al-Dawlah al-Sa'udiyya* published in 1995. These essays reveal a different side of Mas'ari and his views on Saudi Arabia's global policies. Mas'ari suggests that by ratifying the United Nation charter, Saudi Arabia has violated the teachings of Islam. This is because, in his view, the UN charter endorses a system of state-based sovereignty that contradicts the universal vision of Islam. Furthermore, in his view, the UN covenants violate Islam by granting equal rights to men and women. Thus he calls on the 'ulama to denounce the Saudi state as un-Islamic.[28] Mas'ari's hatred of the UN became obsessive, as revealed through a series of articles in *al-Huquq* calling for "the destruction of the United Nations."[29]

Saudi Arabia and the Gulf States

Within the CDLR's weekly publications, Mas'ari also criticizes Saudi Arabia's alliance with other "un-Islamic" states of the Gulf region. A long discussion is dedicated to the charter of the Gulf Cooperation Council (GCC). In it Mas'ari asserts that most of the internal laws of these states are not Islamic and are therefore a violation of God's teachings. He also criticizes Saudi internal laws, including commercial laws that allow for the accrual of interest. Like other Saudi radicals, he severely criticizes the Saudi alliance with the U.S. and the decision to house U.S. troops in defense of Saudi Arabia.[30]

The United States and Saudi Arabia

The CDLR's discourse on the United States is at best ambivalent. In its Arabic publications, it attacks the American presence in Saudi Arabia and frequently refers to this presence as occupation. Yet most of the CDLR's discourse on the royal family's hold on power appeals to the U.S. administration to pressure the Saudi government to open up the system and allow for greater power sharing. Furthermore, the CDLR's discourse on human rights is yet another way of linking with the larger strategic goals of stated U.S. policy emphasizing democratization and human rights. In its English publications and to some extent in its Arabic ones, the group attempts to highlight the differences between Saudi Arabia and the United States and makes it seem as if America is no longer interested in the royal family and could work with any alternative regime. For example, in the news section of *Ash-Shar'iyya* (no. 6, vol.1, December 1995), the CDLR offers 20 news items. Four focus on Saudi-American relations and the distrust between the two countries concerning the Riyadh bombing. This news is further accentuated by reports from the Western media. In two news items that address division within the family, the CDLR suggests that the Americans would certainly have a say in who should be the next king of Saudi Arabia. Many of the CDLR's publications focus on how Americans would not wish Crown Prince Abdullah to be king. They attribute this to the influence of Saudi Arabia's ambassador to Washington, Prince Bandar bin Sultan, and his father, the minister of defense. This discourse has gained some currency in Arab circles outside Saudi Arabia. By circulating this discourse inside the kingdom, the CDLR leaders hope to create divisions within the royal family concerning who is pro-American and who is not. The CDLR promotes a perception that the United States is against Abdullah and that CDLR members themselves, though they hate the royal family, are more willing to deal with Abdullah than to deal with King Fahd and his full brothers (generally known in Saudi Arabia as the Sudayri Seven). This particular issue emphasizes the differences between al-Waleed bin Talal, one of the world's richest men, and Prince Salman, the governor of Riyadh.

Human Rights

Like many Islamic organizations throughout the region, the CDLR pays special attention to the issue of human rights, especially as a means of enlisting the support of nongovernmental organizations, such as Amnesty International and Human Rights Watch, to pressure the Saudi government to release Islamists from prisons. However, a gap is evident between human rights as stated in the Universal Declaration and Shari'a rights as constructed by the CDLR. This difference becomes obvious when the English publications are compared with the Arabic ones. References to human rights in the English edition become references to Shari'a rights in Arabic. The conflation of the two serves a clear political purpose: it enlists the support of Western governments, Western media, and activists who might pressure the Saudi government for further reforms.

The group's initial publications suggest that the CDLR is a indeed a human rights organization. In its first communiqué, the CDLR provided an Islamic rationale for itself and outlined its mission in a way that was compatible with human rights agendas. "There is ample evidence from the Islamic tradition (al-Kitab wal Sunna) urging Muslims to protect the rights of human beings," the first statement of the communiqué reads. The group also lists six different hadith (sayings of the Prophet Muhammed) that support the idea of alleviating injustices whenever they are found and address the issue of cooperation between Muslims. Of course, this activism, according to the CDLR, is to be carried out by the learned men of religion rather than liberals and secular forces. Thus the group's spokesman states, "We declare here that we are ready to contribute in any way to alleviate injustices and protect the rights that *Islam* [emphasis added] has guaranteed to human beings."

As the group embarked on this task, a great deal was revealed about Mas'ari's conception of human rights. In his writings, Mas'ari condemns the Universal Declaration of Human Rights as anti-Islamic since it calls for absolute equality between men and women. The organization's second communiqué, issued May 26, 1993, stated, "The committee clearly realizes the difference between the meanings of human rights in Islam and the meaning with regard to other ideologies."

Furthermore, as I pointed out earlier, Mas'ari has attacked the Saudi government for joining the United Nations because, in his views, the UN charter contradicts the basic teachings of Islam. Mas'ari's not only wants Saudi Arabia to withdraw from the United Nations, but he also calls for the destruction of the United Nations.[31] Thus Mas'ari's Saudi Arabia is likely to be not only a pariah state that does not recognize the existing covenants but also one that rejects international law altogether.

In spite of this, some members of the movement have attempted to focus on the issue of human rights in Islam. In a book entitled *Huquq al-Insan bayn 'Adl al-Islam wa Jour al-Hukkam* (Human rights between the justice of Islam and the tyranny of the rulers), Abdullah al-Hamid, one of the CDLR's founding members, argues against the state's right to search and seizure and for respect of individual privacy and security.[32] Nevertheless, he does not endorse some basic freedoms, such as freedom of belief and freedom of expression outside Islam. Of course, these two principles are central pillars in the international human rights platform, and without them, the argument of the Saudi Islamists appears to be no more than an attempt to protect themselves from the state. Nothing in their discourse would guarantee the rights of those who disagree with their own interpretation of religion.

Thus, it is clear that the Universal Declaration of Human Rights is not the frame of reference for Mas'ari's or the CDLR's conception of rights. The group may conflate the global discourse of human rights with Islamic rights, but they are not identical, nor even compatible in the CDLR's view. To be fair, this disparity was not an issue initially. Apparently this theoretical debate was not a central component of the underlying criticisms that led to the organization's creation. Instead, the founders wanted to use the organization as a practical model to demonstrate that protecting Muslim rights is possible. The debate about human rights and Islam was left to the 'ulama. Despite the secondary role of human rights in the CDLR's initial critique of the Saudi state, however, the group adopted its discourse for tactical reasons.

The Split within the CDLR

Until February of 1996, the CDLR appeared to be a very effective media organ publicizing the problems of the Saudi government, despite its mixture of silliness and serious reporting. Nevertheless, the organization had its own contradictions that gradually led to a split within its ranks. These contradictions include differences in ideological orientation among the top leaders, the London Islamic culture itself, and the group's penetration by the Saudi intelligence. The story of the split has both negative and positive implications for the Saudi opposition.

On March 4, 1996, the CDLR suffered an internal division between its two main leaders, Muhammed al-Mas'ari and Sa'd al-Faqih. One of the outcomes of this split was the formation of a new group called the Movement for Islamic Reform In Arabia (MIRA) headed by al-Faqih (Chapter 3 discusses this group). Mas'ari and those who remained with him kept the original name of the organization. Both Mas'ari and al-Faqih claim to represent the movement inside the kingdom. After the split, there were noticeable changes in the CDLR's home page and in the organization as a whole, although we must be careful not fall in the trap of analyzing the CDLR on the basis of what is published on its Web site. Since the Internet is more accessible in English and most Arabic texts are difficult to access, the conclusions that I draw here are based on study of the English discourse only. The group's Arabic discourse, as presented in the Arabic newsletter, may reveal a different set of priorities.

Although it is difficult to identify the main reasons behind the split, it might be instructive to look at how the parties constructed the events that led to it. According to Mas'ari, on March 4, 1996, the CDLR decided to "dismiss Sa'd al-Faqih" from his post as a director of its London office, replacing him with Sheikh Kassab al-Utaibi. The decision was unanimously approved by the Shura Council of the CDLR and supported by Sheikh Abdullah al-Mas'ari, the head of the organization in Saudi Arabia.[33] Mas'ari gave four reasons behind the "dismissal" of al-Faqih: First, "al-Faqih's political program and agenda is in direct conflict with the 'Islamic program that the organization has pledged to follow.'" Second, the committee needed to reorganize in view of the political circumstances and the threat posed by the government. Third, the committee needed to reevaluate its reform program. And finally, the reconciliation efforts to contain the differences between the two had failed, and thus it became obvious that a formal split was in the interests of the organization. After providing these reasons, Mas'ari also implied that the Saudi government had orchestrated the group's division.[34]

To begin with the English discourse, the Web site was rarely updated after the split. Except for a few advertisements soliciting money from supporters, no new news items or analysis was added. The organization depended on mass electronic mail, yet my analysis of six months of dispatches suggests that Saudi Arabia was no longer the main focus of the group's critique. Most of the electronic mail coming from the CDLR was not signed by Muhammed al-Mas'ari but by Muhammed Jalal-Abadi, a Bengali writer. The issues focused on Israel, Zionism, Jewish influence in the West, and Jewish hatred of everything Islamic. This is partly because Mas'ari lost much of the Saudi audience and financial backing after the split and wished to compensate for this loss of support by appealing to a wider Muslim audience. Indeed, in an e-mail fund-raising appeal dated May 29, 1998, the CDLR states that Mas'ari's personal debt exceeded £200,000 and that he had been forced into bankruptcy. The new focus can also be attributed to Mas'ari's interest in Hizb al-Tahreer,[35] and the Muhajiroon in London, groups of immigrants from the Arab world and south Asia who made London the center of their activities. The governments of Egypt, Tunisia, Algeria as well as Saudi Arabia have complained to the British government about London-based activists who send money to their supporters at home.

After the split the Arabic component of the CDLR's discourse, as presented in *al-Huquq,* was still active. However, the newsletters were neither as regular nor as well written, and they now focused on different issues. The first newsletter after the split restated some of the organization's goals and added new ones. Together they indicated the direction Mas'ari hoped the organization would take as a Saudi opposition group, as opposed to the more general Islamic resistance group that it became. The CDLR sees the Saudi system as deviating from Islam, and thus the group must work toward changing the system by all possible peaceful means. The CDLR aspires to provide a sophisticated framework to organize and mobilize people all over the kingdom with no discrimination on the basis of region. The organization is committed to its initial principles, with the Memorandum of Advice as a reference. Yet it also welcomes any new ideas from anyone in the kingdom. It is for Saudis of all social classes and professions. The group does not accept any dialogue with the government unless the government agrees to the Memorandum of Advice as the basis for this dialogue or before it releases all political prisoners in the kingdom. The group welcomes any alliance with all organizations on the basis of Islam to resist and undermine the current government by all peaceful and legitimate means.[36]

A review of a 120 e-mail dispatches written in English reveals yet another side of Mas'ari after the split. In these dispatches, it is obvious that he has moved away from his Saudi focus to engage in more broadly Islamic issues. Although they were sent from the CDLR's e-mail address, these dispatches are not signed by Mas'ari himself, but Muhammed Jalal-Abadi of the Bangladeshi Muslim Literary Circle in Great Britain. Mas'ari seems to have become part of a larger umbrella of a Pan-Islamist movement known as Al-Muhajiroon. He is now spokesman for the Rally Against Oppression in addition to being the secretary general of the CDLR. He is part of a troika of Muhajiroon leaders in Britain that includes Sheikh Omar Bakri Muhammad and Maqbool Javaid.[37] The main focus of the dispatches has been a constant attack on the United States and its global policies. Many are also obsessed with the "Zionist conspiracy" or attacks on the United Nations as an instrument of imperialism. This anti-Jewish focus undermined Mas'ari's credibility with the British press and alienated many of the Western supporters to whom his English-language message originally appealed. Furthermore, a review of some 49 issues of CDLR's weekly publication *al-Huquq* (nos. 91, March 20, 1996 to no. 140, January 14, 1998) after the split also reveals changes in the organization's orientation.

The split in the organization certainly has weakened Mas'ari's position in any upcoming negotiations with the government. The image of the organization was further tarnished by open exchanges between Sa'd al-Faqih and Muhammed al-Mas'ari; both men used the Arabic press to accuse one another of misconduct. The men's public image has been damaged not only in the eyes of Western and Arab reporters but also in the eyes of their followers. This conflict has made the group seem disorganized and unprofessional and revealed that there is not enough ideological or strategic common ground to preserve even a minimal level of agreement within the ranks. This has made the government more relaxed in its assessment of the group.

Constructed and Reproduced Images

Central to the CDLR's activities is the construction of an image of Saudi Arabia that the Western press processes uncritically; the CDLR then sends that image home, as representative of what the Western media says about Saudi Arabia. This recycled narrative that gains legitimacy through its mobility within different media organizations makes it difficult to distinguish just who is the author, the CDLR or media reporting. Thus the CDLR has been very adept at using the Western press, both as a source and as an outlet. A very important section of *Ash-Shar'iyya* includes translated articles. Because Saudi Arabia is very low in the U.S. news agenda, and because of the relatively few academic experts, the news media has seized on the opposition. Thus an incident like the bombing in Riyadh or Khobar is overreported. The impact of this reporting gives the Saudi opposition an exaggerated sense of its size and power. Its image in the Western media is certainly greater than its actual size on the ground. This is why the magazine dedicates six pages to reports about Saudi Arabia in the Western media. To maximize the role of the opposition, it collects any news item about the Saudi opposition in both significant and non-significant Western publications. Thus, Arabic readers have a very different sense of the magnitude of the Saudi opposition. Most issues of the magazine include translated articles from Western publications such as *The Times* of London, *The Guardian,* the German *Der Spiegel, Newsweek, The Economist,* the *Washington Post,* and the *New York Times.* The reports selected for translation emphasize that Saudi Arabia is under attack from the Islamists and that the stability of the regime is in question. Since the non-Arabic news media rely heavily on the reports of the CDLR and the opposition to furnish the substance of their coverage, and the CDLR, in turn, relies on the Western media for corroboration, a fantastic dynamic of news laundering develops. The story of instability goes out from the CDLR office in London to experts and journalists who write a story to the *New York Times* or *The Times* of London; then the CDLR translates this story into Arabic, as if it were the Western journalists' independent assessment. This process of recycling narratives exaggerates the size and impact of the Saudi opposition and accentuates the role of the global media in highlighting or dismissing an opposition group. Certainly the Saudi opposition is neither the largest nor the most dangerous opposition force in the Gulf, yet it is quite prominent in the Western media. The global and the local narratives have thus converged, despite the lack of congruency between their aims and values.

After analyzing the activities and organization of the CDLR and the ideological orientation that informs its narrative, it is very important to focus on Mas'ari the man, his background and his life as he constructs it, to identify points of strength and weaknesses of the group's political program. To begin with, currently Mas'ari's connection and power base inside the kingdom is limited at best. My overall impression is that the Islamists in the kingdom constitute separate islands connected by a general enthusiasm about religion and social norms that are being undermined due to the influx of foreign values via foreign workers and foreign media. Cells do exist, but they are small in terms of hardcore activists. Nonetheless, the overall religious mood in the country exaggerates the linkage between these groups. So far, Mas'ari does not appear to have the organization necessary to pose a serious security threat. After the split, he lost much of his appeal even as a propaganda threat to the Saudi monarchy.

Mas'ari's objectives and political program seem to be contradictory. On the macrolevel, his objective is to lead the Islamists of Saudi Arabia. However, he is not clear about the direction he would like to take this group, nor is he sure that all of them would follow him. He talks about a country that he would like to build—at least theoretically—where the concept of citizenship is the criterion and there is "no difference between men and women." When I asked him about actual procedures and implementation of this goal, he stated only that "during elections—men and women vote, but separately." Beneath this rhetoric, however, is a man driven by parochial concerns and objectives. Mas'ari strives to achieve recognition both inside and outside Saudi Arabia. Ultimately, he may be satisfied by a position similar to that given to his colleague, Ahmed al-Tuwaijri, a membership in the Shura Council.

His discourse is designed to build political capital both inside Saudi Arabia and beyond; however, Mas'ari is also very good at squandering this political capital. He knows that the royal family is strong and that the "opposition is too fragmented to take power."[38] Yet his program does not depend on a plan of action; rather, he counts on the internal contradictions of Saudi Arabia that, in his judgment, will lead eventually to the demise of the royal family.

In spite of the degeneration of the organization's discourse and the lack of focus in its message, announcing the death of the CDLR as a political organization or of Mas'ari as an activist would be a grave mistake. Mas'ari is too complex to be taken for granted.

Government Response to the CDLR

Regardless of the problems of the CDLR and the Saudi Islamic movement at large, these groups have managed to pressure the government into implementing limited reforms. Because Saudi Arabia is a rentier state that does not depend on its people for legitimacy or taxes, there was a widespread perception that it is not likely to respond to Islamist demands. Contrary to this theory, the regime was somewhat responsive. The royal family did take two significant steps in direct response to the Letter of Demands and the Memorandum of Advice: It codified the basic laws and established the Shura Council.

Conclusion

As the global media focused on Saudi Arabia during the Gulf War and after and as the CDLR relocated to London, local Saudi issues became the concern of people beyond Saudi Arabia. However, in the same way that globalization of the media was instrumental in magnifying the size of the CDLR, it has also contributed to its demise. The CDLR was effective in its early years in attacking government policies domestically and internationally and captured the attention of most observers because of its innovative techniques and use of postmodern technology to resist a quasi-modern or premodern state. Media outlets were enamoured with the CDLR and were ready to believe what it disseminated about Saudi Arabia because of the novelty of the movement and its approach. Yet the CDLR's critique of the Saudi state focused on its betrayal of its foundational Islamic principles. The Saudi violation of Islam, according to the CDLR, included the kingdom's alliance with the United States and its allowing of foreign troops inside Saudi Arabia, but it also criticized the government for the absence of a constitution and basic laws allowing freedom of expression and association. As the ideological transcript of the group emerged through its publications, it would seem that the state envisioned by Mas'ari would be more restrictive than the current regime. According to Mas'ari, his state would allow freedom only within the context of the Hanbali school of jurisprudence. Members of the Shi'a minority of Saudi Arabia would not allowed any influential positions and would be second-class citizens to an even greater degree than they are now. Mas'ari's state is based on Islam, with only very little attention given to tribalism in Saudi Arabia, although many would argue that tribalism represents the building blocks of that society. Islam is the cement that binds these building blocks together, and a state made up of cement alone might not stay together for very long. Moreover, Saudi society differs from Hijaz in the West to the Eastern Province; each area has its own local cultures and outlooks. Nothing in Mas'ari's program engages the different regions in different discourses to create antistate feelings on the basis of regional differences. His treatment of all Saudi Arabia as if it were Najd might be perceived negatively in the other regions.

Gradually the novelty of the CDLR dissipated because the elements that contributed to its rise in the first place faded. The movement is no longer the charismatic new postmodern phenomenon coming out of the desert land of Saudi Arabia. The romantic story of a movement bringing down a 200-year-old dynasty with a fax machine has become less believable as time goes by. The split within the movement between its founders and the rise of a rival movement made this vision even less conceivable.

As Saudis became familiar with the satellite dish and the new means of communication, Western ideas no longer seemed so threatening. The U.S. troops in Saudi Arabia contributed to a great wave of opposition in 1990–91; now the troops have been moved out of the urban areas into the desert, away from the Saudi public's gaze. Furthermore, with the attacks on Americans in Riyadh and Khobar, the confrontation between the opposition and the government shifted from words to bombs, something that Saudis have little experience with and seem repelled by. Although these acts emboldened some Saudi radicals, it made many shy away from the opposition movements. Talk is one thing; killing people is something else. Discontent with foreign influence symbolized by the physical presence of U.S. troops on Saudi soil and the cultural penetration associated with it has gradually eroded, especially as satellite dishes became more popular and the country became more involved in global discourse.

The CDLR could not cope with the new global spaces. In London, Mas'ari gradually abandoned the Saudi issues in favor of more global issues to appeal to émigré communities there. He joined al-Muhajroon organization, led by the Syrian Omar Bakri. As part of this organization, Mas'ari gained credibility with the immigrant communities in London but lost credibility in the eyes of reporters, analysts, and his home base inside Saudi Arabia. The group's growing tendency to mix unsubstantiated, trivial allegations with serious and credible charges further undermined the credibility of its criticism of the Saudi government. Thus, as the group sought to satisfy various audiences, it lost its core message and confused its main constituency. Local Saudis turned away from the CDLR as they started to learn more about the group through Mas'ari's speeches and writings. Because of his lack of personal credentials as a religious scholar or as a man of important tribal prestige, Mas'ari seemed a less attractive alternative to the current regime. As the local constituency lost interest and the money dried up, Mas'ari focused even more on his pan-Islamic activism. Finally, as his position weakened due to the split within the organization and his mounting debts, he seems more open than ever to the idea of negotiating with the government. His only conditions are the release of prisoners and acceptance of the Memorandum of Advice as the basis for negotiations, conditions similar to those set by the Shi'a organization before it reconciled with the government. As chapter 7 shows, the government was flexible with the Shi'a and accommodated most of their demands. Will the same happen with the CDLR? The likelihood of this happening depends on Mas'ari and his group as well as on the dynamics of the opposition groups themselves.

CHAPTER FIVE

Sa'd al-Faqih and the Movement for Islamic Reform

My experience in Saudi Arabia in the past 20 years or so convinces me that our country will witness major and fundamental changes in the near future. This, however, doesn't mean the rebirth of a true Islamic state [caliphate] as I envision it. For such radical transformation to take place, generations and generations of young motivated Muslims have to take on the responsibility of this serious task. Yet I'm convinced that I will witness part of this change in Saudi Arabia in my lifetime.

—Sa'd al-Faqih, interview London, June 11, 1997

Social and political changes in Saudi Arabia have been the order of the day since the unification of the kingdom in 1932. However, unlike trends of the past, Sa'd al-Faqih foresees Saudi Arabia yielding to "the larger global trends that will not only impact Saudi Arabia, but the Islamic umma at large."[1] The story of the evolution of the current Saudi state is certainly linked to its contact with the outside world. The Ministry of Foreign Affairs, established in 1930, and the Ministry of Finance, established 1932, were responses to the increased dealings between King Abdul Aziz and the outside world. Almost all other would-be ministries were departments under the Ministry of Finance. The oil industry led to greater differentiation in the system.[2] The encounter with the modern world and its technological development has been central to political change in Saudi Arabia. This is not to argue, however, that the modern Saudi state is a product of ARAMCO. Such an attempt trivializes one of the most indigenous processes of state building in the region. Nor am I going to overemphasize the local character, as many nationalist historians do. The point here is that the articulation and the dialectical relationship between the local and the global processes is what matters, regardless of the particular weight given to any of these factors. The story of the Movement for Islamic Reform (MIRA) and its place between the local and the global force us to rethink Saudi Arabia and its opposition. Previously, Saudis viewed all modern and technological innovations with extreme suspicion; they feared the encroachment of modernity on their traditional life and religious values. Because the Saudi government considered such innovations integral to building a modern Saudi state, it had to maneuver cautiously to balance religious and worldly interests while also preparing to pay the political price of any resistance to such modernization projects. This was the case when King Abdul Aziz introduced the telegraph and the radio in the 1940s and 1950s. Similar conflicts arose with the coming of television in the 1960s and introduction of the satellite dish in the 1990s. Historically, traditional Islamic opposition in the kingdom has criticized the introduction of these modern technologies and blamed the government for facilitating the erosion of Islamic values. MIRA and its leader, Sa'd al-Faqih, represent the antithesis of the traditional Islamist trend in Saudi Arabia, for instead of resisting technology introduced by the state, they have adopted it as means of resisting the status quo. In a significant departure from the past, they use the most sophisticated information technology, such as the fax machine and the Internet, to bring about social and political change. Their final goal is the much-anticipated Islamic state.

History of the Movement

MIRA is the most sophisticated and effective of the Saudi opposition groups. It emerged in March 1996 as a result of a split in the Committee for the Defence of Legitimate Rights (CDLR). Such a split signified the deep rift between the CDLR's leaders, Sa'd al-Faqih and Muhammed al-Mas'ari. Al-Faqih created MIRA and became its director, while Mas'ari continued to be CDLR's spokesperson. Al-Faqih sees the split as due to differences between him and Mas'ari over "policy and methodology." Al-Faqih wanted the CDLR to focus on Saudi Arabia only, while Mas'ari wanted to forge alliances with other Islamic movements in the region, creating a larger Islamist movement with a wider focus and agenda. This, according to al-Faqih, was "a breach of CDLR's policy by individuals whose names had become synonymous with the organization." Even if we assume that before the split the CDLR reflected the new Saudi opposition internally, strangely, the split did not result in any visible cracks in the opposition movement inside the king-dom, due to the loose nature of the Islamic organizations there. Certainly the split within the CDLR is in keeping with Islamists' politics outside Saudi Arabia; the splintering of larger groups is the norm from Algeria to Egypt.

This split has led to a conflict between MIRA and the CDLR as to which group is the actual representative of the Islamic movement inside the kingdom. Al-Faqih insists that MIRA is and that it is the legitimate repre-sentative of the Islamic movement that started during the Gulf War. To make his case, al-Faqih constructs a narrative that makes him the legitimate heir of the original CDLR and Mas'ari a renegade and irresponsible leader. He presents MIRA as one of the stages in the evolution of the reform move-ment under the guidance of Safar al-Hawali and Salman al-'Auda. Accord-ing to al-Faqih, "The movement did not start with this name but started since the beginning of the reformist efforts after the Gulf War, and the men who lead it today are the same men who presented the king with the Let-ter of Demands and are also the authors of the Memorandum of Advice. They are the organizers of the CDLR. This is why we speak on behalf of this trend and follow its platform."[3] After the Letter of Demands, which re-vealed the movement's effectiveness in gathering signatures from prominent Saudis, the group moved to present its detailed argument in the Memoran-dum of Advice. Furthermore, after detecting the government's reaction to the memorandum, the group moved to build institutions and organizations that led to the emergence of the CDLR. The CDLR, as I have shown in chapter 4, continued to operate until the split between Sa'd al-Faqih and Mohammed al-Mas'ari in 1996. This event was bound to happen, for the two men are different from each other in ideology, upbringing, outlook, sensibility, and organizational affiliation. Unlike the ambitious Mas'ari, al-Faqih is very clear about his limited mission and sees himself as committed to the group that began with the Letter of Demands and the Memorandum of Advice. As one of the five founding members of the domestic Islamist movement, al-Faqih abides by the discourse of the movement, and today he considers MIRA as the third phase in its development in Saudi Arabia. More specifically, he views the role of MIRA as the "media arm of the [Sunni] reform movement" inside the country.

Who is Sa'd al-Faqih?

Sa'd al-Faqih was born in 1958 to a conservative family. Tall and thin with a black beard, a sign of religiosity, he is a surgeon by profession who until 1994 was a professor of surgery at King Saud University, the most prestigious uni-versity in the country. Later he decided to enter the realm of politics and cast himself as a major opposition leader against the Saudi government. I talked

with him for a total of ten hours in London on June 11–12, 1997. Al-Faqih
is a complex opposition figure who is not easily understood, since he defies
stereotyping. To seriously analyze his political thought, his movement, and
his political program, we have to understand the forces that shaped him. Here
I outline some of the most salient experiences that have had an impact on al-
Faqih: his family background, his life in Iraq until the age of 16 and the experience of immigration, his education and his medical practice in the
kingdom, his encounter with the West through his two trips to Britain, and
finally his life in Saudi Arabia during the Gulf War.

Family

Al-Faqih's family moved to Saudi Arabia in 1974, when young Saʿd was 16
years old. His family provided a source of influence on his personality today,
particularly his religious side. Yet he considers himself neither a fanatic nor
very religious. Religion for him was something to provide guidance in life on
the basis of high principles and well-founded morals. "Simply, I was someone who prayed and practiced the basic pillars of the religion," he says.
Within his family, al-Faqih considers his father to have had the strongest influence on him. His father supported and encouraged him to pursue not
only his schooling but also a more general education that made him the cosmopolitan man he is. Although his father had limited formal education, this
did not dissuade him from "reflecting on issues of power and authority." Al-
Faqih learned about authority, politics, and power from his father, who
taught him also about dignity and self-respect. His father also encouraged
young Saʿd to participate in boy scout camps, a Muslim Brotherhood activity. These trips allowed him to travel and see Riyadh and Jeddah for the first
time while he was a teenager living in Iraq. There he mixed with the youth
and attended Islamic conferences. Although these activities seemed empty of
any political overtones, they certainly made an impression on young Saʿd.
While his father allowed Saʿd the freedom to travel at a young age, he also
imposed restrictions.

The influence Saʿd's father has had on him is a mixed blessing. Although
it has provided the support that made al-Faqih what he is today, it could
also prove fatal to his political career. In a society where family is the ultimate unit where loyalty lies, Saʿd's father could also become a source of political pressure. The father wanted his son to study medicine because it is a
profession that "obliges others, prince and pauper alike, to respect you."
Even as an older and mature political activist, al-Faqih is still tied to his father and speaks of him with great reverence and respect. Saʿd recalls that
early on, he wanted to study engineering, but his father wanted him to
study medicine. He says: "I studied medicine to please my father. Looking

back, I know I have succeeded in proving myself and pleasing him as well."
Respect for the profession was evident in al-Faqih's family. Sa'd's older
brothers, Mohammed and Salah, are very successful Saudi doctors. In fact,
his older brother Salah is well respected by the royal family and has operated on some of them as well as on many of the kingdom's official guests.
Another influence on al-Faqih's life is Salah. He grew up looking up to him.
Salah, according to Sa'd, was very much influenced by the preaching of the
Muslim Brotherhood. He opposed the Nasserites. After the Arabs were defeated by the Israelis in 1967, he felt vindicated because Nasserism was
proven intellectually bankrupt. Al-Faqih shared most of his older brother's
Muslim Brotherhood orientation. The influence of the Muslim Brotherhood on Sa'd appeared when he was a high school student. His school, al-
Najat, was predominantly under the influence of the Muslim Brotherhood.
Later, he started reading the works of Sheikh Sayyid Qutb, the militant
leader of the Egyptian Muslim Brotherhood. In our discussion, al-Faqih
was particularly enthusiastic about two books: *Ma'alim fil Tareeq* (Sign-
posts) and *Hatha al-Deen* (This religion). Al-Faqih considers the latter to be
a very successful presentation of Islam as a divine message sent not to an-
gels but to fallible human beings. Al-Faqih also has been influenced by Islamic history books, namely the sera (biographies of early Muslim leaders).
"These readings inspired me to follow the lead of such memorable Muslims
as Omar ibn al Khatab and Khalid ibn al-Waleed."

His family's influence on his upbringing cannot be ignored in any attempt to understand al-Faqih's political thought. Familism appears to be a
very strong component in his ideological orientation. In light of this, it is
probable that al-Faqih could give up his whole London-based resistance operation to please or avoid the criticism of his father or an older brother or
any important figure in his family.[4] In his case, familism as ideology could
prove more powerful than Islamism. This familism, including the desire to
please one's father and to comply with conventional norms, hampers the efforts of most Arab activists to propose any serious departure from tradition.
However, as I listened to al-Faqih, I realized that he is more complex than
this formula suggests. Although during our first interview I was left with the
impression that familism is much more important than Islam in al-Faqih's
mind, on our interview on the next day, he surprised me by describing himself as a man with a streak of stubbornness and a desire to challenge authority. "I remember when I was young, I was the only one challenging my
father, although he was a man of a very strong personality both in the house
and outside. Nobody dared to disobey any order of my father; but I did. I
was rebellious by nature," al-Faqih says. This, of course, seems to contradict
the image he gave earlier of a man who obeys his father and went to medical school to please him. Nonetheless, al-Faqih sees no contradiction in this.

He sees fearing the father and rebellion against him as the law of nature. "Father-son relationships are always ambivalent," he says. This ambivalence, I would argue, still persists in his character today. Yet al-Faqih asserts that this ambivalence does not prevent him from being dedicated to his cause. He states that he has already been exposed to family pressure: "I was exposed to heavy pressure from my father and brothers to abandon my mission. I refused even the slightest change of the details of my program."[5] Nonetheless, the power of the ideology of familism cannot be overstated.

Politics, Medical School, and the Medical Profession

Both medical school in the Saudi capital and the practice of the medical profession in Saudi Arabia contributed to the making of al-Faqih as a political agitator. Al-Faqih attended medical school in Riyadh from 1974 to 1981. During these years Islamic activism outside Saudi Arabia grew with the rise of the Islamic groups in Egypt in 1971 with the coming of Sadat into power and the victory of Islamic politics in Iran in 1979. During that same year Saudi Arabia witnessed the most violent and significant stability tests when Juhaiman al-'Utaybi and his men took over the Grand Mosque in Mecca. Another upheaval took place in the Eastern Province when the Shi'a population, emboldened by the Iranian revolution and the Khomeini message, poured into the streets and protested against what they saw as discriminatory policies of the "Sunni" Saudi state against its Shi'a citizens. All these events contributed to the politicization of the universities in general. The defeat of Juhaiman, however, and the success of state in portraying the takeover of the Grand Mosque as sacrilege undermined what could have been a very dangerous trend. Even Islamists such as al-Faqih saw Juhaiman's takeover of the Grand Mosque "as a stupid move in addition to being wrong religiously." Al-Faqih argues that had Juhaiman chosen another target, he could have been more successful. As for the Iranian revolution, al-Faqih seem to have been impressed by it. "Despite my view of Khomeini as an extreme Shi'a, I was greatly impressed by his success in playing the political game skillfully and mobilizing the people in the correct time and with the most effective means."[6] Clearly, Saudi Arabia at that time was not immune to the Islamic activism outside it. Al-Faqih witnessed these events and was certainly influenced by them.

Through his work as a doctor in Saudi Arabia, al-Faqih learned about the shortcomings of both Saudi medicine and Saudi society. The connections between the inefficiency of the Saudi health care system and his political activism are clear in al-Faqih's mind. As a surgeon, specializing at one time in transplantation, he found that the system does not take into consideration either the welfare or the will of the people. He characterizes the health care system in Saudi Arabia at the level of both prevention and treatment as inefficient. "There was a clear lack of a national strategy or plan to provide sound and basic health services in the village, city, and country as a whole." Instead of providing such medical services, al-Faqih claims, corruption was the order of the day. "This was especially pronounced in the field of organ transplants," he says. In a country such as Saudi Arabia, with its limited population and quite traditional culture, a doctor of organ transplants already faces many challenges, as few viable organs are available. However, since there is no firm national strategy to manage and organize the distribution of any organs to the four or five transplants centers, the doctor's task becomes almost impossible. Moreover, most countries seek to provide health care plans which will cause such centers to specialize. Again, this is not the case in Saudi Arabia, where each center competes to do transplants of all organs. In the process, billions of dollars are wasted, as transplant centers are plagued by a lack of efficiency and competition for increased funds. Politics became intertwined with medicine. Al-Faqih, then, felt a need to change the health system fundamentally. This feeling put him on the path of politics. To al-Faqih, there was very little difference between what is happening in the medical field and what is taking place in the political system at large. The medical field is a microcosm of the general condition of the state and the society of Saudi Arabia.

Encounter with the West

Al-Faqih's encounters with the West also have had an impact on both his life and his political program. He begins by recalling his first trip to Britain and its impact upon him.

> I traveled twice to Great Britain, once when my mother was ill. I accompanied my mother in her trip in 1978. This was my first encounter with the Western way of life.... In Britain I enjoyed the British systematic thinking and their systems of transportation and communication. I have always thought, for example, that the Western postal system and the way streets and addresses were ordered is vital to any infrastructure. You know, in our countries, no such thing as an address exists, for we use natural landmarks for that purpose. There is absolutely nothing wrong with putting names on streets and numbers on houses. We spend billions of riyals on other matters when even a simple address system is not developed yet. That trip actually made me think that there must be a lot wrong in my country.

Al-Faqih's second visit to Britain in 1988 helped him not only in understanding the British medical system but also in discovering his Islamist orientation. Like Mas'ari, he took advantage of the freedom of association in the West to mix freely with other Muslim activists. "During that trip I was inside the British system working as a surgeon and I was able to see how the country was run. My work in medical practice especially in the field of surgery taught me how to be decisive with a clear aim. It also forced me to practice efficiency and professionalism." Indeed, one major characteristic that has impressed many who dealt with al-Faqih, including this author, is his professionalism. He is forthcoming in providing researchers with data and in granting them unlimited time for interviews. Al-Faqih prides himself at learning the best traits of Western culture while rejecting the worst.[7]

After returning from Britain, Sa'd was appointed assistant professor of medicine at King Saudi University, where he taught graduate students and worked as a consultant for the government on medical issues. Although Sa'd never liked to give orders to others, neither does he like to take orders. "I have never allowed even the head of the hospital nor the chief of staff to interfere in my work," he says. This style may weaken Sa'd as an effective leader of the movement. While Sa'd is good in his field, he lacks Mas'ari's charisma and charm as a political leader.

Al-Faqih's views of the Western world and its way of life have evolved over the years, becoming more complex as well as more critical. After he left for London as a member of the CDLR and later MIRA, he seems to have formulated different views of the Western world as an autonomous social and cultural formation as well as views of the way it relates to the Arab and the Muslim worlds. The West in its current state, al-Faqih argues, lacks a solid moral frame of reference to guide its people in their conduct, morals, and everyday life. His central criticism of Western societies is this absence of moral guidelines and the lack of communal life. "It is puzzling that such societies does not seem to have any moral obligations to prevent people from enjoying the euphoria and excitement of sex, alcohol, or drugs. It seems that the main purpose of living is enjoyment for enjoyment's sake." He is also critical of what he sees as "indulgence in self-centered themes, whereby individuals seek to maximize their own enjoyment at the expense of the larger society." It is obvious that al-Faqih detests the West's extreme individualism that comes at the expense of communal life. "Western societies, which created democracy and liberal ideals suffer from utter lack of any collectively or solidarity." This makes al-Faqih suspicious of Western societies and their style of governance. He asks, "What use is their democracy to a society which is so fragmented?" He adds, "Experiencing living in the West at different phases allowed me to witness severe decline in the values and morals of their society."

In the face of this decline of values, al-Faqih makes the case for the importance of the Islamic movements on global scale. He sees the new Islamist trends as a way for Muslim societies to reassert their identities and finally become victorious. "This new era of strong Islamic presence on the world arena is likely to lead to a clash between these two forces: Muslims and the West."

If anything will challenge Western culture, it will be Islam, according to al-Faqih. "This challenge comes from the fact that both civilizations subscribe to different frames of reference." Al-Faqih argues that although there are differences between the French, British, and American experiences and indeed there might be clashes between these subcultures at certain moments, because they share the same frame of reference, they are unlikely to undo each other. Al-Faqih also argues that even the clash between Marxism and liberalism is still within the domain of the Western tradition and thus the two ideologies are not incompatible. In the case of Islam, however, al-Faqih points out, there are serious philosophical and epistemological differences. "On a philosophical level, the main differences between the West and Islam is that the Western culture has sought to obtain self-rule for the individual as an end result. In Islam, on the other hand, the end result is establishing and guaranteeing God's dominance over the individual and community as a whole. Many Muslims fall in the trap of judging their own societies from a Western frame of reference." These differences are enough to bring about this clash. In this regard al-Faqih is still faithful to the views of Safar al-Hawali and Salman al-'Auda, two men who seem to thrive on an impending East-West conflict. Al-Faqih's life is of course made of many elements. His life in the West and his views of Western societies are only some elements of this very complex political and religious activist.

Al-Faqih's Position in Saudi Society

Like al-Mas'ari, al-Faqih is to some degree an outsider in Saudi society. Although he does not acknowledge any direct influence of the first 16 years of his life that he spent in Iraq, at least the immigration had an impact on his political thinking. Al-Faqih may have his own reasons to minimize the impact of his first 16 years of life; nevertheless, readers should know something about his early life. Al-Faqih was born in the town of al-Zubair. There he attended al-Najat school, where the teachings of the Muslim Brotherhood were emphasized. His life in Iraq certainly contributed to an identity question that he has to deal with throughout his political career. Although al-Faqih is a Zubairi originally from a Najdi origin, he asserts that he is related to the royal family. The grandmother of late King Abdul Aziz is Latifa al-Faqih, a cousin of al-Faqih's grandfather.[8] Yet supporters of the regime and opponents of the Islamists view al-Faqih as coming from a marginal family.[9] This perception of marginality may prove an obstacle to al-Faqih if he is to

present himself as an alternative to the Sauds. In a society where identity, genealogy, and place of birth are very important, I wonder how al-Faqih would
deal with this question later on in life. He seems cognizant enough of his position as an immigrant. He is very evasive when asked about his immigration
from Iraq to Saudi Arabia, especially now, when tension between Iraq and
Saudi Arabia is high. Al-Faqih repeatedly returns to the point that his family originally moved to Iraq as part of a larger immigration wave from central Arabia to the Levant. Indeed, during the first Saudi state, many Najdis
settled in al-Zubiar and al-Basra.[10] These Sunni Wahhabis remain in Iraq to
this day. He attributes his family's treasuring of their Saudi identity to the
fact that al-Zubiar was surrounded by non-Sunnis (Shi'a) and thus they were
not integrated in the larger society, unlike other Najdi tribes who migrated
to areas where the inhabitants were primarily Sunnis. "There were many
families which came to al-Zubiar in the past two centuries, and there were
also ones like my own which inhabited the area for fifty or sixty years prior
to my birth," he says. Whether this theorizing of genealogy will take hold
whenever al-Faqih returns to Saudi Arabia is another question. It is very important to note that in spite of their marginality, many Zubairis have been
included in the cabinet, including Muhammed Aba al-Khail, the former
minister of finance; Sulaiman al-Sulaim, the former minister of commerce;
and Abdurrahman Assuwailim, the former deputy health minister. In the
army, some Zubairis have been appointed as senior officers, such as Abdullah al-Hamdan, a former head of the air force. Al-Faqih's origin in Najd is
more respectable because of his tribal origin more than that of Mohammed
al-Mas'ari, a khadiri (nontribal). Indeed one of the jokes about al-Faqih is
that the highest point he reached in his political career is to be a second man
to a khadiri, a reference to al-Mas'ari.

The Gulf War

Al-Faqih's political activism came as a result of the Gulf War, which he sees
as an event that transformed his life and took him into another phase. Since
the war was not discussed openly in the Saudi media, most serious discussions of its implications took place in the informal gatherings of friends. In
most Arab states, it is in these informal institutions where the substance of
politics can be found. However, to be privy to this shilla (group) discourse,
one has to be a Saudi first and trusted one after that. Al-Faqih was part of a
shilla whose members he described as people who "adopted different ways of
thinking about themselves and the world. Their analysis of politics went to
the heart of the matter, instead of the usual sidetracking which plagues most
of these discussions in Saudi Arabia." Members of this group gradually
moved from discussing events to becoming political activists. As al-Faqih ex-

plains, its purpose was to transcend the Islamic movement's negative attitude toward political change. "Our purpose was to utilize the natural support that Islam enjoys in the society to bring about the hegemony of religion and its dominance."[11] The goals were clear: "to have a specific mission, to map out the forces under the banner of the Islamic movement, and to understand the environment in which this plan will be executed." To bring about a qualitative shift in Saudi political thinking, the group focused on the issues of the 'ulama, the state, and politics. Its aim was to change the dominant language of Saudi politics from the rule of habits to the rule of religion. The first step toward this change was to present the king with the Letter of Demands. This letter formed the basis for what came to be known as the Memorandum of Advice, a 42-page double-spaced document signed by about 400 activists. Although Sheikh Abdul Aziz bin Baz, Saudi Arabia's Grand Mufti and the head of the Council of Higher 'Ulama, endorsed the Letter of Demands, he did not endorse the Memorandum of Advice.[12]

The Movement and Its Ideology

The movement's ideology consists of various statements, speeches, books, and sermons of the various Islamists of Saudi Arabia during the Gulf War and after, and most recently a draft political program. The latter, completed in May 1998, is a mixture of the Memorandum of Advice and what the group learned during the past six years.[13] This 46-page document addresses nine areas of concern for the movement, which are very similar to the Memorandum of Advice discussed in chapter 1. The nine-point program covers: 1. Shari'a and justice, 2. The current political system and its limitations, and the alternative system, 3. Foreign affairs, 4. National security issues, 5. The economic system of Saudi Arabia, 6. The society, 7. The information system, 8. Protection of individual rights, 9. Strategies for political and social change. In spite of this elaborate draft document, the group's ideology remains the sum total of its episodic discourse and its reaction to events. Some of this discourse may lose currency as the distance between the event and the social reality becomes greater; other elements may continue over time. To trace the ideological underpinnings of this group, we have to recall some events that shaped the movement. No event in Saudi history exposed the Saudi state as much as the Gulf War did. It made the shortcomings that culminated in the writing of the Memorandum of Advice very obvious, namely, the gap between Saudi discourse and institutions and the reality of the Saudi life. This gap between institution and ideas was central in shaping this group's ideology as well as the nature of the Saudi protest at large. Thus, as a result of general feeling among Islamists that the Saudi system needs reform, students, university professors,

and religious activists gathered together to discuss the affairs of Saudi Arabia. They described the state of affairs as follows: "What is un-Islamic dominated the social life, although it is contrary to what the society is all about,
and what is good and Islamic receded in the society, contrary to the fact
that it is rooted in the society and its people."[14] As the group discussed
these issues, they realized that the Islamic movement in Saudi Arabia, although strong, was fragmented and that Islamists seldom were capable of
transcending their small circles. Even when they did—as in the case of the
preachers who used cassette tapes to sensitize the larger society to their
call—they lacked any strategy for change. They also react to events.[15] The
group that met during the Gulf War and, as still part of MIRA, developed
a three-element strategy for action: to define short-term and long-term
goals; to size up the group's weight in Saudi Arabia and that of the Islamic
trend at large; and to map out the movement's friends and enemies in Saudi
society and to understand both the global and the regional context and
their implications for the reform movement. As the group itself admits,
"We did not have the means to launch such an ambitious plan, and thus it
needed a lot of work to reach these goals." The group's main purpose has
been to create a qualitative shift in Saudi society and to resocialize Saudis
into a different set of priorities and issues. The main issues that group
wanted to focus on were those concerning "religion and the 'ulama, politics
and governance, and cleaning people's minds from ignorant ideas cloaked
as Islamic." This forced the group to think about how to reach a larger
number of people and how to focus its message to replace old ideas with
new and Islamic ones. Their starting point was the Letter of Demands that
was signed by many prominent Saudis and was delivered to the king and
later published. This publication opened the door to the larger effort of the
Memorandum of Advice. According to al-Faqih, the Letter of Demands
shows the public that something can be done and that one can be responsible for whatever consequences might follow. After it was signed and delivered to the king, the letter shattered an age-old concept of the "secrecy of
advice for those who lead the nation." This led many people to believe that
the Islamists were leading the process of reform. Yet it is important to note
here that the Islamists' Letter of Demands came *after* the liberal forces presented their own letter of demands. Contrary to what al-Faqih claims, the
liberals were first in demanding reform, although they did not follow up
and left the arena to the Islamists who seized the moment and developed
the Letter of Demands into the document they called the Memorandum of
Advice. Until that time, the group's aim was reform. However, the discourse
of the movement and its leaders have changed over time, especially when
the CDLR was formed and when its leaders left the country for London.
However, with the Memorandum of Advice the group used another strat-

egy. The same group of five met and recorded a tape that later came to be known as "the Supergun" to propagate the concepts included in the memorandum and make them understood by the man on the street.[16] Because it directly criticized the royal family, government ministers, and others, the two-hour tape attracted the attention of both Saudis and Western reporters alike.[17] The popularity of the tape and its reception in Saudi Arabia and in the West gave the Islamists the chance to present their Memorandum of Advice with very little fear, as the interplay between the Islamists and the Western media may have protected them from royal wrath.

Like many of the post-Gulf War movements and organizations in Saudi Arabia, MIRA uses the Memorandum of Advice as the main reference for its political program. Al-Faqih claims that MIRA is the legitimate heir of the original program and that the CDLR as it exists after the split is far from that program. MIRA espouses a political program that emphasizes the following features: (1) the group's political project is religious in nature; (2) in this project the Shari'a is supreme; (3) leaders of this political program should follow the teachings of the 'ulama; (4) Saudis should be resocialized about the "true" nature of the Saudi political system; and (5) the leaders must adopt realism in implementing this political program, taking into account the complexity of the Saudi political environment. MIRA clearly sees no alternative to the Shari'a as the main frame of reference for Saudi society. It also sees a central role to the 'ulama. However, the movement adopts a middle ground "between the [government] 'ulama, who appease the rulers but are rigid in applying Islam on the larger society and [the liberals] who are critical of the government without applying these principles to themselves and the larger society they live in."[18] To this group, the 'ulama are represented by Sheikh Safar al-Hawali and Salman al-'Auda, who practiced what they preached. Al-Faqih himself accords al-'Auda greater importance than Hawali. Perhaps because the movement focuses on Saudi traditions, it does not advocate Western democracy as the model.

Yet the political aims of MIRA are not clear. Some of its newsletters seem to suggest that it is reformist rather than revolutionary. For instance, in its weekly Nashra (newsletter) of July 14, 1997, the group responded to the government increase in the membership of the Consultative Council from 60 to 90 members by republishing the 1992 Letter of Demands,[19] suggesting that it thinks that the regime's reforms fall short of what the letter has specified. Here the group appears hopeful for greater reform. Yet the Nashra of June 16, 1997 seems to suggest that this group is revolutionary, bent on overthrowing the regime. Here the group reprinted an earlier article in which it tried to answer whether it is reformist or radical. In this letter, the group says that reform does not apply to the Saudi system. It believes this system is falling apart and should be eliminated. The system's collapse would be better for the society than its continued existence.[20] Thus the ideology of the movement and its main political program remain unclear. While some central strands can be identified, the discourse of the movement remains episodic.

Some of the group's ideology can be identified from the various publications, pronouncements, and public stances of its leaders. Yet such pronouncements are not the final word. As described in its weekly newsletter, MIRA presents itself as a Salafi organization. The term "Salafi" or "Salafiyya" is a complex one, usually translated into English as "fundamentalist" and "fundamentalism" respectively. However, the literal translation of "Salafi" is "one who follows the way of the Salaf" (those who preceded him, or his ancestors). Whenever it is used in Arabic, it is usually followed by the word "al-Salih" (those who advocate enjoining good), suggesting that they are not embracing all the ancestors and their ways. More specifically, the word "Salaf" refers to the four caliphs and the four schools of Islamic jurisprudence: Maliki, Shafi'i, Hanbali, and Hanafi. MIRA narrowly follows the most conservative of these schools of jurisprudence, the Hanbali school, which Sheikh Mohammed bin Abdul Wahhab revived in the eighteenth century. In addition, MIRA anchors its interpretations and discourse in the writings of other Hanbali 'ulama, such as ibn Taymiyyah and ibn Qaym al-Jawziya.

The mission of MIRA and its basic ideological contours appear in its publication entitled *Risalat al-Haraka* (the message of the movement) and to some extent in another broadcast on the Internet entitled *Qadhiyat al-Isbou'* (the weekly issue). The existence of sound capability on the Internet has made it easy for MIRA to broadcast its message in Arabic. Previously this message was available only as text. Earlier text-based messages on the Internet were in English only; Arabic was image-based. Both *Risalat al-Haraka* and *Qadhiyat al-Isbou'* aim at presenting "the views of the movement's leaders, their position on events and their public policy, and its approach and means of dealing with issues."[21] Many of the movement's ideological strands appear in al-Faqih's comments on events. Another purpose of the broadcast is to resocialize Saudis into the movement's ideology and broadcast MIRA's reform project to people inside Saudi Arabia.

Al-Faqih insists that the London wing of the movement is merely the media arm. "The London office is not the movement, nor is its body or its organization. The movement is inside the kingdom," he says in direct response to Mas'ari's claims to be the leader of the Saudi opposition. Unlike Mas'ari, al-Faqih argues, "I will never be seduced by the glow of television and the media and forget my role as a spokesman for the larger movement inside. I'm not aspiring to lead; I will remain faithful to our leaders, the 'ulama, and will remain loyal to their circle."[22] However, the lack of media attention may limit the effectiveness of the movement. Moreover, al-Faqih refuses to think of his movement as an opposition within the Saudi context. In our interview he stated, "We are not the opposition. We are in harmony with the history of the Arabian peninsula and we represent the mood of the society. If there is an opposition to the values of Saudi society, it is the state." He also refuses to be compared with other Islamic movements in the rest of the Arab and Muslim world. "Those who attempt such a comparison are ignorant of the basic facts about Saudi society."

Cyberresistance and MIRA's Home Page

MIRA has benefited tremendously from the new spaces accorded to its members both in London and in cyberspace. MIRA has utilized cyberspace, in particular, in ways no Saudi opposition have utilized it before. MIRA's home page, which can be accessed at www.miraserve.com, provides downloadable information, both text and audio data. The audio is in Arabic and directed to the Arabic-speaking audience. One program consists of questions and answers with the head of MIRA, Dr. Sa'd al-Faqih. This part of the home page is called the Itha'a (broadcast). There is also text-based material in both English and Arabic. MIRA's Arabic newsletter also is available by dialing a telephone number in the United States. This number changes constantly due to security threats. After dialing this number, step-by-step instructions in Arabic detail how to get the newsletter automatically. MIRA also advises its members in the kingdom on how to use the Internet. For instance, in its May 20, 1996, issue, MIRA instructed its supporters on how to get on-line through universities and research institutions or through commercial servers like CompuServe. It says: "One can also avoid being detected by the Saudi intelligence, if one subscribes to a server in a neighboring Gulf country such as Kuwait or the Emirates. Visiting our home page is not a security risk. Those who use the Internet can also talk to each other free of charge as long as your computer has a microphone and the special software needed for this activity."

Al-Faqih tells followers back home that they can access MIRA by an 800 number from inside Saudi Arabia or from outside the kingdom in other Gulf States. In addition to the Web site, al-Faqih is also entertaining the possibility of a broadcast version of electronic resistance via one of the satellite channels that beams radio broadcasts directly to Saudi Arabia. According to al-Faqih, thus far the group has met some difficulties in securing a channel due to the "nervousness of satellite companies." Al-Faqih believes that the theme of tapes, leaflets, faxes, the Internet, and then radio broadcasts are stages of evolution in one process: breaking the wall of secrecy in the kingdom. He believes that the royal family is very vulnerable to successful mass message delivery in and out of the kingdom. He claims that this was why very few people in a small office in London could be successful as the group's media arm.

One of MIRA's tools to disseminate information is its weekly newsletter. The issues it discusses reflect MIRA's priorities and agenda. This section provides a content analysis of MIRA's on-line newsletter for the past two years. The contents of MIRA's home page are very sophisticated. Aside from the basic introduction about who they are and the aims of the organization, it provides analytical articles on relevant subjects, such as royal succession, the economic crisis in the kingdom, and the history of dissent in Saudi Arabia. The Arabic version of MIRA's weekly newsletter, *al-Islah,* provides news from the kingdom, foreign media reports about it, and an analysis about the current situation. Because *al-Islah* is designed to address a local audience, its discourse has the movement's Islamic coloring but is more organized and more moderate in tone than that of the CDLR. The local leadership trusts MIRA, evidenced by the fact that Salman al-'Auda and Safar al-Hawali send their writings from prison to be published in MIRA's newsletter. A recurring theme of the newsletter is the movement's commitment to following the fundamental ideals of Islam. For examples, the newsletter repeatedly supplements its message of commitment to the "salafi" principle with multiple hadiths and verses from the Quran. According to al-Faqih, the English section is not designed for English-speaking Muslims; it is prepared for Western media and think tanks. The MIRA Web site provides a monthly publication, *Arabia Unveiled,* and a weekly publication, *Arabia in the Media.* The latter is a collection of whatever has appeared in the Western press about Saudi Arabia that week with separate MIRA comments on it. The Arabic and English sections on the Web site differ in subject of interest rather than in position or opinion.

Despite the newsletters' overwhelmingly religious tone and political rhetoric, at times they reflect the realities of the Saudi state and its opposition. The fourth issue is a step in that direction, for its main article did not focus on the reform movement. It discussed challenges facing the Saud regime, which entailed issues such as corruption, economic austerity, the royal succession question, Saudi-U.S. relations, and confrontations that may arise from all of these elements. The same issue also included news summaries of events taking place inside the kingdom. Perhaps we can conclude that the initial issues of the newsletter presented readers with the agenda of the reform movement as a Saudi opposition movement that is part of a larger coalition and based on the ideals of the fundamentalist principles. The fourth newsletter changed that pattern.

The following issues discussed the overarching theme of the collapse of the Saudi state and the reasons behind regional and global support for the continued hegemony of that state. Such discussions entailed multiple dimensions of oil politics, U.S. military presence in the Gulf, disparities of wealth and power in the region, and a narrative of colonial history. The Islamist discourse is not the central issue in the newsletter. One issue, dated April 29, consists solely of a poem dedicated to dissidents in prison. The eighth newsletter discussed the terrorist bombing in Riyadh and the effect of the government's arrest campaign on the stability of the country, as the government increasingly violated human rights to maintain order. Various articles also discussed the relations between the Saudi state and the United States and the influence of such a relationship on the sovereignty of the Saudi state, the strategic and security arrangements in the country, and policy ramifications for the Saudi people. The ninth issue returned to the reassertion of goals, which characterized the early editions of the newsletter. Again, a clear religious overtone dominated, emphasizing the movement's agenda. While the tenth issue presented some mention of Western media coverage of Saudi events and news, newsletters remained dedicated largely to local Saudi concerns.

Following the bombings in Riyadh and later at the Khobar Towers, the newsletters were dominated by information on the government's plot to crack down on various Islamic groups even though they were not responsible for the bombing. The newsletters also conveyed increased frustration with the close relationship between the Americans and the Saudi state. Reporting on the royal family's corruption scandals also continued. The newsletters also focused on Arab/regional issues, which of course were of great pertinence to Saudis. Such issues included the oil-for-food deal with Iraq, human rights violations in Kuwait, and the suppression of Islamist groups in North Africa. For example, newsletter number 16 included a letter issued by MIRA to the Group of Seven industrial countries summit in Leon, France. It was intended to address leaders/presidents of those countries in light of developments in the aftermath of the Khobar bombing and to highlight the unjust effects of U.S.-Saudi relations on the Saudi people. In general, however, the inflammatory language of the newsletter undermines much of its effectiveness.[23] In addition, other newsletters, especially number 17, for example, sought to present information on the Western coverage of these bombing for the first time. Throughout its dispatches, MIRA attempts to consolidate its place as part of a larger opposition movement in Saudi Arabia. Nonetheless, its is not reluctant to acknowledge the fragmentation and division plaguing the Saudi opposition. The early issues of the newsletter perceived this fragmentation as part of the transition phase, claiming such disagreements are "good for the movement and not at all bad."[24]

Indeed, the Web page provides information on government efforts to undermine the Islamic movement inside; it does not indicate the actual size of this movement and how many individuals are connected to MIRA. Does MIRA's information reach the Saudi Islamists and does it influence their political activities inside the kingdom? These questions require answers to seriously assess the group's ability to challenge the government.

Power Base: Leadership and
Audience Inside Saudi Arabia

It remains unclear how many Saudis share al-Faqih's perceptions. When I asked him about the group's base of support inside the kingdom, he answered, "I have no way of knowing how many people would have access to our message." Indeed, very few know the exact number of the movement's followers inside the kingdom. According to al-Faqih: "The message reaches at least 300 people inside Saudi Arabia, these are the fax numbers I have." Of course, these 300 dispatches may be copied and sent to other people. Many people in Saudi Arabia say they receive copies of al-Faqih's faxes. The question is, however, if they await these dispatches eagerly or perceive them to be "junk" mail. Another question is how important the information provided is and whether it competes with other sources coming into Saudi Arabia, such as the BBC radio or the multiple channels of the satellite dishes that permeate the Saudi society. Of course, faxes are not the only means for Saudis to get information from or about MIRA. They may access the Internet and see MIRA's Web page. Yet this is, of course, limited by the restrictions imposed on the Saudi media in general and the Internet in particular. Furthermore, Saudis have access to MIRA's Web page via an international line outside Saudi Arabia. Through my interviews, I realized that although MIRA's Web page reaches many people outside the kingdom, it reaches few inside it. It was very difficult for me to assess the movement inside Saudi Arabia, because very few people were willing to talk about being part of the Islamic movement. Nonetheless, I have interviewed some contacts provided by al-Faqih himself. From these interviews it became obvious that the movement does not have an organizational structure as such. That is, although people may claim to be part of this movement, none of the respondents could address the issues of leadership and decision making. One can speak of an executive director of MIRA in London, but one cannot find a leader who dispenses decisions and orders for members of the movement to follow. According to al-Faqih, more than 300 Islamist leaders in Saudi Arabia are under arrest. These are people who became close due to the similarity of their ideology and their critiques of the government, but they are not bound together in an organization with a clear command structure. Al-Faqih also speaks of about 1,000 or so "Arab Afghans," Saudis who fought in Afghanistan and who are currently in prison. However, these people may be connected more to the Advice and Reform Committee (ARC) under the leadership of Usama bin Laden than they are to MIRA. Nonetheless, they are part of the general Islamist mood in Saudi society. I will discuss this group in detail in chapter 6. However, at the level of both organization and arrests, there are very few Saudi Islamists in comparison with the Islamists of Egypt or Algeria. In spite of this, al-Faqih claims that they are very strong organizationally. "Horizontally we are strong. There are thousands who support us. Support that requires sacrifice, however, is very weak."

In spite of these weaknesses, the movement's impact on the political language of Saudi Arabia cannot be ignored. The fact that al-Faqih does not have a large following does not necessarily mean that his critiques of the current Saudi system are irrelevant. Al-Faqih's critique and his strategies could be used effectively by a more charismatic leader under different conditions. However, as it stands, it very important to know to what degree al-Faqih's views on governance, democracy, and the issue of minorities are a departure from the current system. Assessing the mobilizing potential of these ideas and their impact on the stability of the current system is of paramount importance.

Al-Faqih's Critique of the Current Saudi System

Al-Faqih's criticism focuses on three aspects of the Saudi system: the royal family and its style of governance, the 'ulama, and the judicial system. Al-Faqih's selective emphasis on these three areas at the expense of other areas mentioned in the Memorandum of Advice is not accidental; Western journalists and analysts reporting on Saudi Arabia usually focus on these areas. To some degree, although not at the scale of the CDLR, MIRA seems to pay more attention to this global audience at the expense of the local constituency. In this respect, its local appeal is likely to be weakened.

"True political reform will inevitably entail a restructuring of the Saudi regime itself," says al-Faqih. He further elaborates: "All the problems of the regime are linked to the royal family and its monopoly on power. This is a fundamental problem that every Saudi opposition seeks to eradicate."[25] Al-Faqih's antiroyal stance is conveyed in a book that summarizes his arguments.[26] His main criticisms center around the following issues: (1) the concentration of power in the hands of the Sudairi branch of the family; (2) the reliance on the United States for protection; (3) the reliance on patrimonialism rather than meritocracy in the appointment of cabinet ministers and other high officials; and (4) the personalization of politics and the condescending attitude of members of the royal family toward the public. On the latter point, al-Faqih claims that the royal family sees itself as racially superior to others. This racial and socioeconomic superiority, according to al-Faqih, is asserted by the family's absolute control over the country's polit-ical, economic, and information system.[27] In addition, the royal family hates the Islamic movement. Although he raises some interesting points about the way the family rules in Saudi Arabia, al-Faqih's criticism is not shared by many inside the country. Those who benefit from the current system dismiss his criticism as mere envy and zealotry.

In addition to his hatred of the royal family, al-Faqih is very critical of the role the 'ulama play in justifying the Al Saud's rule, particularly Sheikh Abdul Aziz bin Baz, the Grand Mufti. This criticism is part of a larger argu-ment that contends that the current system in Saudi Arabia does not con-form to the rules of the Shari'a (Islamic law). Like Mas'ari, who published a book asserting that the Saudi state is an infidel state rather than an Islamic one, al-Faqih also published a book making similar points.[28] Al-Faqih's book, however, is milder and more measured than that of Mas'ari. For in-stance, he avoids the idea of complete takfeer (accusing Saudis of being non-Muslims, a point that Mas'ari makes explicit in his book). Al-Faqih begins his critique of the 'ulama by pointing out that there is no clerical or religious hierarchy in Islam. Nonetheless, he does not believe that anyone capable of reading and understanding the Shari'a can be an alim (learned man of reli-gion). For al-Faqih the true alim is "the person who speaks the truth to those in power." Sheikh bin Baz falls short of meeting this criteria, according to al-Faqih, because of his criticism of the Islamists such as Hawali, al-'Auda, and those who launched the CDLR. Al-Faqih further adds that the true alim is the one who is faithful to the teachings of the Shari'a and not influenced by worldly concerns. In our interview, al-Faqih said: "Bin Baz and the other 'ulama might be men of great personal morality and knowledge, but they do not always have the courage to speak the truth when confronted with worldly power."

As an evidence for the 'ulama's corruption, al-Faqih asserts, "Almost all the fatwas issued by the 'ulama at times of crisis supported the state." He enumerates the fatwas concerning the arrival of American troops to the kingdom, against the CDLR, against the Memorandum of Advice; and that allowed the state to arrest al-'Auda and Hawali. Furthermore, he accuses both bin Baz and bin Otheimeen, of standing by the state in spite of its vi-olation of Islamic law.

When I stated that these 'ulama are respected and revered in Saudi Ara-bia, al-Faqih replied that they were revered because of their personal piety and because, until the Gulf War, they had not been confronted by an issue that would put their reputations on the line. When they faced a choice be-tween the state and Islam, they obviously chose the state. Al-Faqih accuses both men of hypocrisy because they portray Saudi Arabia as if it were a Rashida state (based on earlier models of the Islamic state). Thus he believes that it is a mistake to rely on the established 'ulama because they have participated directly in perpetuating the current state of injustice.[29] These 'ulama, according to al-Faqih, are not the right ones. If there are 'ulama to be trusted to speak truth to those in power, they are people like Hawali and al-'Auda.

Al-Faqih's critique of the religious establishment is both substantive and procedural. In terms of substance, he thinks that the basic problem with the current institution is that it is a mirror image of the relationship between church and state in medieval Europe. The religious establishment, according to al-Faqih, is removed from the lives of the people, and its main function seems to be to establish the legitimacy of the ruling elite. Its leaders issue fatwas that reflect the wishes of the ruler but never criticize his practices, even if they are anti-Islamic. Al-Faqih thinks that the Council of Higher 'Ulama (the fatwa institution that has become part of the Ministry of Endowments and Islamic Affairs), the Institution for the Promotion of Virtue and the Suppression of Vice, and the judiciary all require reevaluation. He states that the first section of the Memorandum of Advice focuses on the reform of the religious establishment, criticizing the current institutions because those who work in them are appointed by the ruler, who interferes in their work. This is why their fatwas are merely a defense of the ruler. This was evident in the fatwas issued from the Gulf War until the Khobar bombing. Al-Faqih also is very critical of the Institution for the Promotion of Virtue and the Suppression of Vice and considers its use by the royal family to be highly hypocritical. In fact, al-Faqih does not believe that there is any need for this institution in an Islamic state because almost all state institutions, from the police to the judiciary, should promote virtue and fight vice. Furthermore, al-Faqih considers the offices of da'wa as a hindrance to Islam, because he believes that tying the da'wa to an official institution limits it. He does not believe that the current regime is capable of implementing the necessary reforms. This can happen only if there is a radical political change. He cannot conceive of any change within the religious establishment outside a larger and more comprehensive program for change. He writes: "The issue of Da'wa cannot exist within a system that does not allow for freedom of expression and freedom of association and building institutions of civil society." Al-Faqih cannot excuse bin Baz or the other Saudi alim linked to the state. In his eyes they have sold out. He proposes the 'ulama of al-Sahwah (the awakening) as alternatives. These 'ulama, of course, would include Safar al-Hawali and Salman al-'Auda on the top of the list.[30]

Another important focus of al-Faqih's criticism is Saudi Arabia's judicial system. Again this is part of his critique of the "un-Islamic" nature of the regime.[31] According to al-Faqih, the justice system of Saudi Arabia has three major problems: the Shari'a is not fully applied; is not an independent body;

and is chaotic administratively. Al-Faqih accuses the justice system of deviation from the Shariʿa laws and claims that under the current system, the
judges are obliged to apply laws that are not Islamic. Worse, the judges
themselves are subject to the whims of the executive branch of government.
Furthermore, the special committee set up to deal with commercial law has
the judges' authority although the laws are un-Islamic. He believes that even
if the justice system used experts in modern issues, this would be unacceptable under Islamic law. For him judges should be Islamists. These secular
laws are not the codification of the religious laws as some claim, al-Faqih argues, but they are based on the desires of the ruling family. He further adds
that even among the ʿulama of Saudi Arabia it is unacceptable to codify the
Shariʿa, because the Shariʿa is broader than codified laws. Moreover, he feels
that under the current system, Shariʿa is not applied equally: It prevails over
those who are weak and form the working classes, but it is not applied
against those who are in positions of power or protected by the royal family.
The judiciary lacks independence because the king or any prince can call a
judge and alter the sentence at any time. It would be very difficult to reform
all these things without a radical change of the system.

Let us now turn to the features of the new system that MIRA and al-
Faqih envision.

Governance and the Islamic State

In most of its publications, MIRA is very careful not to endorse models of
governance derived from the Western experiences. MIRA's leader argues
that, in terms of procedures, any political system should be adjusted to suit
the needs of the people, their traditions, and their environment. "We don't
have to borrow a complete model. For example, the procedures of the American political system are acceptable within Islam. Philosophically, however,
in an Islamic system the Shariʿa must be supreme. This is our major difference with Western-style democracy." To ensure the supremacy of the Shariʿa,
al-Faqih argues for the institutionalization of these ideas in a form akin to
the current Council of Higher ʿUlama. The main task of this council is to
ensure that all the laws are in keeping with Islamic law. Indeed, such an institution exists in the current Saudi system. Yet al-Faqih asserts that unlike
the current system, the council will be elected to reflect the consensus of the
society (the umma). Elections are one way to reach such a consensus, but
this does not preclude other mechanisms. "Procedural issues are subject to
the wishes of the public." In al-Faqih's envisioned state, all segments of society are represented in the political system. The institutionalization of these
ideas would certainly take time. Al-Faqih uses the current Iranian model to
make a point about the gradual institutionalization of his ideas.

In addition to elections and representation, al-Faqih's political system allows for both freedom of expression and freedom of assembly. "Let people talk. All people, Jews, Christians, and others, should talk." He restricts this, however, by insisting that free speech should be subject to the confines of the Shari'a. Freedom of both assembly and speech seems to be a tactical tool to bring about the collapse of the current political order. "If people are allowed to speak freely and assemble freely they would expose the corruption and demonstrate against the current system. As they demand a trial of any of the symbols of the regime, Prince Sultan for instance, change is likely to follow." Nevertheless, al-Faqih remains ambivalent about freedom of speech, assembly, and elections, saying: "You have to remember that elections and other things require some time." In his ambiguous language there are many unanswered questions about his conception of democracy and who should be included in the process. One important issue that can be used as a measure for al-Faqih's commitment to pluralism is his stance on the issue of other Islamic minorities. The Shi'a of Saudi Arabia provide a test of his commitments.

For al-Faqih, the Memorandum of Advice is the framework for any reform program. "The Memorandum of Advice represents a complete program that discusses ten major points for reform. Chief among these reforms are reforming the justice system and the courts, the economy, the military, the public administration, foreign policy, and the general condition of Saudi society." Although the memorandum is five years old and was presented when the group was inside the kingdom, al-Faqih still sees it as the only document that all Saudi Islamists agree on. Yet he thinks that any attempt to open up the system will lead to removing the ruling family from power. For example, he suggests that permitting the freedom of expression and association that his group demands would undermine the corrupt system of patronage and kickbacks that keeps the ruling family in power. If intellectuals, clergy, and journalists were permitted to object to corruption in military spending, for instance, there would be a public outcry, for various important princes would be put on trial for misuse of public funds. This in turn would so damage the royal family's prestige that many people would openly advocate getting rid of the monarchy itself. For this reason, al-Faqih feels, the Sauds are highly unlikely to allow any meaningful reforms.

Many wonder if his program is a reformist one or a radical one that advocates the overthrow of the monarchy. Al-Faqih refuses to answer such specific questions. His program is based on two stages: establishing freedom of expression and freedom of association as principles and establishing institutions that represent the nation and its belief system. This includes an independent judiciary, the absence of secret police, and a significant role for the 'ulama as the custodians of the system. Al-Faqih does not give any details of how the 'ulama would rule or how these institutions would work. He says,

"The lack of details is because we don't have enough experience yet. However, we see that as a result of an open debate we can arrive at a consensus about how these institutions should work."

Furthermore, al-Faqih believes that an Islamic state should have a leader, an imam, whose duty is not merely to lead prayers and interpret the Shari'a but to apply Shari'a law in consultation with the 'Ulama "in order to alleviate injustice and give citizens the right of equal justice." The test of whether an imam is a true Islamic leader or merely a person seeking power for himself is his success in administering a state based on Shari'a law rather than personal or tribal favoritism; it must be a state in which the citizens feel free and secure. However, there are also objective criteria for determining whether a state is Islamic. First, he says, an Islamic state would not commit acts specifically prohibited by Islam—such as permitting usury or allying itself with non-Muslims to fight against Muslims. As for the argument that Saudi courts are currently based on Shari'a law, al-Faqih observes that since the judges are appointed and dismissed by the ruling family, they are tempted to make decisions based on what will please that family, not on what the law actually allows: They feel pressure to find people with connections to the royal family innocent and to find guilty those who oppose the regime. An Islamic state would follow the laws made by God, but people would be free to disagree and experiment concerning secular matters in the day-to-day running of the government. For instance, how and where a road should be built is a secular matter, but the degree of proof needed to convict someone of a crime is specifically stated in Shari'a law.

MIRA and Minorities: The Shi'a of Saudi Arabia

The relationship between the Sunnis and the Shi'a is difficult to analyze because of the Shi'a concept of taqiyyah (hiding their belief for fear of persecution) and the Sunni politics of display, where the overemphasis on outer appearance in a stylized formal presentation distorts reality. Given those two processes of masking, we are left with impressions and guesses about the actors and their orientation toward the political system and toward each other. One obvious fact, however, is that the two groups do not trust each other. Al-Faqih and his group's attitudes toward Shi'a are no exception. In general terms, al-Faqih accepts the idea of dialogue with others who differ with him both within the Islamic world and outside it. "Lately, I have decided that there is enough room for ijtihad [modern interpretations of Islamic traditions]. I think that our attitude is one of openness and dialogue." He then quoted verses from the Quran in which God told the Prophet to argue politely and in good faith with those with whom he has differences. Al-Faqih accepts that Muslims may criticize each other, but feels they do not have to pronounce each other heretics on the basis of their disagreements. "We condone the freedom to criticize certain acts, but we don't accept that Muslims accuse other Muslims of kufr [being non-Muslims]." Al-Faqih is aware of the political costs of dismissing Shi'a as non-Muslims. In fact, he seems willing to accept a tactical alliance with the Shi'a to overthrow the regime. But because of the 1993 Shi'a agreement with the government, al-Faqih dismisses the potential of such an alliance out of hand. His position is further complicated by his followers' attitude toward the Shi'a. MIRA's followers inside the kingdom distrust the Shi'a greatly. "The reform movement thinks that the Shi'a are not their allies. They don't trust the Shi'a." Al-Faqih cites the Islamists' response to an interview that al-Mas'ari gave to the Iranian Broadcasting Corporation before the split within the CDLR as an example. "Mohammed al-Mas'ari was strongly criticized by those inside who accused him of speaking to the rafida [those who rejected Islam, a Shi'a designation that the Saudi Islamists use]." Although al-Faqih himself is willing to accommodate the Shi'a, he cannot convince his followers to do likewise. "I told them that the Shi'a are less dangerous than the British. However, people inside see the Shi'a as traitors. One cannot afford to lose these people who represent the core of our movement." In spite of this circular narrative, it is obvious that an alliance between MIRA and the Shi'a is almost impossible. This becomes clearer if one knows that the Shi'a themselves do not trust the Sunni Islamists. One incentive for the Shi'a to strike a deal with the government was the rising tide of the Sunni Islamists. This pushed the Shi'a to seek government protection. This point will be elaborated upon in detail in chapter 7. Indeed, al-Faqih believes that Shi'a prefer the Saudi regime to the Sunni Islamists. He also believes that Iran would prefer the current Saudi system to the Sunni Islamists because this would make Iran the only credible example of an Islamic state in the Islamic world. A real Sunni state would be a serious threat to Iran, al-Faqih asserts.[32]

Conclusion

It is obvious that MIRA is the most mature of the Saudi opposition groups. Unlike Mas'ari and the CDLR, who became overextended over the years and squandered their efforts on the Islamic politics of London, MIRA remains faithful to the Saudi cause. However, like the CDLR, MIRA has problems with exaggerated reporting, something that is likely to undermine its cause. For example, on March 21, 1998, al-Faqih rushed to announce the death of King Fahd. This reliance on unverified information has become typical of both groups. Al-Faqih may have had probable cause to think that the king was likely to die any moment, but to announce it on the home page without verification was very amateurish.[33]

Furthermore, while MIRA's agendas and concerns may be able to change the political language in and about Saudi Arabia, the group does not represent a threat to the royal family and its stay in power. Some future movement could have this potential if it does not start from zero, but builds on al-Faqih's efforts. Thus far the trends and the record of the Saudi opposition do not indicate that this is likely to happen. For instance, there is no evidence that the liberal princes benefited from the activities of the Arab nationalists. Also there is no evidence to support that the Shi'a movement has benefited from the royal opposition or from the communists. It is also obvious that neither MIRA nor the CDLR started from where the Shi'a left off. Had these groups utilized the experiences of other opposition groups to inform their own programs, the current opposition could be more effective. The lack of any coordination between these groups makes them all vulnerable to the regime's strategies of segmentation and fragmentation. And virtually all of these groups do fragment. This lack of coordination between the groups is one of their major weaknesses, and MIRA is no exception. It is surprising that only now, after about six years of work, do al-Faqih and MIRA come close to the Shi'a Reform Movement in terms of the quality of reporting and political analysis.

Moreover, al-Faqih still has a long road ahead of him to appeal to other Saudis from the various regions in the country. At this stage, he does not provide a viable alternative to the royal family. His vision of the Islamic state does not differ significantly enough from the existing order to justify regime transformation. Moreover, he has to gain trust to implement his reforms of free speech and free elections. Saudi liberals, his natural allies in this cause, do not trust his statements and suggest that they are merely tactics to mobilize support. Moreover, he wants to maintain the Council of Higher 'Ulama and implement the Memorandum of Advice. The state has already responded to these demands and may have succeeded in taking the wind out of MIRA's sails.

Al-Faqih's discourse is neither radical enough to attract those who are likely to take up arms against the regime (the bin Laden followers) or moderate enough to appeal to Western governments. On human rights, for example, his rhetoric neither fully endorses the internationally recognized principles such as the Universal Declaration on Human Rights nor is significantly different from that of the Saudi government. This ambiguous position is not likely to have any impact except to change the language of the debate about the nature of the Saudi state and how to reform it. It is not likely to undermine its legitimacy, and al-Faqih's attack on the integrity of the 'ulama is likely to cost him politically, because inside the kingdom, Saudis still admire bin Baz more than they do al-Faqih. MIRA may be the most serious movement and its legacy may contribute greatly to the coming opposition to Saudi rule, but as it stands, the movement's role is likely to remain strong at the level of cultural change but weak in motivating people into action. This is a major difference between this movement and the Committee for Advice and Reform, led by Usama bin Laden and the subject of the following chapter.

CHAPTER SIX

Usama bin Laden and the Advice and Reform Committee

"Good Gracious! Anybody hurt?"
"No'm. Killed a nigger."
"Well, it is lucky, because sometimes people do get hurt."

—Mark Twain, *The Adventures of Huckleberry Finn,* Chapter 32

"What matters is that in Riyadh and Khobar no Saudi was hurt, only Americans were killed."

—Usama bin Laden, Interview, *Al-Huquq,* 1997

Central to Usama bin Laden's politics is the division between the world of "us" and the world of "them," Muslims/non-Muslims, believers and non-believers, Saudi/non-Saudi. The circle grows smaller or wider depending on the conflict and the combatants. Although his activities seem to blur the borders between the local and the global, his rhetoric and his intellectual production work as a divide between "us" and "them." Like the racialism of the American south depicted by Mark Twain in the opening quote, Usama bin Laden's xenophobia excludes the different others from the realm of humanity, thus his reaction to the killing of Americans in the Khobar bombing. What drives this callousness in this particular case?

Unlike previous Saudi opposition leaders such as Salman al-'Auda and Safar al-Hawali, who are elaborating a transcript and a discourse that shields Muslims and their culture from the Western onslaught, bin Laden is willing to use violence to prevent the "West" and its values from dominating Muslim lives.[1] He also differs from them in another respect. While their opposition exists in global media space and cyberspace, bin Laden's exists not only in these spaces but also in the worlds of weapons and high finance. What went into the making of Usama bin Laden, and how are we to understand him? In discussing the previous opposition leaders, I focused on the domestic factors that figured so prominently in their discourse. In the case of bin Laden, however, an analysis that emphasizes only domestic variables within Saudi Arabia is less useful. Bin Laden lives both inside and outside of Saudi Arabia, on the borderline between domestic and international politics. Thus we cannot understand him without understanding global and local politics simultaneously. We have to understand why he was driven out of Sudan, why he was stripped of his Saudi citizenship, why he is under the protection of the Taliban fighters in Afghanistan, and why the American and the Saudi governments are after him. This puts us face to face with a different kind of opposition, and the domain of analysis has to be broadly defined to include not just the Saudi political system and Saudi society but borderline politics and the global system. This transnational component of the Saudi opposition forces us to refine our concepts as well as our tools.

Although bin Laden's Peshawar and Afghani experiences appear novel to some and may lend support to the current global moment, Wahhabism was a force in Afghanistan and its politics two centuries before bin Laden. In 1824 the Wahhabi sheikh Saiyid Ahmed declared a jihad against the infidels in the Punjab region. In fact, he was fighting the British in the same way that bin Laden was fighting the Soviets in his time, both movements fueled by Wahhabism. In 1830 the Wahhabis occupied Peshawar and built a state there; their coins carried the name of Ahmed. The Wahhabi resistance against colonialism in India is very well documented, especially during the uprising of 1857 to 1859. The Wahhabi movement also influenced other movements in North and West Africa. Bin Laden's activities are thus in many ways a continuation of a historical pattern.[2]

No matter how seductive the historical continuity, bin Laden is also shaped by various other forces. While some factors relate to bin Laden as a person and the local politics of Saudi Arabia, other factors relate to the rise in the politics of identity on a global scale and the position of Muslims in this new world. Still others relate to U.S. politics in the Middle East and the Muslim world or to the new information age and the nature of the media. As these factors converge, there is a dialectical process in which Western governments and media agencies shape bin Laden's image to serve their own interests, and bin Laden draws on these constructed images to highlight the "anti-Muslim" nature of U.S. foreign policy. As Muslims watch the Arab-Israeli peace process deteriorate and sanctions are imposed on numerous Muslim countries such as Iraq and Libya, anti-American sentiments intensify. Bin Laden manipulates these sentiments and presents himself as a defender of the faith against an aggressive West.

The role of Western governments and media in this dialectical process made bin Laden a household name both in the United States and abroad due to his presumed connection to the Riyadh bombing and the bombing of the Khobar Towers. Although bin Laden never directly admitted responsibility to the two bombings, the media assumed that he was the mastermind behind these attacks. Some U.S. government officials have supported this media image by casting bin Laden as terrorist financier.[3] Although bin Laden has never been charged with an offense in the United States or Britain, the governments of both countries consider him a dangerous person and seek to convince others that he poses a global threat. The Saudi government and media likewise exaggerate the image of bin Laden and his ability to cause damage, thereby further enhancing his global importance.[4]

While bin Laden's image is clearly influenced by Saudi and Western governments and media, he plays an active role in the dialectical process of image-making. As is the case with many radical leaders, exposure on CNN and through other media outlets gives both the leader and his followers an exaggerated sense of their own importance. Bin Laden, for instance, believes that he and his followers brought down the evil empire of communism in Afghanistan. He thinks he is also capable of defeating the leaders of the capitalist world. As he attacks the United States and threatens its interests, he attracts more media attention. His image from his hiding place in Afghanistan becomes larger than life. Moreover, he also plays on U.S. foreign policy in the region in order to influence the image of the United States and Western world. In the same way we know of bin Laden here through the Khobar bombing, he and many Arabs knew of the United States through its support for Israel. Images, no matter how distorted, have shaped bin Laden's understanding of the West and the West's understanding of bin Laden.

Currently it is difficult to tell the difference between bin Laden the image and bin Laden the man. This chapter attempts to sort out the two and analyze the impact of their interplay to assess both the man and his organization. But, first, what is the Committee for Advice and Reform, and who is Usama bin Laden?

The Launching of The Advice and Reform Committee

The Advice and Reform Committee (ARC) is an umbrella organization for many radical groups in Saudi Arabia that have been active since the early

1980s. Its members took advantage of government support for the Muslims in Afghanistan to gain military experience. Khaled al-Fawaz, bin Laden's representative in London, is an activist who was born in Kuwait in 1962 and returned to Saudi Arabia in 1979.[5] Like al-Faqih, he returned to Saudi Arabia at the time of political turmoil: the Iranian revolution, the Juhaiman takeover of the Grand Mosque, and the disturbances in the Eastern Province. Al-Fawaz's family comes from al-Zubair region in Iraq, as does al-Faqih. Bin Laden is also a marginal figure in terms of tribal genealogy and place of birth. Saudi Arabia is not his deera (land), although he was born in Riyadh. His family comes from the Hadramout region of southern Yemen. In spite of his family's incredible wealth, he is considered non-Saudi and for this alone even the poor of the Najd look down on him. Thus the theme of marginal figures using religion to establish their own position in a society dominated by tribalism and Islam continues in this case as well.

Further damaging to bin Laden's standing in the community is that this money came from his family's connections with the royal family. Most of the wealth of the bin Laden Group is the direct result of major state contracts, such as the reconstruction of the Muslim holy sites in Mecca and Medina.[6] Because the family acquired its wealth as a result of its relationship to the state, they were willing to denounce and disown bin Laden when he became an opposition figure. For the family business, good relations with the royal family were more important than Usama. When he left Saudi Arabia, he took his share of the $260 million family fortune with him and used this money to maintain his position as a financier and philanthropist in the eyes of his followers.

Many describe Usama as a very gentle and pious man. His volunteering for the jihad in Afghanistan to fight on the side of Muslims against the communists came from his deep religious convictions. A fellow Afghan volunteer said, "He was a hero to us because he was always on the front line. He not only gave his money, but he also gave himself. He came down from his palace to live with the Afghan peasants and the Arab fighters. He cooked with them, ate with them, dug trenches with them. That was bin Laden's way." His involvement with the conflict in Afghanistan started in the early 1980s, when, with the help of the Saudi government, he set up the Islamic Salvation Foundation to recruit Arabs to the Afghani cause. Through his personal contacts and funds, he was able to recruit fighters from various Islamic countries including Saudi Arabia, Egypt, Turkey, Yemen, Algeria, and Lebanon. As he started his operation in Afghanistan, bin Laden used his company to build bomb shelters, strategic roads, and hospitals. All of these activities influenced those around him, and many "Arab Afghans" supported him as their leader. As a guerrilla commander in Afghanistan, bin Laden is proud of two particular battles, Jaji in 1986 and Shaban in 1987. Later, his battle against communism went beyond the Afghani conflict to include Yemen and the struggle of the government of the north against the communists of the south. In fact, in some of his communiqués, he chastises the government for its "support of the infidel communists in southern Yemen" against the Islamic north.[7] In both Afghanistan and Yemen, he acted on his ideological convictions and thus won the confidence of his followers.

The group's objectives are revealed in a second document entitled *Ta'reef wa Tabiyyin* (Description of the organization and its goals), which gives the reasons for establishing its office in London. "Due to the government ban on freedom of expression, the group finds it necessary to set up its operation abroad."[8] Al-Fawaz asserts that ARC was in the making even before the CDLR or any other group came into being. "We were there, working secretly since the early 1980s," he says. "But because we did not want the government to find out about our activities, we delayed the declaration of the organization." Al-Fawaz believes that the members of ARC were disappointed that the CDLR came into the open when the society at large knew little of the whole Islamic project. It is also surprising that al-Fawaz and the bin Laden group did not know of Mas'ari and his group. "We knew of Sheikh bin Jibreen, one of the founders of this committee, and Sheikh Abdullah al-Mas'ari, Mohammed's father, but we were not sure," he said in our interviews. "We thought at first that this may be a ploy by the regime to take the wind out of the sail of our movement, but by the time we realized that these were our brothers, they were taken into custody." However, as soon as the group made it to London, al-Fawaz and bin Laden did not mind cooperating with the CDLR. Bin Laden's group had their reservations about the CDLR and the whole reformist project and its pioneering approach to change the situation. "We know that the way of positioning the governed is not the right approach. We think that the government is not an Islamic one," al-Fawaz continued. He believes the tactical mistake of the other groups is that their demands are limited. "Suppose Abdullah becomes king and releases the prisoners and controls corruption, what is left in the program of al-Mas'ari and those who signed the petitions?" It is very illuminating that these groups are not as connected with or knowledgeable of each other as many would have supposed.

The group's sense of self and mission is defined as follows: "The Committee for Advice and Reform is an all-encompassing organization that aims at applying the teachings of God to all aspects of life."[9] The group's approach to social and political change is based on "a comprehensive understanding of Islam, the holy book and the Prophet's tradition as it was interpreted by our Sunni predecessors." This is central, since bin Laden presents himself as the legitimate heir of Sheikh Mohammed bin Abdul Wahhab. The organization has four aims: (1) to eradicate all forms of

Jahiliya (pre-Islamic or non-Islamic) rule and apply the teachings of God to all aspects of life; (2) to achieve true Islamic justice and eradicate all aspects of injustice; (3) to reform the Saudi political system and purify it from corruption and injustice; and (4) to revive the hezba system (the right of citizens to bring charges against state officials), which should be guided by the teachings of the top 'ulama. Although the goals do not make it clear that this group is out to destroy the current political structure, in interviews members are very clear that the system cannot be reformed and has to be changed completely.

Nonetheless, the early documents published by this group were not as confrontational as bin Laden's later messages, which advocated war against the "American-Israeli alliance and its local supporters."[10] These earlier messages emphasized a multitier approach to political change, including education, da'wa, and building alliances with other Islamic forces. In the second document after the announcement of the operation of the London office, the group emphasized educational means to achieve its mission. The group strives to use all modern technological means in order to educate the public about the Saudi political system and its problems. Second, it aims to use da'wa (missionary activities for the propagation of the faith) to promote virtue and suppress vice. Third, the group counts on "the cooperation and support of all Islamic forces that share the goals of the organization." Finally, this committee specifies that all means for social change or bringing about their vision of an Islamic state are permissible "as long as they conform to the teachings of the faith." This last statement is vague and could mean that the group intends to use force. The teachings of the religion are open texts that can be interpreted in various ways. Some interpretations could greatly restrict the use of violence; others permit its use. Thus far the teachings and statements of bin Laden seem to endorse a more violent approach to changing the system.

Spheres of Movement and Influence

Bin Laden moves in two spheres of influence, one domestic and the other international. As I will show, it appears that bin Laden's international influence is greater than his domestic one. Yet his discourse focuses more on the domestic constituency. In this regard he is the opposite of Muhammad al-Mas'ari and Sa'd al-Faqih. Both focused on holding the western allies of Saudi Arabia to their professed values of democracy and human rights and engaged the West on this basis. Bin Laden focused on holding the Saudi state to its professed values. His dialogue with the West is confrontational, in part because his knowledge of the West is limited. Again, while al-Faqih and Mas'ari encountered the West through education and lived experiences, bin Laden's encounter with the West was through America's involvement in Afghanistan and its policies in the Middle East, especially its blatant support of Israel. These encounters shaped bin Laden's uncompromising discourse. In the next section I will identify bin Laden's local and global connections to evaluate his power base.

The Local and Domestic Connections

Bin Laden's power base consists of three groups in Saudi society. A very small core group is dedicated to bin Laden as a leader and are bound to him by a bayi'a (oath of allegiance). These few believers are willing to die for him and his cause. However, recently one of his men, Sheikh Abu al-Fadhl, turned himself in to state authorities and gave the Saudi government important information about the group. The next tier of his supporters are people who are not part of his organization but see him as inspirational force and godfather of Islamic activism in Arabia. The third and most dangerous category is represented by the "Arab Afghans," the Saudi youths who went to Afghanistan and have different degrees of allegiance to bin Laden.[11]

Central to the frustration of the "Saudi Afghans" was the disjunction between the rhetoric of jihad that took them to Afghanistan and the total lack of appreciation that they saw when they returned to Saudi Arabia. They were expecting to be treated as heroes who defeated communism. In Saudi Arabia, however, the public did not share this euphoria with the Islamist fighters. Thus, like the Vietnam veterans in the United States, the fighters felt a sense of betrayal. This, in addition to shellshock and other war-related factors, turned these men into social misfits who were looking for another war to fight. Their anger at the Saudi government grew when it rejected bin Laden's offer to fight against Iraq, instead going ahead with its plan of bringing in the U.S. troops. After this refusal, bin Laden left Saudi Arabia for the Sudan and started his anti-Saudi campaign from there. As bin Laden failed inside the country, he looked at the outside world to change the Saudi political order and to continue his struggle for Islam as he saw it.

Borderline Living, Resistance, and Global Constituency

The ideologically and geographically diffuse nature of the Islamist movement(s) has allowed bin Laden considerable flexibility in recruiting warriors and selecting his hiding places and allowed him to exploit the political tensions within the various countries in which he has taken refuge. His supporters range from the tribal leaders of Yemen, to the "Arab Afghans," to the governments of Yemen, Sudan, and Afghanistan, who have at least temporarily given tacit approval to his presence. Yet in the same way that he exploits these states, they also use him. For example, at the behest of the Yemeni government, some Yemeni tribes expressed their willingness to host bin Laden and his troops, which helped to strengthen the Yemeni position in its negotiations with the Saudi government over their border dispute. When both governments were negotiating that dispute, one tribal leader stated in an interview in *Al-Quds al-Arabi* that an emissary from bin Laden had visited his tribe and that it was willing to give him all the support he needed.[12] Similarly, the Sudanese government has used bin Laden to extract concessions from both the Egyptian and the Saudi government. Because of bin Laden's connection with Egypt's Islamic group, Sudan has used him and his "Arab Afghans" to have leverage over Egypt. Sudan has also used him to get aid from Saudi Arabia and to use the Egyptians and the Saudis to pressure the United States to remove Sudan from its list of states that support terrorism. But bin Laden is in control of neither his agenda nor its consequences. Sudan can grant him protection at one time and throw him out of the country when he no longer serves their needs.

Bin Laden's contacts in Yemen, for example, reveal the complexity and the precariousness of these relationships. In direct competition with the Saudi government, bin Laden has developed ties with the Sanhane tribe, a branch of the Hashed tribal federation, the tribe of Yemen's president, Ali Abdullah Saleh. Bin Laden also has the support of the radical wing of the Islah party, the Islamist party of Yemen, because the leader of this faction, Abdul Majid al-Zandani, served with him in Afghanistan. Yet compared to the influence of the Saudi government among the Yemeni tribes, bin Laden's contacts in northern Yemen are certainly less than impressive. The Saudi government, on the other hand, has historically cemented special relationships with many Yemeni tribes; some are more loyal to Riyadh than they are to San'a, Yemen's capital. For example, Sheikh Abdullah al-Ahmer, the head of the Hashed tribe, the Islamist party, and the real power behind Ali Abdullah Saleh's regime, is very close to the Saudis. In fact, whenever the Yemeni government is in trouble with Saudi Arabia, Saleh usually sends al-Ahmer to iron out the differences. Thus although bin Laden's family comes from Yemen, it would be a mistake to exaggerate his influence or underestimate the influence of the Saudi government in that country. In fact, my interviews with some of Islah leaders in Yemen support an argument that Saudi Arabia controls both the tribes and the Islamic forces there.[13] Thus Saudi Arabia can threaten the regime of Ali Abdullah Saleh more than bin Laden can threaten the Saudis.

Bin Laden has a very close relationship with the Sudanese government under the leadership of the Islamic Front of Hassan al-Turabi and General Omar al-Basheer. For years Sudan granted bin Laden protection, allowed him to operate from its territories, and celebrated his presence in the Islamic conferences held in Khartoum. For instance, during the 1995 meeting of the Islamic People's Congress there, bin Laden was given an opportunity to present himself as a major leader of the Islamic movement. Under the auspices of Hassan al-Turabi, the real power behind Omar al-Basheer's regime, the congress brought together a host of organizations and their leaders, including: Imad Mughniyah, the second-ranking member of Hizbullah's security service; Fathi Shakaki of Islamic Jihad in Palestine; Mussa Abu Marzuk and Mohamed Nezzal of Hamas; Adnan Saadedine of the Muslim Brotherhood; Sheikh Abdul Majid al-Zandani, head of the Yemeni Majlis al-Shura; Mustapha Hamza; two other representatives of Egypt's Islamic Group; and many representatives from Iran, Algeria, Pakistan, and Tunisia. Bin Laden's presence at the congress testifies to the important role he plays within this diffuse, decentralized network.

But his allies and friends also reveal the complexity and fragility of modern political alliances. Although bin Laden has been under the protection of Afghanistan's Taliban movement since 1996, he also had ties since the early 1980s with its rival, the former president Gilbudden Hekmatyar. It is puzzling that Taliban leaders also have good relations with Saudi Arabia, since the Saudi government probably has more influence in Afghanistan than any other government. Yet bin Laden remains there unharmed. Perhaps the Saudis are not really interested in trying him and are satisfied merely to have him out of the way. Furthermore, the Taliban seem to enjoy U.S. support for their antinarcotics activities. This web of complex relations raises more questions for those interested in the role of nonstate actors in global politics.

Through these connections, bin Laden has made of himself a player in world politics, but like Mas'ari he is also likely to be the victim of these global relations, because the balance of power is not in his favor. His fate may not be all that different from that of Sheikh Omar Abdul Rahaman, the spiritual guide of Egypt's Islamic group. Both enjoyed the support of the Sudan and had some relations with the United States throughout the Afghan conflict. The only difference between the two is that while Abdul Rahaman was fighting a poor state like Egypt, bin Laden is fighting a very rich and powerful state. Symbolically, Saudi Arabia as the guardian of the two holy sites in Islam has more clout among Muslims than bin Laden will ever have. Materially, bin Laden has less money than even a minor prince in the Saud family. Yet bin Laden the man is not as important as bin Laden the agent who both plays on the differences among Arab states and also is used by them.

However, despite his vulnerability, both the nature of the movement and the existence of modern communications technology do give bin Laden's movement considerable power and influence. Now more than ever, networks can be established instantaneously. Bin Laden depends on these transnational networks to circulate his message and fight for his cause. His major contributions within this network are financial, especially running training camps and probably funding actual terrorist attacks. The U.S. government is investigating him in connection with a December 1995 wire transfer of funds from the Armed Islamic Group (GIA) in Algeria to his headquarters in Khartoum, and the Egyptian government has linked him to the assassination attempt against President Hosni Mubarak in December 1995.[14] The U.S. State Department claims that bin Laden runs three camps in northern Sudan that train militants from Egypt, Algeria, and Tunisia.

Bin Laden's Critique of the Saudi Political Order

Usama bin Laden's critique of the Saudi political system is a theme that runs through most of his group's communiqués and declarations. However, the best outline of this critique is summarized in communiqué 17, which the committee issued on August 3, 1995. The title of the communiqué is "An Open Letter to King Fahd." Here the group outlined its main grievances against the regime. These include "the lack of commitment of the regime to the teachings of Sunni Islam," as interpreted by the eighteenth-century reformer Sheikh Muhammed bin Abdul Wahhab, the state's inability to conduct a viable defense policy, the mismanagement of public funds and squandering of oil money, and finally, the dependence on non-Muslims for protection. Bin Laden and the ARC dedicate ten pages to explaining in detail what went wrong with the Saudi policy in these and other areas.

With regard to the state's lack of Islamic credentials, bin Laden starts his attack against state 'ulama who issue fatwas to justify the royal family's hold on power and give Islamic legitimacy to the state's reliance on non-Muslims for protection. Most of the supporting quotes of this section are taken from either the writings of Muhammed bin Abdul Wahhab himself or one of his successors. Thus, in this regard, bin Laden is more radical than the rest of the Saudi opposition, in that he wants to go back to the earlier teachings of Wahhab and his understanding of the relationship between the rulers and the ruled. As I mentioned earlier, bin Laden is critical of the 'ulama appointed by the king and very supportive of the ideas of Safar al-Hawali and Salman al-'Auda. He has devoted specific communiqués to defending these young 'ulama against the state and its 'ulama. Some of his statements are also taken from either Hawali or al-'Auda, especially on the normalization of relations with Israel. He also chastises Sheikh bin Baz for issuing a fatwa that accepts the idea of peace with Israel. Bin Laden is further critical of the way the Saudis handle their defenses and accuses the king and his brothers of squandering money generated from oil revenues. In the conclusion to his open letter, bin Laden advises the king to resign: "We have proven that your regime is un-Islamic. It is mired in corruption and applies non-Islamic laws to certain aspects of the human dealings such as commercial law. It also has failed in the areas of the economy and defense. Thus, you should resign."[15] Bin Laden does not suggest an alternative, however, and seems willing to accept someone from the royal family itself. He uses the model of King Saud's removal from power and replacement by King Faisal, which suggests that he has a special animosity toward King Fahd. However, unlike the rest of the Shura council of ARC, especially al-Fawaz, bin Laden has refrained from criticizing Crown Prince Abdullah. Will the ARC and bin Laden change their position when Abdullah becomes king? The answer to this question depends on the intensity of differences among members of the ARC Shura council. It also depends on the policies Abdullah adopts when he assumes the throne.

Finally, bin Laden is gravely concerned with government suppression of dissent. He claims that all sectors have been wronged but makes particular note of tribal leaders, professors, merchants, and academics.[16] He is particularly angered by the arrest of the "honest" scholars, such as Salman al-'Auda and Safar al-Hawali.[17] These young 'ulama, according to bin Laden, are better than the establishment 'ulama because they speak truth to power.[18] Bin Laden argues against the establishment of an official body of 'ulama to interpret the Shari'a. He considers them apologists for the regime, with their main purpose the masking of the degree by which Saudi policy has strayed from the Shari'a.

Can bin Laden Undermine the Saudi-Wahhabi Alliance?

For the Saudi government, bin Laden poses a threat not through "terrorism" alone but in undermining the regime's Wahhabi and Hanbali base. He challenges the regime by holding its 'ulama to the Hanbali school of jurisprudence that represents the frame of reference for Wahhabism. This is very obvious in two open letters that bin Laden and ARC sent to Sheikh Abdul Aziz bin Baz, the Grand Mufti. Here I summarize his main critique of bin Baz's fatwas. In challenging bin Baz, bin Laden and ARC take a more radical position than any of the other groups I have discussed thus far. Although he refers to the communications between younger 'ulama and their attacks against bin Baz's fatwas, bin Laden's criticism exceeds that of the radical 'ulama. In this regard, he is more dangerous to the hegemonic narrative and institutions of the current state 'ulama.

The first open letter is entitled "An Open Letter to Sheikh bin Baz Refuting His Fatwa concerning the Reconciliation with the Jews."[19] This letter is a response to a fatwa issued by bin Baz published in *al-Muslimoon* in which he endorsed the current peace talks between the Arab states and Israel. ARC and bin Laden accuse bin Baz of giving Islamic legitimacy to "the current terms of surrender signed by the cowardly tyrants of the Arab leaders and Israel." This communiqué also contained messages sent by more specialized 'ulama to bin Baz warning him against the consequences of this fatwa. These 'ulama and activists include Safar al-Hawali, Salman al-'Auda, Abdullah bin Jibreen, A'yid al-Qarni, and nine others.

The case against bin Baz's fatwa was stated even more explicitly in the second communiqué, in which bin Laden outlines five reasons why the fatwa is invalid, according to the consensus of the 'ulama. First, bin Laden states that the current Arab-Israeli peace talks do not meet the conditions stipulated in the Shari'a regarding legitimate contracts between Muslims and their enemies. The parties to such a contract should be recognized as legitimate Muslim leaders through the consensus of the ummah (nation). It is understandable that there would be an agreement between the Muslims and their enemies. However, according to bin Laden, those acting on behalf of the Muslim party are not Muslims. "They are a group of secular leaders who abandoned the faith (murtadoon)." He reminds bin Baz that he himself described the secularists in earlier fatwas as infidels (kufar, plural of kafir). Furthermore, bin Laden states that such an agreement uses international law rather than Islam as its frame of reference and thus will result in giving land to the Israelis. He advises bin Baz to read the agreements signed between Israel and the Palestinians, between Israel and the Egyptians, and between Israel and the Jordanians. The basis of international law, he points out, is the concept of sovereignty in a system of nation states. Under this frame of reference, Muslims are unlikely to win Jerusalem, especially if the Israelis insist that it is going to be their undivided capital.

Bin Laden then uses the work of ibn Taimiyya to assert that bin Baz has no right to issue a fatwa in this matter, since fatwas of this type must be issued by a mufti who is well-versed in the subject under discussion. Since bin Baz did not read the treaties and has a limited understanding of international law and the complexity of the situation on the ground, he should not issue a fatwa in this regard. The letter also states that bin Baz's whole approach to issuing fatwas is wanting, since it aims at pleasing those in power at the expense of Muslim interests, the teachings of God, and the consensus of the 'ulama.[20] Because he follows the whims of rulers whose interests change according to the politics of the situation, bin Baz's fatwas are usually contradictory. Bin Laden thus argues that bin Baz should resign his post as a mufti and repent. He quotes a hadith, telling the sheikh: "Hold your tongue and stay within the confines of your home and cry over your sin." To substantiate this assertion, bin Laden uses the work of ibn al-Qayyim al-Jawziyya, an authority in Hanbali jurisprudence.

In this debate, there is an echo of the 1989 debate between the secular-ist trend and the religious trend in Saudi society. Earlier I identified this de-bate as the basis for the current oppositional discourse within Sunni circles. In the same way that Sa'eed al-Ghamidi accused the secular writers in 1989 of corrupting Saudi society, we find bin Laden accusing bin Baz of catering to the whims of the secular forces of the Arab world that push for recon-ciliation with Israel. Bin Laden's rhetoric also is influenced both directly and indirectly by the sermons and writings of Salman al-'Auda and Safar al-Hawali. Bin Laden directly quotes Hawali in his jihad against America booklet, his book is entitled *Haqa'iq Hawal Azmat al-Khaleej (Facts behind the Gulf crisis).*[21]

Bin Laden's Critique of Saudi Foreign Policy

In the global media scape and its discourse, especially in the United States, bin Laden has been associated with declaring war on America and its troops stationed in Saudi Arabia. Indeed, bin Laden is very critical of United States for its "occupation of the land of the holy places," as he stated in a CNN interview of April 7, 1997. He is also critical of the Saudi govern-ment's complicity with U.S. designs for the Middle East, contending the foreign presence in Saudi Arabia is opposed to Islam and the community of the faithful. "[O]ur main problem is the U.S. government while the Saudi regime is but a branch or agent of the U.S." The U.S. government "has committed acts that are extremely unjust, hideous and criminal whether di-rectly or through its support of the Israeli Occupation." He points to acts of U.S. and Israeli aggression that have resulted in the deaths of Muslims; namely, the occupation of Palestine, the economic embargo of Iraq, and the bomb explosion in Qana, Lebanon, in 1996.[22] Furthermore, he is very crit-ical of the U.S. government pressuring the Saudis to purchase expensive and useless arms while maintaining an artificially low price for oil. In this, bin Laden is echoing themes already raised by Hawali, al-'Auda, Mas'ari, and al-Faqih. These are also the themes elaborated in the Memorandum of Advice in the section that focuses on Saudi defense and foreign policies. Muwalat al-Kuffar (alliance with the infidels) is also a very important sec-tion in bin Laden's open letter to King Fahd. In bin Laden's view, infidel governments include both Western and Arab governments. In his letter to the king, he wrote:

In its foreign policy, your government ties its destiny to that of the crusader Western governments. It is shameful that a government that claims the pro-tection of the Two Holy Mosques pays $4 billion in 1991 to help the Soviet Union before the Soviets washed their blood from killing Muslims in

Afghanistan. In 1982, your government also aided the infidel regime in Syria with billions of dollars as a reward for killing tens of thousands of Islamists in the city of Hama. Your government also aided with millions a tyrannical regime in Algeria that kills Muslims. And finally your government aided the Christian rebels in southern Sudan.[23]

As much as this quote reveals bin Laden's criticisms of Saudi foreign policy, it also shows his loyalties. He was very concerned about the government of the north in the Sudan and its survival against rebel attacks. He was likewise concerned with the Afghani struggle against the Soviets, with the Muslim Brotherhood against the Syrian government, and with the Islamists against the Algerian government. Even when he addresses Saudi involvement in Lebanon, he claims that the Saudis support the Maronite Christians against the Muslims. An interesting point here is that for bin Laden, the Muslims of Lebanon are not just Sunnis but Shi'a as well. Thus, unlike other Saudi Islamists, apparently bin Laden does not discriminate between Shi'a and Sunni Islam, at least in terms of global politics. Obviously, by virtue of being a very conservative Wahhabi, he is likely to condemn the Shi'a of Saudi Arabia, yet for tactical reasons, he seems to be refraining from criticizing them. Bin Laden is also critical of the Saudi support of Yasser Arafat and the "the secular," Palestinian authority at the expense of Palestinian Islamists, especially Hamas. In a letter to the king he states that Arafat is "the colonial administrator who can do the dirty work that the Israelis themselves could not do." He accuses the king of supporting Arafat and the peace process out of deference for American wishes.

Bin Laden's Cosmology and Ideological Orientation

Although there is no clear manifesto for the Advice and Reform Committee, some elements of bin Laden's ideology and worldview can be discerned from his interviews, communiqués, and actions. Central to his view is the question of an ideological authenticity against a perceived Muslim dependency and cultural inferiority to the West. This theme has been repeated before, in the sermons of Salman al-'Auda and Safar al-Hawali and, to some extent, within the central discourse of MIRA and the CDLR. Like almost all Islamist activists, bin Laden constructs an Islamic tradition and history in which Muslims confronted similar issues and threats and came out as winners. This constructed history of the Islamic tradition appeals to the disadvantaged cells and groups throughout the Muslim world.

Bin Laden's cosmology and worldview are shaped by Islamic narrative as handed down, constructed, and reconstituted throughout the ages and by his personal experiences as a mujahid in the Afghan war. He is very critical of all secular ideologies and is willing to risk his life to make sure that these secular principles do not influence Muslim life or dominate their societies. These concerns dominated the Saudi debate both before and after the Gulf War and were prominent themes in the sermons of Hawali and al-'Auda. Indeed, as I explained in chapter 2, al-'ilmaniyyah (secularism) and its consequences for the Muslim world was al-Hawali's doctoral dissertation topic. In interviews, bin Laden quotes extensively from the hadith and Quran and the teachings of early Muslim 'ulama, such as Sheikh ibn Taiymiyya, ibn al-Qayyim, and Mohammed bin Abdul Wahhab. For every modern-day event, he cites a historical precedent to portray his actions as part of being faithful to the teachings of early Muslims. For example, his communiqués identify ibn Taiymiyya as the original inspiration of jihad against a corrupt regime.[24] He questions the House of Saud's claim to the throne on the grounds that it has failed to protect the faithful. This idea of regime legitimacy can be traced from an apologetic doctrine that developed over time under the states succeeding the Prophet and continuing until the eighteenth century. Most important, however, is the great faith he places in the richness of "legitimate" Islamic legal and political history. Islam is "the complete and comprehensive ideology" that has "clarified the dealings between an individual and another, the duties of a believer toward God . . . and the relationship of the Muslim nation and the other nations in time of peace and war." His ideology is not innovation, "not a new thing that we have to come up with."[25] While bin Laden's discourse is based on an interpretation of Islamic history, his power is derived from playing on the current social, economic, and political problems of the Muslim world.

Several pillars of bin Laden's ideology were established and solidified during his eight years fighting in the mountains of Afghanistan. Unlike many nationalist movements in Algeria, Egypt, Palestine, or even Saudi Arabia, where jihad was launched for the good of the homeland, this particular jihad was for Allah and geopolitics. The activists saw themselves as Muslim warriors, facing off with the intrusive atheism of the Soviet Union. Symbolically, the Soviet Union became atheism and the fight against occupation became a struggle against evil. In the process, jihad was semantically transformed; "effort" came to mean "violent struggle." This drastically reduces the flexibility of the term jihad, and thus the doctrine, but it simultaneously unites the bloody reality of a protracted, ugly war with a divinely sanctioned fight between good and evil. Bin Laden has stated "the acme of this religion is jihad."[26] The shift is of awesome importance: Bin Laden perceives the religious-symbolic system of Islam vs. Kufr as the cause and motivation behind the conflict in Afghanistan; the geopolitical dimension is therefore diminished considerably. For him the language and symbols of ideology take precedence over the political or economic realities.

Bin Laden internalized an ethic of jihad that developed during the Afghan conflict based on myth, war, and religious experience. He states: "there is a special place in the hereafter for those who participate in jihad." It is also the mark of the privileged in this life. "Being killed for Allah's cause is a great honor achieved by only those who are the elite of the nation." Second, violence fits within a totality of uncompromising activism to create the righteous society. Bin Laden's most common references to the Quran come from the sections that enjoin piety, activism and the enforcement of morality. A characteristic example is an excerpt from Surat (section) Al Imraan, 3:110: "You are the best of the nations raised up for the benefit of men; you enjoin what is right and forbid the wrong and believe in Allah." Bin Laden defines jihad very narrowly in a way that confirms the worst of Western stereotypes of Islam as "a violent religion"; in fact, the term is broader and all-encompassing, from the betterment of someone's personal status to the improvement of a nation to defend itself against its enemies. Bin Laden's mujahedoon are intensely loyal to him and to their comrades-in-arms.

Experiences of an almost mystical peace further affirm bin Laden's belief in his cause. Although a puritanical Wahhabi, he sounds like a Sufi whenever he speaks of the great peace ("sekina") that filled him in battle: "Once I was only 30 meters from the Russians and they were trying to capture me. I was under bombardment but I was so peaceful in my heart that I fell asleep."[27] Success, however, may be the most important proof. As bin Laden said in his CNN interview, "Slumber and fatigue vanished and so [did] the terror which the U.S. would use . . . or the Soviet Union used by attributing itself as a superpower." Bin Laden can point to an array of successes against superior forces since Afghanistan: Somalia, Bosnia, Eritrea, and Beirut, with ongoing jihads in over a dozen countries.

Conclusion

Central to bin Laden's opposition is his conception of the Saudi state as part of the larger web of global relations. Thus he believes that disrupting this web, preferably by severing Saudi Arabia's ties to Western powers, could weaken the domestic position of the royal family considerably. Indeed, with his loyal "Arab Afghans," he may be able to mount a serious violent campaign to achieve this purpose. Yet despite the major strength represented by this loyal following, bin Laden also has major weaknesses. He is not only vulnerable to potential policy changes on the part of the Taliban movement, but he also occupies a marginal position in Saudi society and lacks a political program.

Like Hawali and al-'Auda and the Saudi nationalists of the 1960s, the thrust of bin Laden's oppositional discourse and activities focuses more on external factors than on domestic ones, in this case the presence of U.S. troops in Saudi Arabia. Unlike Mas'ari, who tried to shame the West into acting in accordance with democratic and human rights principles, he views efforts to persuade the West to alter its policies toward the Saudi regime as ineffective. He thus turns instead to violent measures in an effort to directly undermine the Saudi regime's international support base. He justifies these measures via an ideological discourse that presents the House of Saud as unable to defend the Muslim state and links the regime's complicity to corruption in the government and society at large. He is critical of the 'ulama and their inability to demonstrate God's teachings to the rulers and wider society. His communiqués emphasize the image of a Saudi state that has abandoned its duty to enjoin what is right and forbid what is wrong.

Despite his sweeping criticism of the Saudi state, however, bin Laden lacks any clear program for political change. Like Mas'ari after the split in the CDLR, he views himself as part of the larger Islamic movement, which transcends national boundaries. His discourse is more episodic than systemic. He reacts to events rather than taking the initiative on the basis of an a priori conceived political program. Bin Laden may want to establish a theocratic state in which the Shari'a is supreme, yet there is nothing in his written or spoken statements that delineates the shape or instrumentalities of that state. However, unlike al-Faqih and Mas'ari, he is willing to use force to achieve this objective, and he also has a stronger power base. His "Arab Afghan" followers gave him their allegiance and pledged to die for his cause; neither Mas'ari nor al-Faqih commands this type of following.

On the global level, however, bin Laden's future may be uncertain. In spite of his success in maintaining his position as a global actor, he is likely to face two main problems. First, the Taliban protection is not likely to continue forever. Taliban as a movement is subject to global pressures, especially from the United States and Saudi Arabia. Previously, under pressure from both countries, Sudan expelled bin Laden from its territory. Under similar pressure, Taliban may behave likewise. Taliban is already in contact with the U.S. government, and the Saudis also seem to have influence on the movement. There may come a time when Taliban is asked to turn bin Laden in. Moreover, since the conflict between Taliban and its rivals in Afghanistan has not yet been settled, bin Laden's future is uncertain if any of those rivals gain control. Furthermore, although his personal wealth has helped him to move around and support his troops, time is his enemy. Eventually, his money will run out, and he may face the possibility of living in debt, as Mohammed al-Mas'ari does.

Finally, bin Laden previously worked in Saudi Arabia for his family's business, a construction company that took pride in building numerous projects essential to the maintenance of the modern Saudi state and its global image, especially expanding the two holy mosques. Could he reverse course and become a force of destruction? This may be true on the global level. In this media age, if bin Laden is to kill others, it will not be for Islam and Jahad, but for air time on global television screens. However, domestically, it would take more than bin Laden to tear down this 66-year-old state. It would require stronger Islamic credentials, a prominent tribal lineage, and large tribal following. Bin Laden's image may be great in global spaces, but locally he remains a marginal figure who in a local division of the world into "us" and "them" is a "them" to most Saudis.

CHAPTER SEVEN

Sheikh Hasan al-Saffar and the Shi'a Reform Movement

It is best whenever the people assume a role in managing their affairs and solving their problems. This is the way a people may learn and grow. Of course, private/civil performance is much better and of higher quality than government. Whatever is done by private hands is the result of self-motivation and drive, whether this stems from personal interest or from noble, voluntary feelings. The government's work, on the other hand, is bureaucratic and follows a pattern of routine. . . . Thus in developed and advanced societies there is an abundance of civil organizations, institutions; they are the ones which solve societal problems and ills.

—Sheikh Hasan al-Saffar, "Al-Mujtama' al-Ahli" (Civil society), January 1997

Read in isolation, these words appear to echo the familiar Western discourse on "civil society," the widely extolled yet ambiguous buffer between democratic leaders and those they govern. Yet this tribute to civil society is not the work of a Western activist or scholar. Rather, it is an excerpt from a taped sermon given by Sheikh Hasan al-Saffar, the spiritual leader of the Shi'a Reform Movement in Saudi Arabia.

Considered within its political, geographical, and historical context, this sermon is part of a dramatic shift in the movement's ideological discourse and strategy of resistance. This change in discourse, as reflected in al-Saffar's writings and taped sermons, represents a shift from radicalism to moderation and from confrontation to accommodation. However, it would be a mistake to confuse tactical shifts with the demise of strategic goals. A better approach would be to analyze these changes within the broader context of local, regional, and global realities, both on the part of the Shi'a opposition and on the part of the Saudi state.

In this chapter I trace this ideological and tactical shift and examine its ramifications both within Saudi Arabia and without. I also analyze Shi'a discourse within its historical and political context, as reflected in 3 books and 12 taped sermons of al-Saffar. By exploring the overlap and interpenetration between "the local" and "the global," I identify the intentional and unintentional consequences of this dialectical process. As al-Saffar's works reveal, leaders of the Shi'a Reform Movement are acutely aware of this local-global linkage and seek to use it to their advantage. In an effort to gain support, bolster their credibility, and strengthen their bargaining position vis-à-vis the regime, they have tailored their message to appeal to wider local, regional, and international audiences. This message incorporates issues that resonate beyond the Shi'a community, such as civil society, democracy, "pluralistic politics," dialogue among Muslim sects and between Muslims and non-Muslims, state intervention in the social life of citizens, "freedom of expression and belief," "human rights," and the position of non-Muslims in a Muslim polity.

Faced with the transformation of Shi'a discourse as well as other changes in the political and economic environment, the Saudi regime has responded with a tactical shift of its own. As it seeks to deal with the consequences of the Gulf War and rise of internal opposition from Shi'a, Sunni, and secular groups, the monarchy is reassessing the efficacy of exclusionary policies. During this ongoing process of reassessment, it has taken some steps toward a more accommodative, less confrontational stance regarding certain internal opponents. While the regime has not abandoned exclusionary politics, it is renegotiating the balance between coercion and compromise. In the case of the Shi'a Reform Movement, the state has granted limited concessions, and the movement has shifted toward more moderate discourse.

The Local Context

Before looking at the taped sermons and written works themselves, it is important to consider the atmosphere in which they were produced. On the most immediate level, the writings and sermons of Sheikh al-Saffar and the leaders of the Shi'a movement are directed at a local audience and address local problems, such as the Shi'a's relationship to the Saudi regime, at the

Sunni opposition movement, the Committee for the Defence of Legitimate Rights (CDLR), and to liberal opposition groups and the more radical Sunni preachers, such as Sheikh Saffar al-Hawali and Salman al-'Auda. Thus we need to review the history of the Shi'a reform movement and to consider the specific actions of the Saudi government to which the movement is a response. This historical background will focus on the changing nature of Shi'a resistance to Saudi rule and Shi'a strategies either to cope with the restraints or to build alliances with other opposition forces inside the kingdom. The sociopolitical conditions of the Shi'a in eastern Saudi Arabia establish a context for al-Saffar's sermons and writings.

As a minority, the Shi'a in Saudi Arabia experience the same sociopolitical disadvantages as other powerless minorities throughout the world. The Shi'a feel that unlike other groups in the kingdom, they are victimized by both Sunni anti-Shi'a feelings and certain state policies that discriminate against them.[1] Perhaps it is their exclusion from power, more than their religious beliefs, that has prompted their leaders to rethink their political position as well as their theology. However, during the 1980s, their information/propaganda centers in Europe and the United States emphasized government harassment of their community, especially after they rioted in 1979.[2] During that decade, Shi'a communities in the towns of Safwa, Sihat, and Qateef suffered from the lack of economic development: "Compared with other towns in the Eastern Province, the Shi'a towns of Al Qatif and Al Hafuf were depressed areas. The Shi'a lacked decent schools, hospitals, roads, and sewerage and had inadequate electrification and water supplies."[3]

Beyond inequitable distribution of social services, Shi'a leaders also claim that the Saudi government consciously tries to repress any manifestation of Shi'a culture. Some Shi'a leaders claim that they are forbidden from building mosques, funeral homes, or community halls.[4]

Many of the Shi'a complaints focus on what they perceive as repressive state policies that curtail freedom of religious expression and association, condone employment discrimination, and infringe on personal status decisions.[5] Some of these complaints were part of their demands when they conducted negotiations with the state in 1993. Major among the Shi'a complaints was the harassment they suffer from the Sunni religious police (mutawi'een), who warned the Shi'a imams not to use the Shi'a prayer call, which includes the phrase "I testify that Ali is one of God's believers" and have threatened "severe punishment for noncompliance."[6] Shi'a books and audio cassettes are banned, as are pictures of Shi'a religious leaders. Anyone possessing such items may be imprisoned.[7] Some of these cases have been documented by human rights organizations.[8] However, not all these discriminatory practices are a reflection of official state policies. As described earlier, the mutawi'een is a group that exists on the border of state and society and the formal and informal politics. Thus it becomes very difficult to lay the blame for their practices on either the state or Sunni religious institutions.

Many of the practices of discrimination have lessened considerably since the government and Shi'a agreement in 1993. In fact, two Shi'a leaders were included in the new Consultative Council. However, even moderate leaders such as Sheikh Hasan al-Saffar and Tawfiq al-Sheikh, although happy about government response to some of their demands, still hope for more, warning that if the government reneges on the 1993 agreement, the Shi'a population will be taken over by the more radical Hizbullah activists. The Shi'a claim also that discrimination is still common in any position of leadership.[9] These local conditions undoubtedly play a central role in shaping the ideological discourse and tactical decisions of the Shi'a Reform Movement. As an overview of the wider historical context reveals, however, external as well as internal events account for the movement's recent shift.

The History of the Shi'a Movement: Shifts in Tone and Tactics

Since its inception in 1975, the Shi'a Reform Movement in Saudi Arabia has demonstrated an impressive ability to cope with local, regional, and international changes. As internal and external factors have changed, so too have the tone, emphasis, and scope of Shi'a discourse. Al-Saffar embodies a general trend in the movement's direction. He has adopted a more moderate tone than his predecessors, emphasizes issues that appeal to a wider audience, and expanded his scope to encompass regional and international issues. Tracing the phases of the movement's shift enables observers to situate al-Saffar's works within their historical context and better understand their implications for Shi'a and non-Shi'a communities.

During the movement's first phase (1975–80), leaders adopted a militant stance and demonstrated limited understanding of the regional and international implications of their activities. Ideologically, the main aim of the movement was to purify Islam from "Sufi practices and the selective usage of religion to bolster a certain regime's legitimacy."[10] At that stage, radical discourse dominated the movement's publications. The monthly *al-Thawrah al-Islamiyya* (The Islamic Revolution) was its main voice. Events in 1979 helped to further radicalize the movement, namely the coming of an Islamic government in Iran, the uprising in the Eastern Province, and the takeover at Mecca's Grand Mosque. Leaders of the Shi'a movement, including Sheikh al-Saffar, followed the Iranian line. Until 1985 the discourse was uncompromising. In an interview, one of the movement's leaders stated that the Shi'a position toward the Saudi royal family was one of "no negotiation with a regime that violates Islamic teachings."[11] In fact, Shi'a considered the regime "illegal":

We cannot negotiate with a regime that has no regard for the rule of law. The change that we want is to let the people choose the regime that they want to live under. Also, we want a regime that is not dependent on the capitalist world, and we want to reduce American influence in Saudi Arabia. Since the regime will not accept any of these changes, there is no reason to negotiate with it.

However, a notable shift had occurred in Shi'a discourse by 1988, signaling an end to the revolutionary rhetoric in favor of a broader agenda of democratization and human rights. Shi'a criticism began to focus on the regime's human rights abuses and on the absence of a constitution and national assembly. The new agenda called for broader participation of citizens in running the affairs of their government, for limiting the absolute power of the king, and for curtailing police power to detain and arrest those who even verbally criticized the regime.[12] Increasingly, opposition leaders pushed for collective action and popular empowerment, seeking to limit citizens' dependence on the Saudi state.

In 1990 Sheikh al-Saffar published *al-Ta'adudiya wal Hurriya fi al-Islam* (Pluralism and Freedom in Islam), a work that greatly influenced the reform movement's political discourse and agenda. By addressing the Islamic basis of freedom and pluralism, al-Saffar carried the movement to a new and more sophisticated plane. His book paved the way for a transitional period that led the movement away from the rhetoric of revolution and the influence of Khomeinism[13] toward a more moderate discourse anchored in the ideas of the contemporary Iranian philosopher and university teacher Abdol Karim Soroush.[14] Since the appearance of al-Saffar's book, Muslims in various Arab countries have written extensively on the subject of Islam and democracy.[15] Likewise the subject has preoccupied many scholars and policymakers in the West. While published in response to local realities, *al-Ta'adudiya* thus had regional as well as global ramifications.

The moderating trend heralded by al-Saffar led to the emergence of a new magazine titled *al-Jazeera al-Arabia* (The Arabian Peninsula), which was published from January 1991 to August, 1994. Compared to *al-Thawrah al-Islamiyya*, *al-Jazeera al-Arabia* appeared to be a more substantive publication focused on reporting events in the kingdom and providing serious analysis. The magazine's purpose was not to incite a revolution against the royal family; instead, it focused on human rights, tolerance, problems of public administration in Saudi Arabia, government corruption, and abuses of civil rights.[16] The magazine's credibility caused many, including the Saudi government, to take the Shi'a Reform Movement seriously.

The shift apparent in the reform movement's publications extended beyond the level of ideological discourse. Sheikh al-Saffar was instrumental not only in changing the tone of the movement's publications but also in redirecting its political strategy. In June 1992 he signaled a willingness to negotiate with the government, stating:

> We do not refuse any initiative for a dialogue between us and the government as long as we are talking about issues. So far the government wants us to return to the country with very little regard for our political demands. I can tell you now that we will respond positively to any initiative that includes political reform and an end to discrimination on the basis of religious orientation, regionalism or tribalism.[17]

Together, these shifts in tone and tactics helped bring about a change in the Saudi government's response to Shi'a opposition. One year after al-Saffar made this statement, the government provided an initiative acceptable to the Shi'a opposition, and on September 27, 1994, four Shi'a opposition leaders returned from London and the United States to Saudi Arabia. This delegation included Tawfiq al-Seif, Ja'far al-Shayib, Sadiq al-Jubran and Isa al-Muz'il.[18] They met with King Fahd, Prince Sultan, Prince Salman, and Prince Mohammed bin Fahd, the governor of the Eastern Province. Furthermore, the king himself visited the Shi'a areas and promised to improve conditions there. Concessions by the Saudi state on an ideological level led to a meeting between al-Saffar and Sheikh Abdul Aziz bin Baz, the Sunni Grand Mufti of Saudi Arabia. This is very significant because bin Baz previously refused even to shake hands with Shi'a in general, let alone their political leaders.[19]

Of course, the shift in the Shi'a movement was not solely responsible for this new response on the part of the Saudi state. Government openness toward the Shi'a came at a time of momentous political change. Locally, the royal family had come under severe criticism by Sunni religious groups concerning its use of Western soldiers in the holy land. Presumably the government hoped that accommodating the Shi'a would free them to focus on the potentially more threatening Sunni opposition. Moreover, the Persian Gulf War and uprising of the Iraqi Shi'a against Saddam Hussein helped change local perceptions of Saudi Shi'a. During the Gulf War, Saddam courted the Saudi Shi'a, but they refused to cooperate with him. Consequently, Saudi officials wanted to reward the Shi'a leadership for being responsible citizens.[20] Moreover, unlike their Sunni counterparts, especially Salman al-'Auda and Saffar al-Hawali, the Shi'a leadership exercised some restraint in their criticism of the royal family during that time of crisis. Thus the change in the Saudi government's attitude toward its Shi'a opposition was not a function of the shift in al-Saffar's discourse alone but also the result of internal and external pressure on the government. Nonetheless, al-Saffar's conciliatory discourse undoubtedly reinforced the government's decision to reevaluate the balance between inclusionary and exclusionary policies.

In the wake of reconciliation between the state and Shi'a opposition, members of the reform movement returned to Saudi Arabia from abroad. Their reconciliation and return did not, however, signal an end to Shi'a resistance. Instead, it represented a change in tactics from direct confrontation to creative resistance. In addition to the taped sermons and the writings of Sheikh al-Saffar, the movement's new strategies also included the publication of two quarterlies, al-Kalima (the word), a magazine dedicated to broadening the movement's dialogue with other groups, such as the Muslim Brotherhood and other moderate Islamic organizations throughout the Muslim world, and al-Waha (the oasis), which informed its audience about the long-ignored and suppressed history and culture of the Shi'a of the Eastern Province. The latter also included poetry and fiction written by Shi'a from Saudi towns such as al-Ihsa, al-Qateef, and Sihat among other places, thus giving the publication a literary as well as a politically oriented focus and broadening its potential base of support.[21]

In addition to written publications, al-Saffar's taped sermons also provide insight into the movement's changing orientation. The tapes under discussion here were recorded when members of the movement returned to Saudi Arabia after their reconciliation with the government. Interpreted in juxtaposition with other Shi'a writings in al-Waha and al-Kalima, the taped sermons and the writings of Sheikh al-Saffar show a greater openness toward internal and external forces and the desire to begin a dialogue with Sunni and secular opposition groups. These sermons seriously attempt to anchor concepts of pluralism, freedom of expression, belief, and a theology of resistance squarely in the Islamic tradition, both Shi'a and Sunni. They also show greater willingness to embrace Western concepts and reconcile them with indigenous ideas.

As the epigraph on civil society reveals, the latest phase of Shi'a discourse draws heavily on the discourse of mainstream scholarship. By retelling the Shi'a narrative of resistance in language that originated in the West and has a hegemonic hold over Western scholarship, al-Saffar intentionally blurs distinctions between "the global" and "the local." While his message still addresses the immediate, local context and is grounded in Islam, it also appeals to a wider audience. Within Saudi Arabia and the region, this audience includes Shi'a and non-Shi'a who long for political reform, expanded personal freedom, and greater equality. Within the West, this audience includes Muslims and non-Muslims who espouse democratic principles and champion universalistic notions of pluralism and civil society. Leaders such as al-Saffar are thus able to retain their legitimacy among Saudi Shi'a while also bolstering their credibility and staking out moral high ground on the

local and international stage. In this regard, al-Saffar is much more successful than his Sunni counterparts. Mas'ari, for example, lost a great deal
of his local power base when he adopted the global discourse of new liberal
economics and human rights. After the split within the CDLR, Mas'ari became aware of the erosion in his local base. Thus he adopted a more xenophobic discourse characterized by anti-American and anti-Jewish rhetoric.
This was enough for the Western media to shy away from interviewing
him. Al-Saffar managed to maintain a balance between the local and the
global that Mas'ari obviously failed to achieve.

Al-Saffar and Western Thought

As al-Saffar weaves democratic and pluralistic discourse into the local Shi'a
narrative, he does not try to distance himself from Western thought. In fact,
he openly embraces the ideas of Western philosophers and comments on
current Western social problems with sophistication and insight. Of course,
he has a specific political reason to do so, namely to reaffirm the universal-
ity of human rights and freedoms and present the Saud regime as an anomaly among world governments. "In general," he tells his audience, "people's
conception of freedom is a function of socialization rather than religion." He
continues:

> In some societies, people are raised with freedom. They drink it in with the
> milk in their childhood. In other societies, the family itself is oppressive and
> thus raises a child whose understanding of freedom is deformed. This child re-
> quires therapy, since these constraints affect his/her growth. This is a medical
> question and you have to ask specialists about it.

Drawing on nineteenth century British philosophy, al-Saffar notes that "The
English philosopher Bentham reached the conclusion that there are no
agreed upon definitions about the limits one should put on freedom. Similarly, John Stuart Mill suggests that different schools of thought have different conceptions of the meaning and limits of freedom."

Although al-Saffar does not spend much of the sermon discussing
Western philosophers and their concept of freedom, he seems to want to
make his audience aware of the existence of different traditions and probably wants them to engage those traditions. Furthermore, we even can
infer that al-Saffar's awareness of the debate on Islam and democracy is behind this inclusion of Western philosophers in his sermon. It is also an attempt to lessen his audience's suspicion of Western ideas by highlighting
similarities between Islamic and Western thought on certain issues. For
him, the differences between Muslims and Westerners on these issues are

minimal, and Muslim perceptions of the gap between themselves and the West are the result of media manipulation rather than experience or knowledge. He continues:

> Freedom in the West is not what our youth are exposed to through satellite dishes and Western media. I advise our youth not to be tempted by this media portrayal of freedom in the West. Instead of paying attention to the Western media, we are better off studying the basis of the West's economic order, its political institutions, and its scientific institutions. These are things that we need to learn from the West, not its worst aspects presented to us through soap operas. Yes, in the West there are no constraints on freedom to act on one's desires and impulses. However, in the West there are voices that are against this, but we don't hear their voices. This is because the media and the big business that controls them find it against their interests to allow intellectuals to speak. Instead they promote sex and violence because it sells.

Al-Saffar explains that the Muslim perception of the West is based on media images rather than firsthand experience, an attitude shared by almost all Muslim modernists, from Mohammed Abdu to Jamal ad-Din al-Afghani. In an effort to offer non-Western Muslims a broader perspective on American society, al-Saffar cites works of recent American political leaders, saying "In Nixon's book *Beyond Peace,* there is a whole chapter on the American family and the need for spiritual awakening. In it Nixon writes about the danger that this monster of desires poses for the future of the American family. He recounts the statistics about crime. In America, they suffer from this kind of freedom." The focus on Nixon's book serves two functions. First, it shows to the audience that the return to family values and religion is not necessarily Islamic and that Westerners themselves share this concern. Second, it is a legitimizing rhetorical move suggesting to Arab secularists that Western and Muslim views are not in conflict. This intersubjective consensus provides the philosophical foundation to deal with the secularists in Saudi Arabia and the Arab world at large. Further, it substantiates the theology of openness that the sheikh emphasizes in his sermons and publications.

Al-Saffar's familiarity with Western thought and incorporation of Western ideas into his own works is one component of the wider doctrinal and tactical shift of Saudi Arabia's Shi'a Reform Movement. It must thus be understood as a response to local, regional, and global realities. As these realities have changed, so too has the movement's message, agenda, and relationship with state and nonstate forces. With this historical, ideological, and tactical context in mind, I now turn to al-Saffar's discussion of pluralism, political participation, separation of religion and state, civil society, personal freedom, and human rights. His treatment of these issues centers on relationships between individuals, groups, and state and society.

Pluralism and Minority Politics:
Explaining Oneself and Understanding the Other

In "The Horizons of Openness and the Limitations of Xenophobia and Intolerance," a taped sermon issued in 1996, al-Saffar examines relations between groups in a pluralistic society. He warns against knowledge based on stereotypes, urging his audience to depend on firsthand information and direct knowledge of the other. Stereotypes, al-Saffar asserts, are based on distorted images of the other and lead to misunderstandings. The consequences of this are harmful, whether within a local Saudi context between Shi'a and Sunnis or within a global context between Muslims and non-Muslims. Thus he prescribes three steps toward creating a more open environment: (1) introducing oneself to the other, (2) listening carefully to the other's conception of the self and of the other, and (3) having a dialogue with the other concerning commonalties and differences. These themes also recur in three other taped sermons: *Al-Taghiyeer al-Ijtima'i* (Social change), *Limatha Yakhtalif al-'Ulama* (Why do theologians differ?), and *al-Amn al-Ijtima'i* (Social security).[22]

By calling for openness and tolerance between different groups and peoples, al-Saffar addresses the concerns of local and global audiences. Locally, he is responding to Shi'a suffering, which stems from secondhand information and stereotypes. The Saudi regime and state-controlled media construct and reconstruct the Shi'a image, portraying the community as a dangerous and heretical fifth column whose members are potential supporters of Iran's anti-Saudi policies. Thus, defaming Shi'a Islam has been central to state efforts to neutralize this allegedly subversive force. Furthermore, the regime has focused on one element of Shi'ism, the concept of taqiyyah, which permits one to pretend to accept the dominant belief while practicing his or her own religion secretly. Using taqiyyah as a pretext, the regime has declared that even seemingly peaceful Shi'a cannot be trusted. This is presumably why al-Saffar encourages Shi'a to look at taqiyyah as a rare practice that Imam Ali Zein al-Abdeen recommended only in extreme cases of repression.

As al-Saffar subtly addresses the concerns of Saudi Shi'a who feel beleaguered by the regime and its Sunni supporters, he explains the importance of openness and danger of xenophobia on religious and intellectual levels. He opens his sermon with the Quranic verse: "We created you male and female, and have made you nations and tribes that you may know one another." Thus he locates the philosophy of openness and difference in the main source of Islam, the Quran. In "The Horizons of Openness" he tells his audience: "These differences among humans, ethnically, linguistically and religiously, represent God's will as well as God's wisdom." Al-Saffar further classifies this difference into two categories: differences that people choose and differences over which people have no choice. The latter category includes ethnicity, color of skin, nationality, and tribal affiliation. Other differences such as belief, religion, and ideology are matters for which humans are responsible. Al-Saffar considers the existence of all of these differences a blessing rather than a hindrance to a healthy society, stating:

> This difference in opinion and belief is a result of God's grace and wisdom. God created humans with minds, and the ability to choose is part of this. Had God wanted people's destinies to be determined, he would have created them with no ability to choose. Even God's words and messages were delivered with the idea that humans have the right to choose. "Remind them," God says. He further says, "no coercion in religion."

Al-Saffar here weaves the question of freedom of belief with that of pluralism in Islam, considering both to be bases of the Islamic community. The main principle for him is not whether pluralism is an Islamic concept but rather how pluralism is dealt with in a heterogeneous society. He says: "If the basis for human activities and associations is pluralism, the question becomes one of how we deal with the differences that exist in the one society and universally. To this I say, there are two options: (1) openness or (2) xenophobia. Either one of these options of course has its consequences." Al-Saffar's openness and his vision of a tolerant Saudi society stand in sharp contrast to the regime's xenophobia and policies of exclusion. The regime's suspicion of everything foreign ranges from the banning of satellite dishes to the summary deportation of Christian expatriates suspected of practicing communal prayers.[23]

One way to bring about greater openness is for Shi'a to speak for themselves. Thus al-Saffar encourages his listeners to follow their imams' advice and introduce themselves to the Sunni community. In "The Horizons of Openness" he says:

> When they [non-Shi'a] know that you are a Shi'a, they will ask, "What is a Shi'a?" Here you have a choice either to introduce yourself or to let someone else define you. Sometimes people have vague or distorted ideas about who you are. It is your duty to clarify this picture. Imam Ali Zein al-Abdeen said, "Those who know me, know me, and for those who don't, I am ready to tell them about myself." Why do we leave a third party to introduce us to others?

As for those Shi'a who do not want to work at introducing themselves and their beliefs to their Sunni counterparts, al-Saffar asks them to see this issue as part of modern practices and not to look at it as a matter of religion. He says, "Look at businessmen and professionals. They carry business cards. These are important to have, especially if people have the wrong ideas about who you are."

The sheikh further warns the Shi'a community of the consequences of apathy. "As Shi'a we have to work hard at this, because there are many out there who work to defame us. They are motivated politically. They want to distort our picture, politically, behaviorally, and religiously." He is referring to cultural violence against the Shi'a of Saudi Arabia in official publications and the fatwas issued by the regime's 'ulama. For example, a September 30, 1991 fatwa issued by Sheikh ibn Jibreen, a member of the Saudi Council of Higher 'Ulama, stated that the Shi'a were rafida (infidels) and that killing them was not a sin.[24] This fatwa, moreover, is a part of a larger pattern.

> There have been many decrees before this one. One example is the fatwa published in a book known as *Fatwa al-Lajnah Al-Da'imah* (Religious decrees of the permanent committee), which states that the Shi'a are infidels. This fatwa was signed by four members of this committee, who include Sheikh Abdul Aziz bin Baz, Sheikh Abdulraziq 'Afifi, Sheikh Abdulla al-Ghudaiyan, and Sheikh Abdulla bin Qa'oud.[25]

At least two other religious decrees are directed against Shi'a: Fatwa No. 1661, which forbids Sunnis from eating Shi'a food; and Fatwa No. 2008, which forbids Sunnis from intermarrying with Shi'a. In both cases Wahhabi 'ulama cite Shi'a deviation from Islam as the main reason for these decrees.[26] Anti-Shi'a sentiments among Wahhabi 'ulama date back to 1927, when they recommended to King Abdul Aziz that if the Shi'a insisted on practicing their religion, they should be exiled from Muslim land.[27]

Anti-Shi'a sentiments also go unchallenged in Saudi publications. The Saudi magazine *Al-Manhal,* for example, ran an article by Professor Mohammed H. al-Ghamari in which he described the Shi'a as "a destructive trend in Islam. Its practices are not different from those of the Jews and the Christians. In fact, there is evidence that the Jews have encouraged Shi'ism as a means of dividing Muslims."[28] The problem is further complicated by the fact that "Shi'a cannot use the press to reply to accusations leveled against them, and complaints to newspapers about the distortion in these stories often leave the plaintiff labeled an opponent of the government and sometimes result in incarceration."[29] This makes it all the more important, therefore, for Shi'a to approach Sunnis on an individual level. Al-Saffar responded to some of the Sunni misperceptions of the Shi'a in another taped sermon entitled "Limatha Nuwali Al Al-Bayt" (Why are we loyal to the Prophet and his family?).

The question of freedom of expression and the difference in opinion among Muslims is central to Saudi Shi'a theology because Shi'a authors have no chance to advance their views on Saudi radio or television or in newspapers. They publish their own books and record cassettes outside the kingdom and then smuggle them in. Currently they publish both of their quarterlies in Beirut. Their monthly *Al-Jazeera al-Arabia* used to be published in London. Media institutions in Saudi Arabia are regulated not only for the Shi'a but also for the Sunnis. Because this tight system of control on freedom of opinion and the press affects both Sunnis and Shi'a, al-Saffar's argument resonates in both communities.[30]

In his sermons, al-Saffar popularizes incidents from the history of governance in Islam to rally his followers and Muslims worldwide to defend their Islamic right to free expression. In "The Horizons of Openness," he says:

> In the early Islamic community differences of opinion were tolerated. During Ali's rule, there were many who had their own interpretations of Islam. Some of them adhered to the opinions of the previous caliphs in both religious and political matters. How did Imam Ali deal with the question of freedom of opinion? Once, the Imam sent his son al-Hasan to tell the people that Tarawih [extra prayer after the last prayer during the month of Ramadan] is not communal. Hasan returned and told him that the people didn't agree with him in this matter. In response, the imam said, "Leave them alone. Let them practice their religion as they understand it."

Al-Saffar emphasizes two points in this quote: Difference of opinion was an established tradition in early Islam, and the ruler may not determine how people understand their own religion. Moreover, he makes the points applicable to contemporary Saudi Arabia by evoking modern repressive apparatus: "Ali did not force the people to do what he saw to be right. He did not send the police to arrest them. These matters should not be enforced by political leaders or the state because the role of a political leader is to regulate public life, not private behavior."

By advocating openness and tolerance between groups within a pluralistic society, al-Saffar addresses local Shi'a concerns using the language of religious and liberal discourse. The call for freedom of expression is echoed in the sermons of Sunni preachers and activists, especially those of Sa'd al-Faqih and Salman al-Auda. On a regional level, the celebration of difference and tolerance also resonates among minority groups and citizens seeking political reform in other countries, especially in Bahrain, Iraq, and Lebanon. Finally, al-Saffar appeals to a global audience by incorporating language that parallels the hegemonic, liberal discourse of the West.

Political Dialogue and Participation

In addition to countering stereotypes and intolerance on an individual level, al-Saffar also encourages his followers to participate in any way possible to make their voices heard by the royal family and government officials. He warns Shiʻa not to follow the example of the Wahhabi propagandists and judge Wahhabis and Sunnis on the basis of uninformed stereotypes, but rather to form an opinion based on genuine dialogue and solid information. This approach for him is a religious duty. In "The Horizons of Openness" he says:

> God will ask you about how you formed your image of the other. One should-n't follow the crowd. You have to wait until you speak to the other person di-rectly. In the same way that we blame people for not knowing us directly through our sources, we are to blame for not knowing them directly and through their own sources. One cannot know about the Shiʻa by reading peo-ple who hate the Shiʻa. Similarly Shiʻa should not rely on books biased against the Sunnis to form an opinion about the Sunnis.

Al-Saffar suggests that although dialogue should focus on understanding both similarities and differences, it primarily must "focus on our common-alties and on our shared values and interests. Cooperation should be the first step. Then we can discuss difference on the basis of good will. This is what I mean by openness." He explains further:

> As religious people, we are obliged to try to understand others, as both state-ments from the Quran and from the sayings of the Prophet indicate. Frank-ness and clarity are more appealing than vagueness and rigidity. Openness makes one's own beliefs more attractive to those who do not already share them. Openness allows others to understand your position, and thus they are more likely to sympathize with it.

Taking the discussion of openness in Shiʻa tradition one step further, al-Saffar then impresses upon his audience the importance of political partici-pation and activism. According to al-Saffar, Shiʻa need to learn from "the tradition of the family of the Prophet, where we find Imam Al-Sadiq dis-cussing religious matters with nonbelievers, even when they accused him of unsound thinking." Even in dealing with rulers and government officials, he advises his audience that a spirit of openness is necessary:

> We can see this in the relationship between Imam Hasan and Muawiyya [the founder and head of the Ummayad state]; despite the traditional enmity be-tween their factions, Imam Hasan visited Muawiyya in Damascus. As we

know, Imam Hasan was not there under compulsion. Imam Hasan and 40 of
his followers would attended the public meeting of Muawiyya to inquire
about the conditions of the followers of Ali in other places and to raise other
political concerns. This delegation also included women such as Sawda bint
'Amara al-Hamdani. They all came to Muawiyya in spite of their political difference and their former injuries in order to negotiate with him. They often
came merely to prove that they still existed, and to introduce others to their
opinions and beliefs.

In this passage, al-Saffar addresses the Shi'a lack of confidence in the government and urges believers to try appealing to the rulers. If the rulers don't
respond to Shi'a demands, at least they will have heard their grievances. Not
only men should make their views known; women also are required to participate. To stress this point, al-Saffar uses the example of Sawda bint 'Amara
al-Hamdani, who went to Muawiyya to ask him for political and administrative reforms in Medina. Al-Saffar explains that:

She went to Muawiyya to complain about the discriminatory policies of the
Medina governor against the Shi'a. What I'd like to emphasize throughout all
of this is that tolerance and openness are at the heart of our belief, and if the
previous Shi'a leaders and communities did not engage others in dialogue,
Shi'ism would have disappeared without a trace.

Presumably, al-Saffar is implying an unflattering parallel between
Muawiyya and the current Saudi regime. At the same time, his message represents a change in the Shi'a response to government policies and to the
question of participation. Perhaps Saudi officials told al-Saffar that the lack
of improvements in Shi'a communities was the result of Shi'a apathy. Such
a response may explain why the sheikh encourages his audience to participate vigorously. His focus on women's roles could also be an appeal to non-
Shi'a women in Saudi Arabia, and perhaps for some sort of an alliance
between the Shi'a and the kingdom's women's movement.

Thus al-Saffar calls not only for openness and tolerance within a pluralistic society, but also for dialogue and active political participation within
this society. Once again he grounds his message in religious tradition while
also incorporating the language of liberal political discourse. He thereby offers guidance to the local Shi'a community while appealing to a wider regional and global audience. His appeal has reached even to the Sunni
community of Saudi Arabia itself. His most recent book, *al-Watan wa al-
Muwatana* (Homeland and citizenship), was well received in the Saudi
newspapers. One columnist wrote, "My heart was filled with joy and
warmth, as I was reading this book and remembering the author, Sheikh
Hasan al-Saffar, his pleasant personality and warmth, his charisma, and his

scholarship. This book transcends the ethnic, tribal, regional, and sectarian differences of Saudi society. It is an enlightened book that advocates the love of the homeland within a larger framework of tolerance."[31]

Precursor for Separation of Religion and State

While al-Saffar stresses the importance of Shi'a political participation and dialogue with the regime, he also advocates greater separation between religion and state. One of the major problems for the Shi'a communities of Saudi Arabia is the government's intrusion into matters relating to the practice of their faith and rituals. Al-Saffar portrays these state practices as an anomaly in Islamic tradition. To make his point, he offers a number of examples supporting the idea that noninterference of the state in the private lives of individuals is an Islamic concept. He recounts the well-known story of Malik al-Ashtar an-Nakha'i, whom Ali sent as governor of Egypt. In his letter to an-Nakha'i, Ali said:

> Know, O Malik, that I'm sending you to a land where governments, just and unjust, have existed before you. People will look upon your affairs in the same way that you were wont to look upon the affairs of the rulers before you. They speak about you as you were wont to speak about those rulers. And the righteous are only known by that which God causes to pass concerning them on the tongues of his servants. So let the dearest of your treasuries be the treasury of righteous action. Control your desire and restrain your soul from what is not lawful to you, for restraint of the soul is for it to be equitous in what it likes and dislikes. Infuse your heart with mercy, love and kindness for your subjects. Be not in front of them a voracious animal, counting them as easy prey, for they are of two kinds: either they are your brothers in religion or your equals in creation.[32]

Al-Saffar's comments on the story emphasize the principle of equality—the Egyptians are brothers, "if not on the basis of religion, on the basis of humanity." In "The Horizons of Openness," he adds, "Ali did not instruct Malik to tell the people of Egypt how to pray or how to conduct their private affairs. Instead, his instructions focused on public, economic, and political elements. Private issues are thus not the business of rulers." Ali's letter further shows respect for local culture. He instructed Malik: "Create no new custom which might in any way prejudice the customs of the past." Al-Saffar's emphasis reveals Shi'a dissatisfaction with Wahhabi attempts to abolish Shi'a cultural practices. This focus on equal rights and equal citizenship is a very important issue throughout the Islamic world. What al-Saffar argues in his 1996 sermons is precisely what Roy Mottahedeh in 1992 hoped theologians would develop if a theology of tolerance based on equal rights were to emerge in the Muslim world.[33]

Al-Saffar also emphasizes that his interpretations of the holy text and Islamic tradition are nothing more than his own ijtihad (interpretation). Since Islam, as al-Saffar understands it, allows for multiple interpretations, Muslims are not obliged to follow any particular interpretation, be they 'ulama or laypersons. Al-Saffar underscores this point by recounting Imam Malik's response to the caliph Abu Ja'far al-Mansour when the latter wanted to adopt a Maliki interpretation of the shari'a.[34] According to al-Saffar's sermon, Malik told the caliph, "There are many sound interpretations of the shari'a and mine is merely one of them." Furthermore, al-Saffar uses the stance of Imam ibn Hanbal, the founder of the Hanbali school of jurisprudence, against the Mu'tazilites, which was the official view of Islam during the reign of Caliph Ma'moun, to support freedom of opinion. This reference is a strategic move to show that Shi'a admire ibn Hanbal, the source of the Wahhabi legal doctrines that dominate Saudi life. His citing of ibn Hanbal is aimed at both the state and its Sunni opposition. Further, al-Saffar demonstrates that Imam Ali's views were not different from those of the Hanbali school: "This is because religious views are private matters, just as Imam Ali said."

While maintaining his support for political participation and state-society dialogue, al-Saffar thus delineates boundaries between private religious practice and public political activity. By portraying maintenance of these boundaries as an Islamic concept, he anchors calls for limited state power in religious tradition. In itself, however, the principle of separation between religion and state is championed by Western governments and pro-democracy activists. Once again al-Saffar's choice of language thus carries meaning for multiple audiences.

Civil Society: A Medium of Participation and Social Change

Al-Saffar envisions civil society as the appropriate medium for collective action on the part of a responsible citizenry. Like Western leaders and activists who extol the virtues of civil society, he views it as a crucial component of the ideal relationship between the state and nonstate groups. The Shi'a community, as one such group, should ideally be protected from unrestrained state power by a buffer of associations. These associations should provide for citizens' needs and facilitate political participation. Situated within an environment conducive to open dialogue and tolerance, civil society is thus presented as a means of popular empowerment. It is closely linked to notions of pluralistic politics, preservation of minority rights, and separation between religion and state.

In "Al-Mujtama' al-Ahli" (Civil society), a taped sermon issued in January 1997, al-Saffar focuses on the need for people to assume responsibility for their own welfare. He recounts the Quranic parable of Zulqarnain, a pious worshiper who protected his people by helping them erect a barrier between themselves and their enemies. Despite his followers' initial reluctance to exert the necessary effort, Zulqarnain convinced them that hard work was their only hope for shielding themselves from harm. Al-Saffar uses this example to offer his listeners several lessons. He concludes: "Firstly, the Quran considers a society that cannot find solutions to its problems a backward one. As long as the means are available to a society to solve its problems, then why doesn't it do so? Therefore, a society's propensity to solve its central problems is the measure of its advancement, of knowledge and sophistication in a society." Further, the people whom Zulqarnain aided already possessed the physical strength and material capability to protect themselves, leading al-Saffar to conclude that "most of the time, a society will have the means for solving its own problems." What society needs, therefore, is "wise/prudent leadership" of the type that Zulqarnain provided. Although al-Saffar cautions that "no leader has mystical, magical, or instant solutions to his society's problems," he asserts that a wise leader "sets a good plan and directs people." By mobilizing and coordinating the labor of others, a leader can help society fulfill its needs and overcome its problems.

While al-Saffar highlights the importance of prudent leadership in this sermon, he also emphasizes that the relationship between leaders and followers is one of mutual commitment and responsibility. He states:

> Many societies today work to solve their problems. They take active measures to find solutions to them. There is a term that is used today: civil society. Its substance is present in our religious teachings, and Muslims in the past lived in accordance with this understanding. This concept means the following: Some people believe that it is up to the government to solve all their problems. But some problems cannot be solved by governments.

Al-Saffar goes on to praise "developed and advanced societies" such as the United States, where "there is an abundance of civil organizations, institutions, etc., which solve societal problems and ills." Lest this praise be misunderstood as unqualified love for all things Western, he also expresses thanks that Saudi society is faithful, religious, and conservative. Like Western nations, however, Saudi Arabia has many needs and faces many problems. Al-Saffar urges listeners to assume an active role in fulfilling these needs and solving these problems by joining together in the spirit of cooperation and philanthropy. Citing past Muslim communities and the contemporary United States as examples, he presents civil society as the ideal medium for coordinating and channeling individual efforts. Indeed, since the return of this group to the kingdom in 1993, more civil society organizations started to emerge in the Shi'a areas of Saudi Arabia, a testimony to the effectiveness of al-Saffar's sermons. They are not just rhetoric but a call for action.

As in his discussion of pluralism and political participation, al-Saffar interweaves religious and liberal discourse in order to define the ideal relationship between the government and its citizens. By singing the virtues of civil society, he once again appeals to multiple audiences. Locally, civil society is a means of popular empowerment for all Saudi citizens, particularly the Shi'a community. This call for empowerment is not, however, presented in a confrontational tone. Rather, al-Saffar asserts that since no government can provide for all of its people's needs, society must share in this responsibility. He thus implies that state and society are working toward common goals that can be achieved through mutual respect, cooperation, and participation. By allowing more extensive development of civil society, the Saudi government would provide its citizens with the space to fulfill their role in this reciprocal relationship. Although al-Saffar bases his interpretation of this relationship on Islamic tradition, he moves beyond the local context by praising civil society in general and choosing the United States as a model for emulation. His implicit support for peaceful avenues of participation, interaction, and change resonates among Western governments and pro-democracy activists.

Freedom, Dependency, and the Politics of Exploitation

Yet another theme central to al-Saffar's sermons involves freedom and its consequences for the politics of exploitation and dependency. He urges listeners not only to take collective responsibility for their needs and problems but also to take individual responsibility for their personal freedom. Drawing on the traditions of Imam Ali, al-Saffar presents unrestrained personal indulgence as a form of enslavement to one's desires rather than genuine freedom. Moreover, dependence on materialism and consumerism—misinterpreted as the "freedom to buy"—makes one dependent on the source of these material goods. Finally, the desire for material goods, power, and pleasure makes people ripe for bribery and corruption. In "The Horizons of Openness" al-Saffar explains:

> Imam Ali emphasizes the linkage between internal and external exploitation, oppression, and even enslavement. For Ali, freedom begins within. If a person is a slave to his own desires, he can be tempted into betraying his external freedom, since he easily can succumb to materialism and to desires for sex and power that the politically corrupt can play upon.

The sheikh employs stories from Islamic history to illustrate his point and to emphasize the linkage between internal and external freedom and its political consequences for impoverished Shi'a communities. He continues:

> When Muawiyya [the first Ummayed caliph] wanted to win Abu Zar al-Ghafari, one of the Prophet's companions, to his side to legitimate his rule, he played on Abu Zar's vulnerable position as a poor man. He sent a slave to Abu Zar with a bag of money, telling the slave that he would be freed if he could persuade Abu Zar to accept the money. The slave used all his best arguments, but Abu Zar replied that as long as he had enough for his next meal, he was rich enough. Finally, the slave told him of the caliph's promise that he would be freed if he could persuade Abu Zar to accept the money. To this, Abu Zar replied, "But if I do this, your freedom would be purchased with my enslavement."

On a local level, the argument in this sermon is directed toward members of the movement who might seize upon this moment of reconciliation with the Saudi government and succumb to their desires by accepting money or government jobs, thus giving up their willingness to work for the larger cause of equality and freedom for the Shi'a. In fact, the sheikh explicitly states: "The government can bribe those who desire money and have become corrupt. Refusing bribery is the first step toward freedom." He also implicitly warns the Saudi government against taking recent Shi'a cooperation for granted. That is, the return of the leaders of the reform movement to Saudi Arabia and their reconciliation with the government should not be misunderstood as a total abandonment of their demands on behalf of the Shi'a community.

This argument also has implications beyond the Saudi context. Not only does it address Sunni-Shi'a relations of dominance but also Western-Islamic societies' relations of dominance. Freedom from within allows for national liberation and allows for undoing the dependency on the hegemon (locally, the Sunni ruling class in Saudi Arabia, and globally, the Western capitalist mode of production and exploitation). In this respect, al-Saffar's theology of liberation is similar to liberation theology in Latin America. It privileges praxis over theory. However, unlike some of the Catholic liberation theologians, al-Saffar does not go so far as to call the existing relations of dominance sinful. In this respect, he is also different from radical Islamists, such as Shukri Mustafa and Abdul Salam Farag in Egypt, who declared the ruling class to be infidels and called for a jihad to overthrow the existing order. (This is more serious than declaring someone to be sinful.) Sheikh al-Saffar merely criticizes in the spirit of reform; in this he is in keeping with the modus operandi of the other opposition groups in Saudi Arabia that petition the king to reform the system. Of course, some groups, such as the CDLR and the Islamist Movement for Change, became more radical when the ruling family was not willing to accommodate their demands, or at least when the king's responses fell short of the kind of reform these groups wanted to implement. At present, however, the Shi'a Reform Movement is moving in an opposite, more conciliatory direction.

By cautioning listeners against perpetuating their own dependency and exploitation, al-Saffar provides a counterbalance to his new tone of moderation and reconciliation. While encouraging open and cooperative relations with the state on the level of political participation and civil society, he warns his supporters to guard against indirect forms of dominance. Because these forms of dominance feed on personal desires for wealth, power, and pleasure, individuals can combat them by placing the collective good before self-interest.

Freedom of Expression and Belief

Despite al-Saffar's calls for reform, political participation, a well-developed civil society, and minority rights, he is not oblivious to restraints posed by current realities. In a sermon titled "Imam Ali's Concept of Freedom," delivered in February/Ramadan 1996, the sheikh demonstrated his awareness of the limitations of freedom in Saudi Arabia, the vulnerable position of the Shi'a, and the limits of what he can address. Al-Saffar sees freedom as a relative concept:

> In this sermon, I will discuss the meaning of freedom within the context and constraints of our public discourse in order to explain what Imam Ali considered to be the meaning of freedom. I cannot speak about absolute freedom, for in our social dealings, we have to consider other people's freedoms as well, and freedom does not mean the liberty to abridge the freedom of others. We must consider where one person's freedom ends and another's begins. There have to be limits to freedom. Freedom is a human desire we all share, but people differ in defining freedom and in determining its limitations.

The kind of limits al-Saffar imposes on freedom are revealing. Due to the particular political culture of his audience, he attempts to quiet the regime's fears by emphasizing that this freedom neither clashes with their traditions as Saudis nor with their religious heritage as Shi'a. While sensitive to the regime's concerns, however, his frame of reference remains Shi'a; he focuses on Ali's conception of freedom and how he practiced it as a person as well as a leader of the Muslim political community. He says, "The question for us is what Imam Ali understood freedom to mean and what he considered its limitations."

Al-Saffar juxtaposes Ali's quotes with verses from the Quran to explain this conception of freedom to his audience. Central to his theme is Imam Ali's advice to "keep yourself above the pettiness of the mundane world."

> What the Imam meant is that one has to be above the temptations of lit-
> tle things. God says, "We have elevated humans." Thus, if a human being
> is degrading his/herself, this is against God's plan. "Do not trade your dig-
> nity for anything else," Imam Ali says. This means that one should not
> trade his/her freedom and dignity for anything of this world, for there is
> nothing that equals freedom and human dignity. He further emphasized,
> "The only price that equals your dignity and freedom is heaven. Do not
> sell it for less than that." For Imam Ali, freedom is the basis of humanity
> as he says, "Do not be the slave of others since God created you free." He
> adds, "O people, Adam did not beget a male or a female slave. All people
> are free."

Al-Saffar is cautious in his approach to issues regarding Shi'a's freedom of religion within a Saudi context. Thus the sheikh seems to address the question in terms of the responsibility of both the Shi'a and the Sunnis to create an atmosphere of tolerance. Here, using the Quran, he moves away from a specifically Shi'a frame of reference to a more general frame of reference accepted by all Muslims:

> Even God Himself did not infringe on people's freedoms in His Book nor did
> He order them to obey His commands. God does not want freedom to be
> confiscated because of His revealed word or because of His teachings. He in-
> structed the Prophet, "Remind them, for you are nothing but a reminder. You
> are not to order them, because you are not supposed to control them." God
> gave humans the freedom to worship. God instructed the Prophet, "Had your
> Lord wished it, He could have made all peoples believers. Thus, do not force
> people to believe."

This makes the concept of freedom central not only to the Saudi condition and the theology of Shi'a resistance but also to Islam to the extent that even God could not or did not interfere or tamper with it. Here al-Saffar's concept of freedom and his advocacy of tolerance and pluralism overlap, because allowing all people the freedom to practice their religion is a central part of the tolerance he extols. The sheikh's discourse goes beyond the Cairo Declaration of Human Rights and beyond the progressive ideas in *Man's Rights in Islam,* a book by Egypt's former minister of awqaf (religious endowments) and then head of Higher Council for Islamic Affairs, Sheikh Zakaria El Berry.[35]

In his sermon al-Saffar continues:

The Quran also teaches, "Whoever wants to believe will believe and whoever wants to doubt will doubt." God instructs the Prophet to respect human beings' freedom of choice. This is obvious in the verse which says, "We have bestowed on people a mind. They either will be thankful or ungrateful." All these sayings ascertain the centrality of freedom in Islam. This is also clear in the saying of the second caliph, Omar, who says, "Why do you enslave human beings who were born to be free?" Although Omar's statement is beautiful, it is different from Ali's understanding of freedom. While Omar addresses the oppressors and slave owners and urges them to free their slaves, Ali urges the individual to struggle to attain his/her freedom and not to sell it under any circumstance or trade it for anything less than heaven itself.

Because al-Saffar recognizes the limitations on his ability to expand Shi'a freedoms and win concessions within the current Saudi environment, he uses accommodative tactics and ideological discourse to push gently against the boundaries of political space. By widening his discussion of freedom to encompass notions of pluralism and tolerance, he highlights concepts that have broad appeal within the Shi'a community and without. He thus holds tightly to the notion of Shi'a rights while advocating preservation of these rights in a nonthreatening manner.

Islam and Politics of Dissent

Despite his awareness of the constraints posed by prevailing political arrangements and his consequent efforts to moderate his discourse and tactics, al-Saffar does not shrink from the politics of dissent. Indeed, his writings and sermons are part of a wider attempt to create a culture that accepts political dissent and differences of opinion.[36] Other members of the reform movement, such as Tawfiq al-Seif, emphasize the same point in the publication al-Kalima.[37] Like al-Saffar, they assert that dissent should be tolerated in an Islamic state. To support this point in his sermon, al-Saffar cites Ali's response to his opposition:

> It was recorded that after the death of the third caliph, Othman, the people went to Ali many times to persuade him to accept the position. Many times he refused, telling them to look for someone else. When they insisted, and he finally accepted, there were people such as Abdullah ibn Omar who refused to support him. Muslims said to Ali, "Shall we bring him to you and force him to take an oath of allegiance?" He replied that the man should be left alone.

Furthermore, Ali did not punish his opponents for disagreeing with him; instead he debated them. Al-Saffar recounts the story of al-Huraith ben Rashid, a Kharjiite, who saw Ali in the mosque surrounded by his followers and told him, "By God, Ali, I won't follow your order or follow you in the communal prayer." Ali responded, "Would you like to debate this issue?" Al-Saffar's comments are revealing: "The man said that he would, but that he did not have time for the debate that day and would come the next day. Instead of having the man arrested, Ali simply agreed to the debate the next day." Although al-Saffar does not equate the Kharijites and the Shi'a morally, he uses their example to show how Ali treated his most ardent opponents. Al-Saffar demands that, at the very least, the Saudis afford the Shi'a the same treatment that Ali gave to his opponents.

Of course, the Kharijites were much more vocal than the Shi'a of Saudi Arabia, as the sheikh indicates. "The Kharijites continued to interrupt Ali when he gave his sermons, crying 'There is no authority but God,' and refusing to recognize Ali's political leadership. Ali replied, 'This is a true statement said for the wrong reasons.' Ali's response to the Kharijites' provocations was to tell his followers, "If the Kharijites are silent, we will let them alone. If they speak, we will debate with them. Only if they spread sedition and corruption will we fight them. I will not prevent them from going to the mosque, nor will I deny them their share of the state treasury." This policy toward opposition is what the Shi'a demand of the Saudi state. They even go so far as to accept punishment if they are seditious.

Saudi Shi'a, of course, want to dispel the Wahhabi accusation that Shi'a represent a fifth column in the kingdom and work for Iranian interests. The Shi'a also are striving to create a Saudi culture that accepts dissent as part of political life. In this respect, al-Saffar's efforts to provide a wider space for opposition in the Saudi context may have regional ramifications. In addition to advocating freer Shi'a discourse in Saudi Arabia, the reform movement has implications for Nasr Hamid abu Zaid in Egypt, Farj Fouda, and Judge Sa'id 'Ashmawi. While answering to local and regional conditions, al-Saffar's calls for open debate likewise appeal to Western and non-Western advocates of democratic freedoms.

Human Rights

Although al-Saffar actively supports freedom of dissent and open debate, he firmly opposes exercising these freedoms in a way that violates the rights of others. In a taped sermon issued in January 1997 entitled "Huquq al-Insan" (Human rights), he outlines his position and offers an assessment of current human rights conditions on a regional and global level. He not only describes the human rights safeguarded under Islam but also discusses those guaranteed by Muslim nations, Western nations, and international law. In the course of this discussion, he draws a clear distinction between the proclamation of rights and their implementation. Criticizing the current disjuncture between principle and practice, he calls on Muslims and non-Muslims alike to take responsibility for their rights and the rights of fellow humans, regardless of race, religion, or gender. As with his other sermons and writings, al-Saffar grounds his discussion in Islamic tradition yet incorporates inclusive language that appeals to various audiences.

Al-Saffar opens his sermon with the Quranic verse, "And we have exalted the descendants of Adam, and we favored them over many of what we created," a verse that he interprets as God's promise to all humans. Human rights, the sheikh asserts, were first set forth by God and thus are central to Islamic belief. He states:

> Allah granted humans this dignity. *He* gave them this status and value—to humans, *all* of them, based on their being human, without any discrimination based on color, race, language, religion, sect, class, or affiliation. Humans, given that they are humans, have dignity and value, which are not granted by other human beings. There is no one who grants others their value and dignity. These are granted by Allah.

Al-Saffar goes on to describe how humans lost sight of their own value and came to "accept enslavement, subjugation, and disgrace." Only with the passing of time did humans gradually rediscover their own worth and "began talking about something called 'human rights.'" Although he maintains that "Islam discussed this issue and laid out systems, teachings, and laws for it," al-Saffar claims that humans only began "to outline and crystallize this idea [of human rights] during the last period—over the last two centuries." As early examples, he cites the U.S. Constitution, ratified in 1776, and the French Constitution, ratified in 1789. He goes on to mention the International Declaration of Human Rights, ratified by the United Nations in 1948, amendments to it in 1966, and the emergence of numerous human rights organizations, such as Amnesty International. Lest these examples mistakenly portray recent advances in the field of human rights as an exclusively Western development, al-Saffar also highlights the Islamic declaration of rights ratified by the Organization of the Islamic Conference (OIC) in 1989, after eight years of preparation and debate. While the sheikh acknowledges that differences exist between the U. N. and OIC documents, these differences are not the focus of his sermon. Rather, he highlights the work of both organizations in order to exemplify heightened awareness of human rights and consequent efforts to safeguard them.

Al-Saffar praises widespread acceptance of human rights on the level of theory and recognizes "the great powers" as "forerunners when it comes to public promotion, discussion, and production of slogans on the issue of human rights and their protection." He differentiates, however, between theoretical advances and actual implementation, stating:

> If one looks at what is happening in the world today, most of the time the issue of human rights is taken advantage of and used for political purposes. The Western states, when they find a state that is not compatible with their policies and interests and is not moving within their orbit, raise their voices with the slogans of human rights against this state. But the state that stays within their orbit, abides by their interests, and follows their lead—let it do what it may with human rights, such behavior does not concern them, and they remain silent.

To exemplify this hypocritical stance, al-Saffar focuses on the Western, and particularly American, failure to acknowledge blatant Israeli abuses against Lebanese and Palestinian rights. Moreover, he criticizes the United States and other Western nations for "producing the torture equipment of oppressive states" and supporting dictators. Al-Saffar thus concludes that a disjuncture between theory and practice will persist as long as nations refuse to place the principle of universal human rights above political or economic interests. Despite advances "from the theoretical and public point of view," he maintains that "human rights are still atrociously violated in many different areas and countries."

Rather than condoning the politicization of human rights, al-Saffar embraces a nondiscriminatory, more inclusive understanding of the issue, which he grounds in the Quran and teachings of Imam Ali. Despite his position as a religious opposition leader, the sheikh does not dwell on the Saudi regime's human rights abuses. On the contrary, he cautions against narrowly defining human rights as "the rights of citizens vis-à-vis the state" and argues instead that they "are in the first place about the interaction of humans with each other." He identifies religion, rather than the state, as the ultimate guarantor of human rights, stating: "Religions and the celestial messages came principally to protect human rights. Therefore, a Muslim must adhere and commit to the rights of his human brothers. At the level of social interaction—without regard to the political side which requires a separate discussion and study—socially, human rights must be protected." By shifting the central responsibility for safeguarding human rights from the state to religion, al-Saffar achieves several objectives. First, his sermon is in keeping with the less confrontational phase of the wider Shi'a reform movement, and second, he indirectly establishes the primacy of religious authority over political authority. Finally, and perhaps most important, he implies that a Saudi regime with genuine religious legitimacy must affirm this legitimacy by respecting human rights in practice as well as principle.

In order to underscore the central place of human rights in Islam, al-Saffar then provides evidence from Shi'a tradition and the Quran. He cites teachings of Imam Ali that emphasize the importance God places on one's just treatment of fellow humans, stating:

> Imam Ali specified "as for injustice that Allah does not forgive, except with the acquiescence of he who is harmed, it is the injustice of people on one another." If one has a flaw in his worship, or falls short in his prayer or fasting for example, Allah may forgive him for such shortcomings. But for a person who continuously violates the rights of his fellow human, Allah will not forgive him for that unless the person whom he wronged permits and forgives.

Al-Saffar likewise cites a hadith based on this theme:

> A woman came to the dwelling of the Prophet, Allah's praise upon him, in Ramadan. It was a Muslim woman, who was of course fasting. She began talking about her neighbor—talking about others. The Prophet turned to his wife and asked her to bring the woman some food and drink. The woman became puzzled, and exclaimed "I am fasting, how can you present me with food and drink in Ramadan when I am fasting?!" The Prophet, praise be upon him, responded: "How can you be fasting when you spoke ill of your neighbor in her absence?" What kind of fasting is this? It is not real fasting.

Drawing on these examples, al-Saffar tells his listeners, "Your religiosity is revealed through your behavior and treatment of others." He thus situates human rights at the center of Shi'a and Sunni belief and deems protection of these rights the responsibility of all Muslims.

Al-Saffar further insists that this responsibility to respect the rights of others extends both to material/physical rights as well as symbolic rights, such as reputation, honor, and belief. Moreover, he deems these symbolic rights "more sacred than attacking one's wealth or body." This assertion clearly has important implications within the local Shi'a context, given the Saudi regime's history of attacking Shi'a beliefs, reputation, and culture. Since Sunni opposition groups are likewise targeted by the regime and official religious establishment, they too can identify with al-Saffar's message.

In closing his sermon, al-Saffar insists that people must not only respect others' rights but also protect their own. He rejects theories that call on people to surrender and passively accept violations of their rights as well as theories that demand that people use all means to reclaim their rights "without consideration for anything else." Rather, he advocates a "third way" offered by Islam, stating:

Islam does not accept that a person surrender to those who attack him. Nor does it accept that one can make an attack. Rather it gives a person the right to respond to an attack on himself. "He who attacks you, attack him as he attacked you." The sanction of an attack is an attack like it. A person should not remain silent when it comes to his rights. Rather, he should cling to his rights.

Even as he insists that listeners defend their rights, however, al-Saffar asserts that this must be done in a way that protects both public and self-interest. Moreover, he informs listeners: "You have the right to forgive, and Islam encourages you to forgive when it comes to your personal rights. But this is not based on the principle of surrender—not on the principle of surrender, subservience, and cowardice." He thus indirectly encourages the Shi'a to continue to push for reform yet also justifies the movement's shift toward more moderate, accommodative policies.

Finally, al-Saffar implies that the Shi'a community's struggle to defend human rights in Saudi Arabia is one in which they had no choice but to take part. He draws an implicit parallel between the current reform movement and the history of Imam al-Hussein, reminding listeners:

And if we look at Imam Al-Hussein's history and find that he rose up and revolted [we must remember that] he did not choose the battle. They were the ones who started and Al-Hussein did not initiate the fighting. At the same time, Imam Al-Hussein rose up because [it] was needed in order to put an end to the legitimacy of that regime [of Yazeed bin Mu'awiyah] and if it wasn't for Al-Hussein's revolution, [that regime] would have become legitimate as well as its decisions and Yazeed bin Mu'awiyah's sayings would have become authoritative for future Muslim generations. Hussein's revolution is what revealed the unjustness of that Ummayid regime.

Al-Saffar's discussion of human rights, like his treatment of other issues, thus reveals his efforts to integrate multiple strands of discourse and appeal to various audiences. On a local level, his insistence on indiscriminate protection of physical and symbolic rights resonates within the Shi'a and Sunni communities. While he abstains from directly challenging the regime's human rights record, his sermon equates just treatment of one's fellow humans with genuine religiosity. By implication, a state with true religious legitimacy would respect the rights of its citizens. Beyond this local context, the discourse of human rights also resonates on regional and international levels. Al-Saffar explicitly recognizes widespread awareness of the issue by discussing its inclusion in Western constitutions and international declarations. His assessment of human rights practices, however, is far from complimentary. While appealing to the human rights principles espoused in the West, he sharply criticizes Western governments' policies. Al-Saffar thus assumes the moral high ground and appeals to human rights ideals without leaving himself open to accusations of selling out to the West.

Rights of Non-Muslims in a Muslim State

Although al-Saffar does not focus specifically on the rights of non-Muslims in "Iman Ali's Concept of Freedom," he does discuss them in other works. Since the sheikh asserts that God granted human rights to all individuals, it is logical that he should insist on protection of non-Muslim as well as Muslim rights within Muslim states. Al-Saffar's treatment of this issue provides yet another example of the multitude of discourses and influences that he draws into his sermons and writings.

Although al-Saffar relies on the same verses that Sheikh El Berry uses in *Man's Rights in Islam,* he adds the tradition of Omar and Ali to emphasize that the political leaders of the Muslim community believed in these ideals as well. Again, the inclusion of Omar is another attempt on al-Saffar's part to move away from the Shi'a specificity to declare that these ideas are part and parcel of the Islamic tradition as a whole. Furthermore, unlike El Berry, who wavered in his justification of the punishment of apostates, al-Saffar seems to make no apology about his conviction in the absoluteness of freedom of belief.

It is important to note that the Cairo Declaration on Human Rights in Islam, adopted by members of the Organization of the Islamic Conference on August 5, 1990, failed to allow for the type of freedom of belief that al-Saffar preaches. In fact, Article 10 of the Cairo Declaration specifically states: "Islam is the religion of unspoiled nature. It is prohibited to exercise any form of compulsion on man or to exploit his poverty or ignorance in order to convert him to another religion or to atheism."[38] Considered within the context of the declaration, however, this article clearly concerns the regulation of missionary activities rather than freedom of belief.

Al-Saffar goes beyond Sunni-Shi'a issues or the position of Muslim minority sects within an Islamic state to include in his "Iman Ali" sermon a discussion of the position of non-Muslims in a Muslim state. According to al-Saffar, Ali not only tolerated dissent among Muslims but advocated more freedom for non-Muslims within the Muslim state:

> In terms of religion, Ali realized that there were different religious orientations. He did not endanger the freedom of non-Muslims living within the Islamic state but rather let them practice their faith as they understood it. These views are not Ali's alone. Prophet Muhammed himself shared these views and even went as far to say "Anyone who injures a non-Muslim is injuring me personally." In a proper Islamic state, the freedoms of non-Muslims should not be infringed upon.

These views are important, because they reveal Shi'a interest beyond local Saudi issues. Because there are no non-Muslim citizens in Saudi Arabia, we can only infer that al-Saffar is addressing a wider audience—countries where non-Muslims and Muslims live together. In this sense, al-Saffar connects with the ideas of Sheikh Yousef al-Qaradawi, a very influential Sunni theologian and a member of Egypt's Muslim Brotherhood. In fact, he draws upon al-Qaradawi's 1983 book, *Ghayr al-Muslimeen fil Mujtama' al-Islami* (Non-Muslims in an Islamic society),[39] which makes the case for the established rights of non-Muslims in a Muslim society on the basis of the Quran, as well as on the practices of earlier Muslims toward non-Muslims. The term "non-Muslim," moreover, does not necessarily refer only to the People of the Book (i. e., Christians and Jews) but also to Sabaeans (i. e., those who belong to other religious orientations). Like al-Qaradawi, al-Saffar sees the issue as one of individual responsibility. In *Pluralism and Freedom in Islam,* al-Saffar borrows heavily from al-Qaradawi on issues of freedom of opinion and freedom of belief.[40] The significant point is the constant sharing of ideas among Shi'a and Sunnis outside Saudi Arabia. Al-Saffar's embrace of the ideas of Sunni intellectuals—Fahmi Howiedy, Yousef al-Qaradawi, and Hasan al-Turabi, among others—has led other intellectuals in the reform movement, such as Tawfiq al-Seif and Abdulla al-Yousef, to endorse the same authors. For instance, in two articles by al-Yousef on freedom of opinion, thought, and belief, published in two issues of the reform movement's new publication *al-Kalima,* one finds numerous citations of al-Saffar, al-Qaradawi, Howeidy, and Soroush.[41] Similar non-Saudi intellectuals are cited in an article by al-Seif.[42]

It is important to note that these discussions on the rights of non-Muslims in Islamic societies have been ignored by Western scholars who write on Islam and human rights. For example, in chapter 7, on non-Muslims, in *Islam and Human Rights,* published in 1991 author Ann Elizabeth Mayer fails to discuss al-Qaradawi's important study even though it was published in 1983 (seven years before her book) and is the most respected and debated work on the subject among Muslim scholars.[43] Indeed, her footnotes for this chapter do not include any Arabic sources.[44]

As an activist and a preacher, al-Saffar and his sermons have dominated Shi'a political language, especially after the group's return to Saudi Arabia in 1993. Compared to other Saudi opposition leaders, he seems to have garnered the greatest number of followers in proportion to the number of Saudis within his religious community. Yet in spite of this large following, al-Saffar is limited by the minority status of the Saudi Shi'a and the actual size of that community. It appears that the strategy of al-Saffar and the reform movement is to live with the current arrangement and to preach more openness and tolerance instead of confrontation. Thus far this approach seems to have been effective; the government has responded to some, though not all, Shi'a demands.

Conclusion and Implications

Tracing the evolution of the Shi'a resistance and its changing discourse and tactics has implications for the study of past, present, and future relations between the Saudi regime and its opponents as well as for the broader study of Islam and politics.

If we look at the implications of the Shi'a movement for the future of the Saud regime, Shi'a discourse challenges Saudi hegemony at the level of both the state and society and exposes its weaknesses. This can be understood only in the context of political space on the borderlines. The Shi'a discourse is a borderline narrative that simultaneously exists both inside and outside Saudi society. In other words, it exists in a space between the religious tribal hegemony of the Saudi state and society and other competing hegemonies outside it—Arab and Islamic discourses in the immediate surroundings and the hegemonic Western discourse of liberalization, democratization, and secularization. Hegemony here is defined in broad terms as an authoritative discourse that people accept as a superior narrative, consciously or unconsciously. Of course, hegemonic discourses do not go unchallenged. Throughout the 1960s, Saudi Shi'a attempted to provide a counterhegemony by linking their discourse to that of Arab nationalism. The failure of this effort to force the Saudi regime to satisfy Shi'a demands led the Shi'a to resort to an alternative discourse, that of revolutionary Iranian Islam. Although events in the Eastern Province in 1979 led the regime to take the Shi'a challenge seriously, the Saudi state managed to ignore their demands with impunity.

Only during the latest phase of Shi'a discourse, stretching from the late 1980s until the present, did the Shi'a seem to succeed in weakening the hegemony of the Saudi state. By interweaving its own narrative of resistance and more inclusive regional and global discourses, the reform movement retained its local legitimacy while also appealing to wider audiences and strengthening its credibility and bargaining position vis-à-vis the Saudi regime. On a regional level, leaders such as al-Saffar incorporated enlightened Islamic discourse that resonated among Shi'a and Sunni communities. On a global level, they espoused universalistic notions of openness and tolerance, political participation, minority rights, personal freedom and responsibility, civil society, and human rights.

Undoubtedly, the shift in Shi'a discourse and tactics both reflected and reinforced other internal and external changes affecting the kingdom. The global communications revolution of satellite dishes, fax machines, and the

Internet contributed to the greater acceptance of the democracy and human rights discourse. In fact, the impact of the satellite dish on Saudi society was so strong that the state chose to make it illegal. Saudi religious police literally fired their guns at the rooftops of homes where these devices were located.[45] Furthermore, the economic and political weakness of the Saudi state as a result of the Gulf War and the state's inability to meet both material and ideological challenges made the regime more vulnerable to Shi'a opponents. As a result, the Saudi king conceded to most Shi'a demands, releasing political prisoners and allowing leaders of the movement to return to Saudi Arabia with guarantees of their safety.[46] The regime's hegemonic hold on Saudi society was further undermined by the rise of Sunni opposition. Thus the regime found itself outflanked by ultra-conservative currents within Wahhabism led by young and energetic sheikhs such as Salman al-'Auda, Saffar al-Hawali, Muhammed Mas'ari, and the more radical Usama bin Laden. This weakness of Saudi hegemony suggests that the Saudi state is likely to grant more concessions not only to the Shi'a but to other social groups.

Al-Saffar's discourse is designed to link with all forces and counterhegemonies both inside and outside the kingdom. In this respect it can be conceptualized as another form of resistance rather than a discourse of coexistence between the Shi'a and the regime. However, we should not rule out the ability of the state to manipulate counterhegemonies and redirect them horizontally instead of vertically. In all scenarios, however, the change in language in Saudi Arabia at the level of state and opposition reveal one certain thing: a change in politics. In this new Saudi politics, al-Saffar and the Shi'a Reform Movement will figure prominently. It also could inform the resistance of other groups opposing the regime.

On a larger level, analysis of these sermons, the writings of al-Saffar, and the history of the Shi'a Reform Movement in Saudi Arabia reveals that Islam is not a static force but an episodic discourse. Islamic interpretations change according to the evolutionary process of political movements, political events, and a group's understanding of the self, the other, and Islam. As demonstrated, the Shi'a Reform Movement emerged from radical origins and initially called for the regime's overthrow. However, as it evolved into a more moderate movement, its leaders moved toward dialogue with the government, Sunnis, and even women. Thus focusing on the Islamic texts alone yields an incomplete understanding these dynamic and changing movements. The most useful way to understand Islam as a social and political text is to study the ways in which Islamists constantly interpret and reinterpret the Islamic message in response to specific political and social conditions. Essentialist analysis that clings to a static, homogeneous view of Arab or Islamic political culture fails to account for change and diversity on the levels of discourse, society, and politics. Hence it is important to analyze al-Saffar's sermons and writings in order to see how the movement's discourse shapes and reshapes itself in response to new conditions.

Although in some respects Islamic discourse represents a counterhegemony, it exists among competing hegemonies on local, regional, and global levels. As revealed through the works of al-Saffar, these multiple discourses interact and influence one another in a dialectical process. Islamic discourse shapes Western discourse if only at the level of its view of Islam, and Western discourse shapes Islamic discourse by forcing it to deal with questions of liberalization and democratization.

These interactions between "Islamic" and "Western" discourses are likely to lead to better understanding of both the self and the other. The interpretations of Islam by Muslim minorities living on the borderlines of their societies are likely to allow greater room for human rights and democracy than even the Muslims themselves may expect. Through their interactions with and their studies of people like al-Saffar, minorities living on the peripheries of both Western societies and Western intellectual communities will come to realize the uninformed character of current Western theoretical debates on "Islam and politics." Thus debates on the compatibility of democracy and human rights with an Islamic culture will move toward a more sophisticated, nuanced understanding of Islamic cultures, societies, and polities.

The Shi'a, however, remain an isolated cultural grouping within Saudi Arabia. Although cultural cohesion of a particular opposition group is usually considered a strength, in the Shi'a case it is more of a weakness, at least domestically. Within Saudi Arabia they live with a sea of Sunni Islam. The Wahhabi theology, which represents an important aspect of the legitimacy formula of the Saudi regime, is likely to further limit the maneuverability of the Shi'a movement as well as the parameters of the regime's response.[47] Also tribally, many of the Shi'a are considered inferior, at least according to the Najdis and the Hijazis. On a regional level, however, the Shi'a can be a powerful destabilizing force. If they were to link with the Shi'a majority in Bahrain, the Shi'a of Lebanon, and the Shi'a of Iraq where the Shi'a leadership is strong, they could threaten the stability of the whole Gulf region. Yet the fact that such a coalition did not materialize during the heyday of the Iranian revolution is another indicator that one is not likely to arise any time soon. Furthermore, the Arab Shi'a are not likely to accept Iranian dominance in the region. Thus, given this limited Shi'a role on the regional level, the Shi'a of Saudi Arabia will remain part of the kingdom's local conditions. They might utilize global and regional factors to maximize gains domestically, but the influence of these factors will remain limited. Locally, the Shi'a's role as a destabilizing factor is further minimized by the rise of anti-Shi'a sentiments among the Sunni opposition groups. As I have shown in the previous chapters, Mas'ari's CDLR, al-Faqih's MIRA, and bin Laden's ARC are far more anti-Shiʿa in their discourse than the regime would ever be. This is probably why we witness more Shiʿa support for the royal family—it can serve to protect the Shiʿa against the rising anti-Shiʿa sentiments in the society at large. Regional as well as local factors thus impose limits on the destabilizing influence of the Shiʿa Reform Movement in Saudi Arabia.

CHAPTER EIGHT

Conclusion

The intensity of the global-local tension has been felt by both the Saudi state and its opponents. Both have been transformed utterly. The Saudi government has been confronted with both real opposition and virtual opposition, that is, by a group of people who engage in Saudi oppositional discourse and sometimes participate in the opposition's criticism of the state. These people are not necessarily Saudis; some are non-Saudis who have commercial or humanitarian interests in the Saudi state and its constructions. To some degree, some of these "virtual Saudis" might be writers and academics who start their research from a normative position of what the Saudi state should or ought to be; those who believe Saudi Arabia should have active civil organizations independent from the state, should have democratic institutions, and should respect the principles enshrined in the Universal Declaration of Human Rights. Thus their analyses could be part of the opposition discourse whether they intend them to be or not. Nowhere is "virtual opposition" clearer than in cyberspace. The presence of these virtual opponents raises the problem of identifying participants in this discourse. Are the members of this opposition "real" Saudi citizens, are they non-Saudis who are genuinely engaged in the Saudi opposition discourse, or are they an unrelated category of individuals who seek, by masquerading as Saudis, to manipulate the discourse in the pursuit of ends unrelated to it? The possibilities are endless: This population may include the state itself masquerading as the opposition, liberals masquerading as Islamists, or another state or any other interested party masquerading as Saudi dissidents. These three categories (real Saudi citizens, virtual citizens, and masqueraders) overlap to some extent. "Real" Saudi citizens may also be virtual citizens; in fact, cyberspace may provide the only place in which they can act as participatory citizens at all. The population of virtual citizens, however, is not restricted to "real" citizens with Internet access; it includes non-Saudi participants who are engaged in, and who shape, Saudi opposition.

An example of these overlapping categories and the complexity of "virtual citizenship" is found in the Web site of the Committee Against Corruption in Saudi Arabia (CACSA, http://www.saudhouse.com/), which maintains the best opposition home page. No one knows who operates this site. A Saudi government official claims that the site was created and operated by a Lebanese journalist who attempted to blackmail the government by offering to remove the site for $1 million.[1] The state, however, would have an obvious interest in portraying its opponents as non-Saudis. Nonetheless, this group can consist of the other possibilities mentioned above. Although the home page has many elements of Shiʻa discourse, none of the Shiʻa I interviewed, both inside Saudi Arabia and abroad, claimed to have any connection to it. In fact, many of them had not seen it. Members of Sunni opposition groups maintained that they had no connection to those who run the site. Then who is posting to and monitoring it? According to its mission statement, the group was initiated by "people with strong ties to the business community in the U.S. and Saudi Arabia."[2] The site could even be operated by a women's group, which would explain why Saudi men know so little about its origin. The committee's stated goal is to expose corruption, human rights abuses, and lack of freedom of expression under "the Sudairi Seven."

An important component of this CACSA Web site is a rich database that contains news centers, copies of books about the kingdom, and a listing of e-mail addresses connected to the king's palace and Saudi ambassadors for those who wish to send their comments. CACSA messages aim at recruiting students worldwide and urges them to spread the message concerning royal family corruption and human rights abuses. The issue of women's rights seems central to CACSA, as are its attempts to reach out to non-Saudis and to pressure the regime from the outside. Besides students, the target audiences of this group are the Saudi elite, journalists, scholars, and policy makers. What is important about this site, however, is that you do not need to be a Saudi to be part of the opposition, and Saudi "netzenship" rather than citizenship is what is important here.

Evaluating Saudi Opposition

Various groups, interests, and circumstances shape the discourse of Saudi opposition and its ability to change the regime. The global-local dialectic, as a context, is also central to the articulation of their interests and demands. To provide a meaningful analysis of these opposition groups, let me summarize the findings thus far.

Safar al-Hawali, the speaker who galvanized the Saudi public during the Gulf War, is not a local Saudi sheikh with a local agenda. In Hawali's sermons, resisting globalization precedes his emphasis on resisting the local political arrangements. Hawali reacts directly to television images and is most concerned about the missionary activities of American televangelists and Christian fundamentalists, whom he considers a danger to Islamic culture. Second, he is critical of U.S. hegemony and politics of domination in the region. He sees America's policies in the whole region as part of a larger scheme to control the Muslim world and its resources. Hawali is also very combative when he addresses the emotional issue of the Israeli occupation of Jerusalem, one of the holiest shrines of Islam. His awareness of global trends and their implication for the Muslim world does not escape even the most uninitiated reader. Thus his criticism of the Saudi government and Saudi elite is part of a larger discourse. Saudi "failure to protect the faith and their inability to confront these new challenges," especially the proliferation of Western thought and culture through the new media such as the satellite dish, is of paramount concern to Hawali and his followers. He sees the influence of the West everywhere in the Arab world. He is critical of other Arab states for their deviation from Shari'a as *the* basis of their constitutions. In his eyes, Arab governments and local elite are implicated in the process of globalization, for they are the local agents who pave the way for acceptance of Western ideas and technologies. Hawali was imprisoned not only because he criticized the local arrangements of state-society relations, but because he criticized the Saudi government's position on globalization and the emergence of forms of global dominance that result. According to a Saudi government official, the regime felt that Hawali was inciting violence.

Salman al-'Auda shares Hawali's global Islamic message and his critique of globalization. And like Hawali, al-'Auda uses the cassette tape to deliver this message. While al-'Auda is concerned primarily with Saudi deviation from Shari'a law, he is concerned also with the impact of globalization in that it pollutes Islamic values and culture. He attacks the secular trend within Saudi society and portrays secularists as a fifth column in the confrontation between the believers and the global trends that aim at destroying the "soul of the Muslim umma." Like U.S. fundamentalists, al-'Auda has been very critical of the United Nations, especially the Cairo Population Conference, which he described as "one which promotes vice and makes what God considers sinful legal and permissible."[3] This attack on the population conference is at the heart of al-'Auda's local strategy of resistance to global intrusion. On the regional level, he is critical of the efforts of other Arab states to normalize relations with Israel.

Unlike Hawali, al-'Auda is aggressive in his criticism of both the 'ulama and members of the royal family. Al-Auda's audience seems to be young

Saudis from the al-Qaseem region and Arab and Muslim students abroad. However, his influence is limited by the fact that in his hometown, Buraydah, he has to contend with a respected establishment Islamic scholar, Sheikh bin Otheimeen, whose reputation exceeds his own. Moreover, bin Otheimeen has stated that al-'Auda has made mistakes and should apologize to other 'ulama for violating the secrecy of advice and for accusing people of things he did not witness. Al-'Auda's message is provocative—indeed, the regime has imprisoned him for his views. However, while some Saudis admire al-'Auda for his courage, few seem to be devoted followers of his ideas.

Unlike Hawali and al-'Auda, who have worked at the local level to resist globalizing trends, London-based Muhammed al-Mas'ari and the CDLR have been directly entangled in global spaces. London, with its own Islamic culture forged from the city's various immigrant communities, has surely influenced the means, the substance, and the aims of Mas'ari's message. During his first two years in London, Mas'ari's message was focused on Saudi Arabia. After his split with the CDLR and his mounting debt (£ 200,000) Mas'ari's audience and message became more pan-Islamic and lost its Saudi focus.

As with the other dissident preachers, Mas'ari's critique of the Saudi state also focuses on its betrayal of its foundational Islamic principles, but his means of communicating with his followers are far more technologically developed. His appeal, however, remains limited not only to a computer-literate audience, but also because his focus on Islam ignores other Saudi realities, such as regionalism and tribalism. Islam may form the ideological basis of the state, but without tribal ethos and familialism it could not remain intact.

Furthermore, the CDLR has not been able to cope with the new global spaces and the complexity of political culture they pose. The Islamic currents in London have pulled Mas'ari away from Saudi-specific issues to more global Islamic issues. This repositioning has to cost him local political capital. He has also lost credibility in the eyes of reporters, analysts, and his Saudi constituency due to the group's growing tendency to mix unsubstantiated, trivial allegations with serious and credible charges. As the group sought to satisfy various audiences, it lost its core message and confused its core constituency. Finally, as Mas'ari's position has weakened after the split within the CDLR, and with his mounting debt, he seems more open than ever to negotiating with the government. His only conditions are the release of prisoners and the acceptance of the Memorandum of Advice as the basis for negotiations.

Sa'd al-Faqih's MIRA organization uses the same technology as the CDLR, but it is more credible and focused in its reporting. Nevertheless, it does not represent a threat to the Saudi state, in part because its vision of an Islamic state does not differ radically from that of the government. Al-Faqih's primary reforms—free speech and free elections—do not have widespread support because Saudi liberals, his natural allies in this cause, do not trust his statements and suggest that they are merely tactics to mobilize support. Moreover, he wants to maintain the Council of Higher 'Ulama and implement the Memorandum of Advice, demands that the state has already accommodated to some degree. Al-Faqih's discourse is neither radical enough to attract those who are likely to take up arms against the regime (the bin Laden followers) nor moderate enough to appeal to Western governments. On human rights, for example, his rhetoric neither fully endorses internationally recognized principles, such as the Universal Declaration on Human Rights, nor is it significantly different from that of the Saudi government. This ambiguous position has little impact except to change the language of the debate about the nature of the Saudi state and how to reform it. It is not likely to undermine state legitimacy. Furthermore, al-Faqih's attack on the integrity of the 'ulama is likely to cost him politically because Saudis inside the kingdom still admire bin Baz more than they do al-Faqih. MIRA may be the most serious current movement and its legacy may contribute greatly to opposition movements to Saud rule; nevertheless, its role is likely to remain strong at the level of cultural change but weak in motivating people to action.

One opposition leader who is focused on action against the state and its allies is Usama bin Laden and his ARC. This group focuses on attacking the presence of U.S. troops in Saudi Arabia. Bin Laden shares with Mas'ari and al-Faqih a critique of corruption in the government and the society at large, but unlike them, he is willing to use force to achieve his objective. Also unlike them, he is linked not only to the world of media spaces but to the world of high finance and weapons. His followers tend to be those who, like bin Laden himself, fought in Afghanistan, but the organization is very loosely knit. Many followers are those who are inspired by his message rather being under his direct orders. Because these followers may act independently, they are difficult to trace and do pose a threat of terrorism. However, they are unlikely to undermine the stability of the regime.

Hasan al-Saffar and his Shi'a Reform Movement differ from the various Sunni movements in that they have a limited goal—the improvement of conditions for Shi'a within the kingdom. Their strategy and tactics have varied over the years. They started as a pro-Iranian revolutionary movement involoved in violent acts against the state and gradually moved to creative resistance. The movement's history and evolution have various implications. First, the change of its language of opposition over the years reveals Islam is not a static force but an episodic discourse. Islamic interpretations change according to the evolutionary process of political movements, political events, and a group's understanding of the self, the other, and Islam. The Shi'a Reform Movement started by calling for the overthrow of the regime, but it has evolved into a more moderate movement focused on dialogue be-tween the Shi'a and the government, between Shi'a and Sunnis, even be-tween Shi'a and women. On a local level, the change in discourse helped the Shi'a movement reach an agreement with the government. The Shi'a of Saudi Arabia do not represent a threat to the regime unless they are linked with other Shi'a groups, from Lebanon, to Bahrain, to Iran. However, the Shi'a question in the Gulf is certainly worth studying as a separate topic.

The Shi'a have made use of the global media during their life in London and Washington, but their experience remains limited compared to that of Sunni groups. They are directly influenced by oil-related issues since they live in the Eastern Province of Saudi Arabia where ARAMCO has its base and where oil is most concentrated, and for that reason they may have been exposed to global trends earlier than the Sunnis of the heartland, though not those of the Western Region (Hijaz). People of the Hijaz have experienced global impacts since Islam began due to the influx of Muslims to Mecca dur-ing the haj (pilgrimage) season. The Shi'a community of Saudi Arabia re-mains the least threatening to the state of all the groups studied here.

Government Responses to New Forms of Resistance

The Saudi government has used various strategies to cope with its opponents, whether they are "virtual" or real. These strategies include accommodating some of the popular demands for reform, competing with the opposition in cyberspace and the "hyperreal" world of television screens, using financial and diplomatic power to limit the impact of opposition both inside and out-side the national boundaries, and using fatwas and publications of the official religious institutions to delegitimize the discourse of these groups.

There is no denying that the kingdom has reformed since the Gulf War. On March 1, 1992, the Saudi government inaugurated the Shura Council, a 60-member consultative group appointed by the king. For the first time, the king decided to codify the Shari'a laws and release them in a form known as the Basic Laws of Governance. These laws deal with administration, local government, and many other issues. The reforms represent a direct response to the demands of the opposition articulated in their Letter of Demands, Memorandum of Advice, and cassette tapes.[4] In 1997 the Saudi government further expanded the Shura Council by 50 percent, to 90 members. The new members included spokesmen for important tribes and major interest groups. Significantly, the council included one of the most radical Islamists, Ahmed al-Tuwaijri, among its members.

Even with these recent reforms, political participation in Saudi Arabia re-mains managed by the state. Under the prevailing system, the state selects council members to represent different tribal, regional, and socioeconomic groups based on the individuals' loyalty to royal interests and technocratic credentials. Were free political participation permitted and council members selected by the groups themselves, seniority would be the determining factor of membership. The state claims that this form of free political participation would be less efficient than its own version of managed participation and would reproduce a "retraditionalization" of the political order.

While the extent of recent reforms is extremely limited, the very structure of the political system presents a formidable barrier to wider political opening. This structure is a series of widening circles, each of which includes an additional element of Saudi society. The innermost circle is occupied exclusively by the king, who, at least in theory, exercises absolute authority over the rest of society. As the circles extend outward, they become more inclusive. The circle closest to the king includes the other members of the royal family, followed by additional circles that include members of the tribal aristocracy, wealthy merchants who lack tribal lineage, ordinary Saudis, and, in the widest and most inclusive circle, foreign workers. While the discourse of absolute authority suggests that the king's authority extends outward across these circles, unimpeded, it in fact meets with resistance at each level. Any efforts by the king to allocate political power beyond a particular circle of society will encounter resistance from within all of the more exclusive circles. Thus members of the royal family will resist any extension of power to the tribal aristocracy, just as the royal family and tribal aristocracy will resist any extension of power to the wealthy merchants. Those within the more exclusive circles strive to preserve their own privileged positions in the social and political hierarchy and thus erect obstacles to political widening. In the extreme case, should the king attempt to extend full political rights to the circle that comprises the entire Saudi society, including foreign workers, he would face opposition from the rest of the population. This model has dangerous implications for regimes that pursue reform, as evidenced by the fate of King Saud. During the 1960s the king agreed to the demands of the "Free Princes" who called for a constitutional democracy. He consequently encountered resistance from within the royal family and 'ulama and ultimately was deposed in 1964. As this example reveals, the current king's ability to use reform as a strategy for dealing with opposition groups is limited by the structure of prevailing political arrangements. The Saudi state thus turns to exclusive and coercive measures in addition to inclusive reforms.

To compete with the opposition in new global spaces and to fend off media wars by opposition groups outside the kingdom, the Saudi government has directly or indirectly purchased major media outlets in various world capitals. Saudi Arabia now dominates the Arabic visual and print media. Arab media conglomerates such as Middle East Broadcasting Corporation (MBC), Orbit Communications, and Arab Radio and Television

(ART) are not run or controlled directly by the government but are owned either by Saudi princes or by Saudi businessmen who have close relationships with the royal family. MBC is part of ARA Group International, a media conglomerate that includes several radio and television companies covering the whole Arab world. MBC and ARA's chairman, Sheikh Walid Al-Ibrahim, is a brother-in-law of King Fahd. Orbit Communication is a three-year-old multichannel pay television service owned by Prince Khalid Bin Fahd Bin Abdullah bin Abd al-Rahman Al Saud, another member of the royal family. ART is a three-year-old entertainment-oriented channel headed by Sheikh Salih Kamil, a wealthy Saudi businessman, and Prince al-Waleed Bin Talal Bin Abd al-Aziz Al Saud, a nephew of King Fahd. On these channels, sensitive issues such as the CDLR and criticism of friendly regimes have been carefully avoided. As owners of these media outlets, the Saudis control the content by punishing those who are critical of Saudi Arabia or who broadcast programs offensive to Saudi social mores. For example, the Saudi Satellite Company Orbit canceled a $150 million contract with the Arabic BBC television network because it aired a Panorama program offensive to the Saudi government, which claimed that the program disparaged Islam.[5]

In addition to purchasing sites of criticism, the Saudis have also struck deals with the actors themselves. In the case of the Shi'a Reform Movement, the king agreed to release members of the movement from prison and offered them jobs in Saudi Arabia. Although this approach has not yet been used with either MIRA or the CDLR, the Saudi government did not hesitate to use its diplomatic leverage to pressure the British government to deport CDLR leader al-Mas'ari from Britain.[6]

The Saudi government has its own home pages, as do many, if not all, Saudi embassies abroad, to counter the effect of Internet-based resistance.[7] However, inside the country, it is difficult and expensive for Saudis to have access to the Internet. Potential users have to register with Saudi telecom, which allows dial-up connections with a foreign service provider. However, many Saudis can pay Internet fees to servers outside Saudi Arabia, either in the West or in neighboring Gulf countries. Nonetheless, the state seems to have bested the opposition in these new global spaces. It has media outlets and its finances far exceeds that of the opposition. What is interesting in this case, however, is that both the state and the opposition have been globalized and the contest has been transported to another site, namely London. It is a conflict between the Saudi state and its opposition on non-Saudi territory.

Theoretical Implications

New means of communication and the local/global dialectic have implications for the substance of the debate on the nature of Islam and Islamic governance. The interactions between the Saudi state and its opponents illustrate that both are forced to contend with different hegemonies and to bargain with different audiences in different landscapes. In the process of bargaining, both lose and gain ideologically and politically, at least at the level of discourse, as the analysis of the opposition home pages and government response to them shows.

The new technology and the "compression of space" have drastically altered the nature of resistance to the state by expanding the domain of political activities beyond national territories. The greater flexibility and extraterritoriality of the new modes of resistance resulting from the mobility of sites of resistance create a marked difference between this new and "postmodern" resistance and the "premodern" one. This is obvious in the case of cassette tapes and cellular phones and the global flow of information via the Internet. These new developments have accorded the opposition an opportunity to communicate with similar groups and to learn new strategies from movements elsewhere. The similarity of the information on the home pages and the sources of this information suggest that these new spaces allow the opposition greater coordination and communication than were available at home. Even if there is no direct communication between groups, information is out there for anyone to see, copy, and download. This information and the debate around it have the potential to provide a basis for a new "imagined community."

A review of the cyberspace resistance home pages of the CDLR and MIRA shows that the structure of the Internet as an environment of communication, the language used, and the diversity of the audience affects the substance of the message. "We have to talk to everybody, including Western governments, journalists, and academics," says MIRA leader Sa'd al-Faqih.[8] Like al-Faqih, Mas'ari also sees other Islamic groups from the larger Islamic world as a target audience.[9] Yet the two organizations are keen on delivering a suitable message to their local audience in Arabic through regular faxes. The dilemma of addressing multiple audiences with different concerns complicates their work.

Both Mas'ari and al-Faqih are convinced that the way to pressure the Saudi government to accommodate their demands is to address its Western allies and patrons. In doing so, both groups anchor their criticism of the Saudi government in the discourse of metropolitan globalization. This global influence is evident in the CDLR's reformism, neo-liberal economics, and human rights discourse. Saudi opposition discourse on their Web sites generally does not question the regime's neoliberal economics but rather the government's mismanagement of the Saudi economy. Thus the home-page technoscape engages both the global idea-scape and the financescape, to name but two. In the human rights sphere, as the two groups move between these multiple discourses, they sacrifice certain components of their Islamic message in favor of a hybrid discourse that attempts to reconcile Islam with the Universal Declaration on Human Rights. In the process, they become agents of globalization by introducing global discourses to their local audience.

In spite of the opposition's setbacks in reaching the local audience directly, cyberspace, the mobility of the resistance site, the compression of space, and the collapse of time pose serious challenges to our understanding of the site of resistance in the age of globalization. The militant preacher or organization no longer speaks from a fixed pulpit in a local mosque. The cassette tape provides him and his listeners with a mobile mosque and a mobile pulpit. The Internet provides him with a global mosque and a global pulpit and the ability to network with like-minded preachers and organizations. Furthermore, the absence of hierarchy on the Internet further complicates the picture. Both state and opposition vie for the same audience. In addition, the philosophy of the Internet is consumer-driven rather than producer-determined. The consumer retrieves what he or she wants; nothing is imposed. The consumer is also interactively connected and can have his or her own home page and become a producer as well. These changes force social scientists to reconsider their concepts, their analytical frameworks, and the explanatory power of these concepts and frameworks in relation to new globalized local phenomena.

Although the global is selectively defined, it reflects itself locally. Reform, in the sense of structural adjustment rather than revolution, is a general global mood. Any opposition group or state that deviates from this is considered either "rogue" or a group that is "out of touch." As chapter 5 reveals, MIRA may be radical, but underneath, it offers a compromising message that focuses on reform rather than revolution. The issues raised in the Memorandum of Advice and the Letter of Demands represent MIRA's core demands. All the requests in these two documents are reformist. They ask for an independent judiciary, freedom of expression, independence of the 'ulama, the establishment of an independent Shura Council, guarantees of human rights, accountability, and the elimination of corruption.[10] MIRA's reformist platform was also obvious in its third communiqué to the Saudi people, dated December 7, 1996, which called on the government to "allow for political participation, listen to the advice of the representative of the people, and to learn that the language of political dialogue [with the opposition] is the only language that will be effective for everyone." Thus, instead of confronting the regime, MIRA and the CDLR have chosen to present the regime's Western patrons with what they regard as detailed and reformist demands consistent with the metropolitan global agenda.

Although text-based messages via the Internet and faxes have proven effective in the "media war" between the opposition and the government abroad, cassette tapes remain the most effective tools inside due to a tradition of oral culture in Saudi Arabia and the limited literacy of the Saudi public. The tape's regional dominance as an alternative medium forces both the Saudi government and its opposition to engage the various discourses of the Islam of other movements and governments. Salman al-'Auda, for example, responded to the writings of the late Sheikh Muhammad al-Ghazali of Egypt and his interpretation of the Islamic tradition. Cassette tapes are a well-integrated phenomenon throughout the region and are a significant means of communication because they are accessible to both the elite and the disadvantaged.[11] The poor, who may or may not be literate, have access to radical ideas via tape-recorded messages. On the other hand, the economically disadvantaged are also disadvantaged in their access to higher forms of media, such as satellite dishes and the Internet. The elite has full access to new global media and to the global space. The poor are more likely to be limited to local radical impulses and to fail to partake in the globalization of concepts and systems of beliefs except those mentioned in the cassettes.

Although the globalizing communication structures and means enhance the opposition's cause by multiplying its access, voices, and channels, it would be a mistake to assume that the new spaces, especially cyberspace, are exclusively oppositionist. In fact, the global space is still dominated by states, albeit with limited sovereignty and limited control over what their citizens are exposed to. In the Saudi case, the global space also complicates the task of opposition. In macropolitical terms, the Saudi state can cast itself as in opposition to the "Western cultural imperialism" that threatens Islam and Muslims. In this sense the state can hijack the rejectionist mood and easily portray other opposition groups as agents of the West. Information sent over the Internet reaches those who are computer literate and English speaking, since English is the Internet's lingua franca. In short, it reaches the technologically adept segments of Saudi society, a group unlikely to rebel openly because of its relatively privileged position. Moreover, this segment of Saudi society has never been deprived of information, since its members could previously listen to the radio broadcasts of the BBC and Voice of America while at home and read English-language newspapers when outside the kingdom. Now, with the introduction of the satellite dish, the English-speaking segment of Saudi society can get news from BBC and CNN television as well as from other sources on the World Wide Web, instead of just the CDLR's or MIRA's newsletter or home page.

The Saudi case reveals problems with the conventional understanding of resistance. It is not enough to explore hidden transcripts to "grasp potential acts,"[12] one has to surf the Internet and home pages of opposition groups.

The Saudi case also reveals that those who are enamored with the totalizing and homogenizing effects of modernity and globalization should take into account the local impulses that replace the grand narrative with multiple and local narratives as a way of resisting a metropolitan globalization. Nor is this the whole story, for domination and resistance in non-Western social formations seen in Saudi Arabia show that even local society engages different trends of the global modes; some forms are part of the Internet and globalization, others are part of the world of cassette tapes and faxes. While the local impulse resists the global narrative, it simultaneously addresses the global arena by adapting the language and narrative of dominant global trends. Thus the discourses of opposition and government interact concomitantly between the phenomenally global and the local. Here it becomes obvious that as the world "opens up," the struggle between governments and opposition is no longer merely local, and that even the local is tremendously mediated.[13] The struggle for hegemony is exported to other venues beyond the boundaries of the nation-state.

In the same way that the dialectic of the global and the local problematizes the category of resistance, it is bound to have implications for other social science concepts, such as political culture and civil society. Traditional political culture studies have to justify where the cut-off point is between the local and the global and between what is "a sign for the real" and what is real. Civil society studies also will have to distinguish between local and global civil societies. Concepts such as the specific territory of the state will have to be reconsidered. In an era in which the discourse of the "sovereign" is simply one among many discourses, and in which these conversations transcend traditional notions of geographic boundary and the physical contours of the nation-state, political scientists will have to reconsider their fixed understanding of the sovereign state. While the local population of Saudi Arabia can vehemently oppose the physical presence of foreign troops on Saudi soil, they cannot prevent the cyberspace presence of foreign, global ideas and trends. Even those opposition leaders who decry Western influences are themselves influenced by global discourses and technologies. Geographic boundaries and notions of state sovereignty, traditionally definers of individual states, seem to dissolve into the cyberspace of an overriding globalization of local concepts and localization of global concepts.

"Islam" as a concept is also a part of the globalizing process, accepting new ideas and attitudes from other cultures and diffusing its own ideas within other societies. Islam as a social and political text is different from the fixed, reified "Islam" that most analysts of Islamic movements discuss. Muslims and Islamists constantly interpret and reinterpret the Islamic message in response to specific political and social conditions and to how other actors in these globalized spaces also shape Islamic discourse. Furthermore, Islam in social science analysis should be written as "islam," and when discussed in multiple contexts we should be discussing islams in the plural. This practice should not have any bearing on the content of Islam as religious belief; it merely addresses the many islams of Muslims. Only then we can produce a meaningful analysis of the social phenomenon where all these islams can be seen as embedded in various cultural and structural relations. Essentialist analysis that views political culture in an Arab/islamic context as static or even views these political cultures as closed systems that only Arabs and Muslims shape does not allow us to understand the process of change on the levels of discourse, culture, and politics. Hence, it is important to analyze Islamist discourse in its proper context and take into account exogenous variables that shape it. It is particularly important to realize that new meanings attributed to the texts and tradition are a response to new political conditions and the new scattered hegemonies.[14]

Although Islamic discourse represents a counterhegemony on a local level, it exists among competing hegemonies locally, regionally, and globally. All of these authoritative discourses interact with one another in a dialectical process and thus influence one another. Islamic discourse shapes Western discourse if only at the level of its view of Islam, and Western discourse shapes Islamic discourse by forcing it to deal with questions of liberalization and democratization.

Saudi Opposition and the Stability of the Political Order

In considering the opposition's ability to undermine the Saudi state, we must look at the cracks or lack thereof in the hegemony of the political order, the power base of the opposition, and how this power base compares with the constituency of the royal family. To begin with, the use of religion in this interchange between the local and the global works to the advantage of the state more than to the advantage of the opposition. This might not be true of other states and other virtual oppositions, but it is certainly a major factor in the Saudi case. The opposition uses Islam as the basis for its dissent even though the royal family has stronger religious credentials than do the opposition leaders. Islam is the only ground on which the opposition can attack the regime and have any significant following within the country, and yet it is a contest that the opposition cannot win. The opposition cannot be more religious than the 'ulama any more than they can be more Saudi than the Sauds. Thus the opposition's use of religion is still part of a dominant and closed discourse that ultimately increases the legitimacy of the 'ulama and by extension enhances the dominance of the royal family.

Just as U.S. militia movements unsuccessfully present themselves as being more patriotic than the U.S. government, the Saudi religious opposition

attempts, and fails, to be more religious than the Saud family. As oppositions, both have the power to harass the state and even commit random acts
of sabotage and terrorism, but neither has the support of the general public
and neither represents a serious threat to the state. The secular opposition in
Saudi Arabia is in much the same position as leftist opposition in the United
States. Just as American leftists are open to the charge of being unpatriotic
and anti-American, the secular opposition in Saudi Arabia is vulnerable to
the charge of being anti-Islamic. Nonreligious dissent is thus even easier for
the Saud family to discredit than legitimate political criticism. The case of
the female drivers who were accused of atheism and immorality is but one
example of how the state can neutralize even the mildest secular dissent.

However, maintaining the public perception that the royal family has
some religious values also imposes limits on the royal family's power. For instance, after the execution of Abdullah al-Hudaif, a young Islamist activist
from Qaseem, the king had a stroke. According to popular rumor, the king's
son went to the family of the executed man and asked them to "yohilo al-
maik" (set the king free from his illness). The action was based on the belief
that God would immediately answer the prayer of persons who had been
punished unjustly and that unless the injured family would forgive the king,
the king would not be cured. Whether this is true or not is less important
than the fact that some people believe it is true. Moreover, it seems that the
royal family is aware of its limitations even when it is under extreme pressure. After the Riyadh and Khobar bombings, for instance, there were no
mass arrests or executions of Islamists, as might be the case in Iraq, or the
demolition of whole villages, as happened to the Syrian town of Hama. The
Saudis executed one person and arrested a dozen or so. Had there been an
Iraqi- or a Syrian-style punishment, the royal family would have lost its constituency. It is that awareness of limitations that allows the family to survive.

Another important element that helps the royal family to survive is the
absence of an alternative in terms of organization. Although it is difficult to
get reliable figures regarding the numbers of followers of each dissident
group, probably none has as many committed followers as the extended
royal family with its thousands of in-laws, clients, and protégés. Even the
wealthiest of the dissidents, Usama bin Laden, lacks the financial resources
of the royal family. And none of the dissidents has penetrated Saudi civil society, as the royal family has done since the founding of the state. The dissidents remain marginal in terms of tribal organization and financial basis.
Moreover, many Saudis, "secular" and religious, seem convinced that the absence of the royal family would mean the total disintegration of Saudi Arabia, since no other family would be able to play the role of arbiter or to
transcend regional or tribal loyalties. As one Hijazi intellectual merchant
puts it, "The absence of Al Saud means la-watan (no country), or the end of

Saudi Arabia as we know it."[15] This threat of disintegration is disturbing for any Saudi to contemplate. In fact, many Saudis argue that the secret of the Saud family's continued dominance is that they made themselves indispensable to the survival of the political order; Saudi Arabia has become, literally and figuratively, synonymous with its royal family.

Thus, despite the presence of vigorous and sometimes violent dissent, the country itself is stable. Since the oil boom, Saudi Arabia has been going through tremendous changes. It has experienced population growth, urbanization, increases in education, and, later, unemployment and economic decline. In 1990 Saudi Arabia was confronted with its greatest crisis, the Gulf War. If as a result of all these changes during the past 25 years and the outcome of the Gulf War there is no more dissent than the current opposition, then the system is likely to survive for quite some time. The Gulf War and its shock, economic decline, and the other factors just mentioned are not likely to repeat themselves again very soon. If the kingdom comes out of the 1990s with only few compromises, then the system is resilient, flexible, and likely to continue.

Moreover, the succession crisis and the coming of Abdullah to the throne is more likely to rejuvenate the regime than destabilize it. Abdullah has the support of both tribal leaders and Islamists. If the Islamists are currently a source of tension, their threat is likely to diminish when he becomes king. As we have seen, none of the opposition leaders has said anything against Abdullah.

As detailed in chapter 1, the creation of the Shura Council and the distribution of the 90 members in terms of regions and tribes has rejuvenated and cemented anew the alliances between the royal family and the tribes and further enhanced the status of the Sauds as the only transregional family. This becomes clearer when one knows that ministers and Shura members are part of the circle of regional princes and governors. Thus each Shura member is a representative of his region and his tribe rather than a national figure who could threaten the Sauds.

Moreover, the Shura system reinforces the loyalty of all government members, making it difficult to oppose the government from within. Each prince nominates some of his people; some receive government appointments and some do not. The same goes for the selection of the ministers. Of course, in addition to nominations based on loyalty to a powerful prince, the appointees are also approved by the mukhabrat, the Saudi intelligence agency. All of this creates a system that is very difficult for a person opposed the royal family to penetrate. If the system is to suffer from any fissures, it would be from within, not without, the royal family. Thus, because the royal family has penetrated all levels of Saudi society, the legitimizing power of religion, the wealth at their disposal, and the familialist ethic that the royal family shares with its citizens, the Saudi monarchy does not face the same "modernization dilemma" that has confronted other Third World countries.

In addition to the strengths of the regime that hinder the opposition's effectiveness, there are also weaknesses within the opposition itself. For instance, these groups' organizational and mobilization skills are far weaker than those of either the Ikhwan of 1929 or of Juhaiman al-'Utabibi of 1979, both of whom the Sauds easily defeated. The lack of any coordination between opposition groups makes them all vulnerable to the regime's strategies of segmentation and fragmentation. And virtually all of the groups have fragmented, as exemplified in the case of the Shi'a movement, where there was a split between the Reform Movement and Hizbullah al-Hijaz. Differences among these groups are greater than what brings them together—nationalism and anti-Western feelings. These differences were the main reason behind the split in the CDLR. The Sunni movement failed to overcome geographical and ideological fragmentation. Moreover, the government has succeeded in co-opting prominent Islamists, such as Ahmed al-Tuwaijri, into the Shura Council. While the groups and their leaders share certain objectives and position themselves in opposition to the regime, their differences stand in the way of unification and hinder efforts to mount an effective political challenge.

As Mas'ari, al-Faqih, and bin Laden seek to overcome these weaknesses and establish their credentials as legitimate reform leaders and defenders of the faith, they actively engage in the politics of personal and collective identity construction. On a personal level, each highlights certain aspects of his identity while downplaying others; and on a collective level, they seek to define their groups' positions vis-à-vis the regime, Islam, and the West. While these efforts at identity construction have shaped the opposition's narrative, the connection to the local context has been weakened in the process. As groups seek to respond to multiple audiences, they become absorbed in overlapping realms of competing hegemonies. On the national level, they must counter the state's hegemonic hold over religious discourse. On the global level, both the Saudi state and opposition groups position themselves in opposition to Western cultural dominance and compete for the forefront role in challenging Western hegemony. Because both the opposition and the state are part of a peripheral counterhegemony to the Western monopoly-liberal hegemony[16] on a global scale, the differences between opposition and the state become very narrow in the eyes of the local constituency. Thus, for the Saudis, it is more of a priority to confront the Western cultural onslaught and monopoly-liberal hegemony than to squabble over narrow differences between a state and an opposition interpretation of Islam.

If these then are the conclusions from studying these various groups, how do we account for the numerous assessments that predict the collapse of the political order? One explanation lies in differentiating between the stability of the order of signs in the culture where the analysis is taking place and the political events taking place in Saudi Arabia or even outside it. As pointed out in the introduction, although Saudi society has indeed changed, so has the sign system within the United States. Saudis appeared different during the Gulf War and afterward. The Arab people as a whole were stereotyped as terrorists in the U.S. media, this discourse was modified somewhat during the Gulf War. U.S. Middle East "experts" explained on television and radio that Egyptians, for instance, were not like Iraqis. American newspapers printed op-eds and editorials distinguishing between Arab allies and Arab enemies. Some Arab and Arab American professors and journalists were even briefly permitted to contribute to the debate through interviews on U.S. television. Later on, as the war ended and new issues emerged, the various discursive communities returned to their previous positions and the Arab and Arab American voices again disappeared from public dialogue. Scholarship and publishing are also affected by changes in the political climate. Thus, when Saudi Arabia was prominent in the news, writers who wanted to pressure the Saudi state for various purposes talked about the eminent collapse of the system. These pendulum swings in the sign system of scholarship and journalistic writing is what have been unstable. To confuse the tremors in the sign system where the analysis is taking place with the stability of the political order is to implode reality into hyperreality, the TV Arab with the Arab, and the stereotype with the real. In the introduction I discussed the numerous problems in the scholarship on Saudi Arabia, Islam, and the Arab world. Unless we let go of stereotypical views and avoid embracing either the system or its opponents in favor of sound analyses, we will always have highly politicized data, analysis, and scholarship. The Saudi case is interesting in terms of state formation outside the colonial experience, the Islamic nature of the state, its diverse regional components, and its position in the world. All these questions require movement away from stereotypes to more serious data gathering, accumulation of knowledge, and sound analysis and method.

The Saudi Political Economy of Signs and Dissent

Another reason that the Saudi opposition finds it difficult to gain mass support is that Saudi Arabia is held together by a network of tribal relations and the ethic of Islamic familialism. This political economy of signs transcends the oil-centered discourse. Saudi Arabia is an oil state and a rentier state, but even more important, it is the result of an indigenous process of state building that produced a sign value different from those produced in the rest of the postcolonial Arab states. It was a familial/tribal/qaraba state before the discovery of oil and probably will remain so after the oil wealth fades. This can be a difficult concept for Westerners to understand, especially since the term "tribe" in English suggests "primitive" people, or at least pre-modern ones. The Arabic terms "'ai'la" (tentatively translates as family and household) and "qaraba" (relations) connote interdependence, accountability, reliability, and continuity—both a sense of purpose and an identity. The reputation of the tribe and the family is something beyond monetary value: The family cannot be lost without losing oneself. It can be understood only within its own specific and historical evolution of a specific political economy of signs.

It is also important to remember that the tribal system of Saudi Arabia is highly functional. First—and especially with the new Majlis al-Shura—all tribal Saudis participate to some extent in their government. However, even before the establishment of the Shura, a tribal Saudi who had a problem with the government could probably persuade a tribal leader to bring up the matter with some member of the royal family. This is certainly not Western-style democracy, but it is not Western-style authoritarianism either. As Diane Singerman has shown in the case of Egypt, there are numerous forms of political participation.[17] The Saudi system does not lack political communication; in fact, it is a society characterized by an obsession with political communication, as we have seen in the efforts of the government and opposition groups to use various technological media to reach multiple audiences. The fact that many of these channels are not easily identifiable to a Western eye does not mean they do not exist.

Second, the whole system is characterized by various forms of 'ai'liya (in the sense of accountability and sponsorship). Someone is always accountable for someone else's behavior. For example, the father is accountable for the behavior of his sons and daughters and they, in turn, are obliged to their parents and accountable to them. The same goes for a tribal leader and his tribe, and the foreign worker and his kafil (sponsor), and a businessman and his prince kafil. It is this kafil system and tribal accountability that puts some limits on the power of the Saud family. The Sauds are, after all, just another tribal family, even if a very prominent and reputable one. Should their behavior become excessively violent or otherwise un-Islamic, the Sauds would lose the reputation that allows them to rule. This is why one does not see the grand-scale human rights violations—at least against Saudi citizens—that are common in postcolonial Arab states. These signs may not make sense in a different context, but much of the content of Saudi politics works in accordance with this political economy of signs.

Finally, the Sauds have used the oil money to reinforce the 'ai'liya/kafil/tribal system of signs, distributing their largesse to those who were already prominent before the oil boom. The newly rich families are thus not exactly "nouveau riche," the money has gone to the oldest and most reputable families and tribes. Thus the "modernizing"—that is, "Westernizing"—wealth, has not led to the Westernization of social structures and values. Saudis have acquired modern technologies without dramatically altering the patterns of their society. In fact, in some cases modern technologies, such as closed circuit TVs, computer technologies, and telephones, enforce an already predominately gender-segregated society, where men can communicate via various channels without actual human contact.

The global revolution in transportation and oil wealth accrued by Saudi elites likewise provides additional safety valves for the political system. The Saudis elite exist both inside and outside the Saudi system or in a middle position between the international economic[18] and communication systems and the local settings. The fact that they invest abroad and acquire labor from other countries makes them function as part of both the international economic political order and the local one. This middle position gives the illusion of participating in both systems simultaneously. Moreover, as elites travel to Western and Arab capitals and spend several months of the year abroad, they are free to engage in unrestrained discourse and behaviors, political participation in the form of a vacation has become part of the Saudi political landscape. After their stays abroad, they can return to the local setting, leaving their oppositional discourse behind in the same way many Saudi men leave their Western suits in the closets of their London apartments. Saudi discomfort with Mas'ari and al-Faqih is that their vacation seem to have been prolonged and that in an un-Saudi manner they bring their practices home via fax and Web sites.

Stability

Islamic dissent has become a general characteristic of Arab politics from civil war-wracked Algeria, to violent sectarian conflict in Bahrain, to low intensity conflict in Egypt. In spite of the severity of the civil war in Algeria, the military regime there is still standing. Similarly, the al-Khalifa state in Bahrain is still functioning. In other cases where the state is threatened by both internal and external pressures, such as Iraq and Libya, the governments remain in place. For the last seven years Iraq has been faced with a strong regime of sanctions from outside and strong ethnic opposition by the Kurds in the north and the Shi'a of the south. In spite of this very powerful pressure, Saddam Hussein's regime is showing no signs of collapse. By comparison, the Saudi opposition is limited and the regime suffers no external pressures. In fact, Western governments favor it. If regimes that are faced with stronger opposition and severe international punishments remain in power, it is unlikely that the current opposition would destabilize the Saudi political order. It is obvious that the modern state in the Middle East is re-silient, and Saudi Arabia is no exception.

Additionally, if the Saudi response to the Islamic opposition is compared with the responses of Syria, Iraq, and Bahrain, the Saudis as a family and government seem to know their limits in relation to society. The state could not arrest thousands and keep them in jail and expect to get away with it, nor could it erase villages. The maximum Saudi response is to apply "Islamic justice" based on the consensus of the 'ulama and execute those responsible for specific acts of violence and no one else. If it exceeded this response, the state could find itself confronting the tribes and other social forces, a contest that would make the kingdom look like the neighboring states. The royal family's respect for this threshold of tolerance is central to its survival.

The Saudi royal family is arguably the most stable institution in the re-gion, at least in terms of longevity. Since 1744 there have been only three Saudi states. The first one collapsed after 66 years; the second continued for more than 20 years; and the third has existed since 1902, although formally consolidated in 1932. Thus the Saudis are not immune to collapse. How-ever, the prior collapses were the result of an external invasion, such as that of the sons of Muhammed Ali that ended the first Saudi state in 1811, or from a division within the royal family. There is no evidence that other forces have changed the order of things in a significant way. Every time a Saudi state has collapsed, a new one has emerged. The hegemony of the Sauds is based on a system that privileges closeness (qaraba) and the ethos of "Islamic familialism," an indigenous world outlook that few Saudi deviate from. Opposition in these new spaces may alter the language of Saudi poli-tics, it may lead to further reforms, but it is not likely to lead to collapse of the state. As the global trends intensify, the language of both opposition and government in Saudi Arabia is likely to come closer rather than becoming farther apart. The language of defending the faith against Western cultural and material domination is likely to capture the imagination of Saudis, op-position and government alike, and thus minimize their local differences. Globalization, "virtual colonialism," and the resulting general confusion about the means of dealing with these new challenges threaten the Saudi po-litical order more than the opposition does. This may be also true for the rest of the Arab world.

Notes

Introduction

1. All the references to the text of these confessions are based on the report of a Saudi daily, *Asharq al-Awsat,* no. 6395, June 1, 1996. p. 14.
2. This military unit was one of many under the leadership of Usama bin Laden.
3. For a critical review of this literature, see Ash Amin, "Placing Globalization," *Theory, Culture & Society: Exploration in Critical Social Science,* vol. 14, no. 2 (May 1997).
4. The idea of a globalized Ibn Khaldun, though not stated in this manner, represents the core argument in Bruce Lawrence's *Ibn Khaldun and Islamic Ideology* (Leiden: E.J Brill, 1984). In this global setting Ibn Khaldun has been used, abused, and contested at the faultiness of theorizing. Ernest Gellner uses Ibn Khaldun to essentialize him and Muslim societies; see Ernest Gellner, *Muslim Society* (Cambridge: Cambridge University Press, 1981). Aziz al-Azmah takes issues with the way Ibn Khaldun was perceived and the problems of Kitab al-'Ibar in *Ibn Khaldun: An Essay in Reinterpretation* (London: Frank Cass, 1982). Ibn Khaldun emerges also as an important source in the work of the Moroccan philosopher Muhammad 'Abed al-Jabri, an intellectual who dominated the Arab scene in the 1980s.
5. Bruce Lawrence, *Ibn Khaldun and Islamic Ideology,* p. 12, footnote 8.
6. David Harvey, *The Condition of Postmodernity* (Cambridge, MA: Blackwell, 1989).
7. Anthony Giddens, *The Consequences of Modernity* (Stanford, CA: Stanford University Press, 1990), p. 21.
8. The globalized world and modernity and their impact on our understanding of social phenomenon are not tied to the works of Harvey and Giddens alone. Other theorists such as Roland Peterson, Ulrich Beck, and Scott Lash

are central to the globalization debate. For a good summary of this debate, see Malcolm Walters, *Globalization* (New York: Routledge, 1995).

9. For a debate on the media, information society, and globalization, see Karamjit S. Gill (ed.), *Information Society: New Media, Ethics and Postmodernism* (London: Springer-Verlag London Limited, 1996); Lance Starte, Ronald Jacobson, and Stephanie B. Gibson, *Communication and Cyberspace* (Cresskill, NJ: Hampton Press, 1996); Sandra Braman and Annabelle Mohammadi, *Globalization, Communication, and Transnational Civil Society* (Cresskill, NJ: Hampton Press, 1996); and Andrew King (ed.), *Postmodern Political Communication: The Fringe Challenges the Center* (Westport, CT: Braeger, 1992).

10. This is Baudrillard's argument. For more, see Jean Baudrillard, "Simulacra and Simulations," in Mark Poster (ed.), *Jean Baudrillard: Selected Writing* (Stanford, CA: Stanford University Press, 1988), pp. 166–184.

11. Arjun Appadurai uses this formulation of a world dominated by five distinct scapes al a landscape: the ethnoscape of global migration; the technoscape of information and technology; the financescape of global capital; the mediascape, and finally the ideaoscape of political discourses. For more, see Arjun Appadurai, *Modernity at Large: Cultural Dimensions of Globalization* (Minneapolis, MN: University of Minnesota Press, 1997).

12. Baudrillard, "Simulacra and Simulations." For more, see Timothy W. Luke, "The Discipline of Security Studies and the Codes of Containment: Learning from Kuwait," *Alternatives,* vol. 16, no. 3 (1991): 315–344. Timothy W. Luke "Security, Sovereignty, and Strategy: Reinterpreting Desert Storm," *Crossroads,* no. 33 (1991): 1–14. Luke also published an important work on resistance in the information age, although it focuses on television in the Western experience. Timothy W. Luke, *Screens of Power: Ideology, Domination, and Resistance in Informational Society* (Urbana, IL: University of Illinois Press, 1989).

13. For more, see Arjun Appadurai, ibid.

14. Aziz al-Azmeh makes a good case not only for the varieties of modernities but also for the variety of Islams. For more, see Aziz Al-Azmeh, *Islams and Modernities* (London: Verso, 1993).

15. For more on the debate of the coexistence of the "modern" in the "traditional" and the traditional in the modern and even the postmodern, see Timothy Luke, "Identity, Meaning, and Globalization: Detraditionalization in Postmodern Space Time Compression," in Paul Heelas, Scott Lash, and Paul Morris (eds.), *Detraditionalization* (Cambridge, MA: Blackwell Publishers, 1996), pp. 109–133.

16. For more on the Saudi role to capture a greater share of the global media market, see Stephen Franklin, "The Kingdom and the Power," *Columbia Journalism Review* (November/December 1996): 49–51.

17. For a discussion of the concept, see Giddens, *Consequences of Modernity,* pp. 21–29.

18. James C. Scott, *Domination and the Arts of Resistance* (New Haven, CT: Yale University Press, 1990).

19. Most Web sites are currently written as English text. Arabic texts are scanned as images.

20. These concepts form the cornerstone of Scott's formulation to understanding resistance. For more, see Scott, *Domination and the Arts of Resistance*.

21. These studies include R. L. Tokes (ed.), *Opposition in Eastern Europe* (Oxford: Oxford University Press, 1979), E. Kolinksy (ed.), *Opposition in Western Europe* (London: Croom Helm, 1988); and G. Rodan (ed.), *Political Opposition in Industrializing Asia* (Sydney: Routledge, 1996).

22. See Lisa Anderson, "Lawless Government and Illegal Opposition: Reflections on the Middle East, *Journal of International Affairs*, vol. 40, no. 2 (Spring 1987): 219–232. Also see Jean Leca, "Opposition in the Middle East and North Africa," *Government and Opposition*, vol. 32, no. 4 (1997): 557–577.

23. This was obvious in Anderson's latest contribution "Democracy in the Arab World: A Critique of the Political Culture Approach," in Rex Brynen, Bahgat Korany, and Paul Noble (eds.), *Political Liberalization & Democratization in the Arab World: Theoretical Perspectives* (Boulder, CO: Lynne Rienner, 1995). The debate on culture in this volume was between Michael Hudson, who argues for "bring [political culture] back in carefully," as he puts it, and the dismissive position of Lisa Anderson. I think there is still more room even beyond Hudson's position to argue for a sophisticated and interdisciplinary approach to political culture. In fact, culture is at the heart of Arab politics. Not wanting to bother with it is not the equivalent of dismissing it altogether as an analytically useful concept.

24. Leca, "Opposition," pp. 557–558.

25. This trend has dominated the study of the Arab world during the 1970s, 1980s, and some of it continues until the present. Native scholars and Western authors alike have embraced the universal assumptions of this school. Examples of the natives scholars include Ahmed Dahlan *Politics, Administration, and Development in Saudi Arabia* (Jeddah: Dar al-Shrouq, 1990); Faud al-Farsy, *Saudi Arabia: A Case Study in Development* (London: Stacey International, 1980); Matrouk al-Faleh, *The Impact of the Processes of Modernization and Social Mobilization on the Social and Political Structures of the Arab Countries with Special Emphasis on Saudi Arabia*, Ph.D. Dissertation, University of Kansas, 1987; and Othman al-Rawaf, *The Concept of the Five Crises in Political Development, Relevance to the Kingdom of Saudi Arabia*, Ph.D. Dissertation, Duke University, 1980. Examples of Western scholars who have used this approach are numerous. The point is that modernization as a hegemonic discourse has influenced not only the orientalist of the Metropolitan West but also the local elite in the way they see their own societies. The interplay between the global-local in this context is also intense and requires further study.

26. Peter Garn, "Political Economy as a Paradigm for the Study of Middle East History," *International Journal of Middle East Studies*, 11 (1980): 511–526.

27. For an excellent overview of these schools and their limitations, see Robert Wuthnow, "Understanding Religion and Politics," *Daedalus* (Summer 1991).

28. One study that used interpretive theory to interpret Saudi politics is Wad-dah Shararh's *al-Ahl wal Ghanima* (Beirut: Dar al-Tali'a, 1981). Another book using interpretive theory mixed with group approach is Raymond William Baker's *Sadat and After* (Cambridge, MA: Harvard University Press, 1990).

29. James A. Bill, "The Study of Middle East Politics, 1946–1996: A Stocktaking," *Middle East Journal,* vol. 50, no. 4 (Autumn 1996).

30. For a similar assessement in the 1980s, see John Waterbury, "Social Science Research and Arab Studies in the Coming Decade," in Hisham Sharabi (ed.), *The Next Arab Decade: Alternative Futures* (Boulder, CO: Westview Press, 1988), pp. 293–302.

31. Some of these exceptions are F. Gregory Gause III, *Oil Monarchies* (New York: Council on Foreign Relations, 1994) and Kiren Aziz Chaudry, *The Price of Wealth* (Ithaca, NY: Cornell University Press, 1997).

32. Two examples of specialists who have never been to Saudi Arabia include Mordechai Abir, *Saudi Arabia: Government, Society and the Gulf Crisis* (New York: Routledge, 1993), and Sarah Yizraeli, *The Remaking of Saudi Arabia* (Tel Aviv: The Moshe Dayan Center of Middle Eastern and African Studies, 1997).

33. For an excellent discussion of the concept of revival, see Eric Davis, "The Concept of Revival and the Study of Islam and Politics," in Barbara Freyer Stowasser (ed.), *The Islamic Impulse* (Washington DC: Center for Contemporary Arab Studies, 1987), pp. 37–58.

34. See Edward Said, *Orientalism* (New York: Vintage, 1978) and *Covering Islam* (New York: Pantheon Books, 1981).

35. This political economy of writing as a disciplinary question has been discussed in general terms by Fredrick Gareau, "The Political Economy of Social Science: Where the Trail Leads," *International Journal of Comparative Sociology,* vol. 31, nos. 1–2 (1990): 49–66. In the context of the Middle East, Judith Tucker raises similar issues. For more, see Judith Tucker, "Middle East Studies in the United States: The Coming Decade," in Sharabi (ed.), *The Next Arab Decade,* pp. 312–321.

36. An example of this is Said K. Aburish's *The Rise, Corruption, and the Coming Fall of the House of Saud* (New York: St. Martin's Press, 1995).

Chapter 1

1. Ibn Manzur, *Lisan al-Arab,* vol. 9 (Beyrouth: 1956), pp. 481–490.

2. See Nazih Ayubi, *Political Islam: Religion and Politics in the Arab World* (New York: Routledge, 1991), especially the chapter entitled "The Politics of Sex and the Family," pp. 35–47.

3. *Al Riyadh,* August 7, 1995, p. 1.

4. Rentier analysis dominates Gulf studies. Some examples of these studies include the work of Giacomo Luciani (ed.), *The Rentier State* (London: Croom Helm, 1987); Hazem Beblawi's "The Rentier State in the Arab

World," in Giacomo Luciani (ed.), *The Arab State* (Berkeley: University of California Press, 1990); Jill Crystal, *Oil and Politics in the Gulf* (New York: Cambridge University Press, 1990); F. George Gause, *Oil Monarchies* (New York: Council on Foreign Relations, 1994); Kiren Aziz Chaudhry, *The Price of Wealth* (Ithaca, NY: Cornell University Press, 1997); and many more. The point is that this discourse has now become a hegemonic discourse that is no longer deterred by alternative hypotheses or alternative data; it is a self-contained discourse that reaffirms its validity and reliability via a detour of narrative.

5. Rayed Kirmly, *The Political Economy of Rentier States: A Case Study of Saudi Arabia,* Ph.D. Dissertation, George Washington University, 1993.

6. Rex Brynen, Bahgat Korany, and Paul Noble (eds.), *Political Liberalization & Democratization in the Arab World* (Boulder, CO: Lynne Rienner, 1995), vol. 1, p. 15.

7. Rayed Krimly, *The Political Economy of Rentier States,* pp. 194–195. My argument runs counter to Krimly's. The main problem with Krimly's dissertation is that, in the first part, he depends very heavily on the work of Mishary al-Nuaim on the pre-oil state without critically interrogating his premises, assumption, or findings. For comparison, see Mishary al-Nuaim, *State Building in a Non-Capitalis Social Formation: The Dialectics of Two Modes of Production and the Role of the Merchant Class, Saudi Arabia, 1902–1932,* Ph.D. Dissertation, University of California, Los Angeles, 1986. In spite of this conflation, the two dissertations are well researched and thought provoking and probably represent the best work on Saudi politics.

8. See Douglas A. Yates, *The Rentier State in Africa: Oil Rent Dependency & Neocolonialism in the Republic of Gabon* (Trenton, NJ: Africa World Press, 1996). Those interested in a brief summary of the rentier state literature should read his first chapter.

9. On the resignation of the government as a result of pressure from the parliament, see *Al-Mujtama'a,* a Kuwaiti weekly, April 2, 1998, p. 10. The Islamist also have been challenging the government since 1986 on social issues, namely the coeducational character of Kuwait University. *Al-Mujtama'a,* July 8, 1996.

10. This discussion is informed by Jean Baudrillard's *The Mirror of Production* (St. Louis: Telos Press, 1975).

11. This discussion has been enriched by the argument presented by Wadhah Sharara's provocative book *Al-Ahl wal Ghanima* (Beirut: Dar al-Tali'a, 1981).

12. Author Interview, Jeddah, July 15, 1997.

13. The Statute of the Provinces, article 4.

14. Ibid., article 16.

15. For a good descriptive information about Saudi Arabia and its people, see Helen Chapin Metz (ed.), *Saudi Arabia: A Country Study* (Washington, DC: US Government Printing Office, 1993).

16. See the Basic Statute of Governance, chapter 2.

17. For more, see interview with Prince Talal bin Abdul Aziz, *al-Quds al-Arabi,* April 17, 1998.

18. Author Interview, Riyadh, July 17, 1997.

19. For the full text of the 'ulama's statement, see *Saudi Arabia* (Washington, DC: Official Publication of the Royal Embassy of Saudi Arabia, Fall, 1990), p. 3.

20. See *Alyamamah,* no. 1181, November 20, 1991, pp. 42–45.

21. For a formal discussion of the Council of Ministers from a modernization and political adaptation perspective, see Summer Scott Huyette, *Political Adaptation in Saudi Arabia: A Study of the Council of Misters* (Boulder, CO: Westview Press, 1985).

22. The fact that members of Al Sheikh family hold various ministries, including the Ministry of Rural Affairs, suggests that this family is not merely involved with religion, as many portray them. In fact, during my stay in Saudi Arabia, I met some members of Al Sheikh family. One works for a major Saudi bank.

23. These data are based on reports in the Saudi newspapers *Al Riyadh,* August 6–8, 1995; information about the most recent council members published by the embassy of Saudi Arabia *http://www.Saudi.net./gov;* and the data collected by Krimly, The Political Economy of Rentier States, pp. 246–251.

24. Author Interview, Riyadh, July 26, 1997.

25. For the names of the members of the council and their personal profiles, see *Al-Jazeera,* July 7, 1997, pp. 8–9.

26. Author Interview with Abdul Mohsan al-'Akas, Khobar, Saudi Arabia, June 20, 1997.

27. This is based on my interviews with eight members of the Shura Council and many interviews with ordinary Saudis.

28. For example, King Fahd inaugurated the second term of the Shura Council. His speech was a list of government achievements. See the text of the speech in *Alyamamah,* July 4, 1998, pp. 7–11.

29. For an excellent study of the first Saudi state, see Abdul Raheem A. Abdul Raheem, *Al-Dawla al-Sa'udiyya al-'Ula 1745–1818* (Cairo: Ma'had al-Bohouth wal Dirasat al-'Arabiya, 1969).

30. The best accounts on Qaseem as problem for the Saudis in the past are those of Sheikh Othman bin Abduallah ibn Bisher, *'Inwan al-Majd fi Tarikh Najd* (The history of Najd) (Saudi Arabia: Matbo'at Darat al-Malik Abdul Aziz, 1983), vol. 2, pp. 250–280. For an excellent modern-day anthropological account of a Qaseemi town, see Soraya Al Torki and Donald Cole, *Arabian Oasis City: The Transformation of 'Unayah* (Austin: University of Texas Press, 1989).

31. For an excellent historical summary of this era, see Alexie Vaseliev, *Fosoul min Tarikh al-Arabiyya al-saudiyya* (Chapters from the history of Saudi Arabia) ([n.p]: Dar al-Fada', 1988). When I met Alexie, he referred to this Arabic book as "al-tab'a al-Muqarsana" (the pirated edition).

32. For an excellent presentation on the Rashidis of Hail from an anthropological perspective, see Madawi al-Rasheed, *Politics in an Arabian Oasis: The Rashidis of Saudi Arabia* (London: I.B. Tauris Publishers, 1991).

33. For a discussion of this period in Saudi history, see Sarah Yizraeli's *The Remaking of Saudi Arabia* (Tel Aviv: The Moshe Dayan Center of Middle Eastern and African Studies, 1997).

34. For an excellent account on the Ikhwan movement, see Muhammed Jalal Kishk, *Al-Sa'udiyoon wal Hall al-Islami* (The Saudis and the Islamic solution) (Cairo: Al-Matba'ah al-Faniyyah, 1981), especially part 6, pp. 549–707.

35. John S. Habib, *Ibn Sau'd's Warriors of Islam* (Leiden: E. J. Brill, 1978), p. 62.

36. For more on the Ikhwan, see Christine Moss Helms, *The Cohesion of Saudi Arabia* (Baltimore: Johns Hopkins University Press, 1981), especially chapter 8, pp. 250–272.

37. Joseph A. Kechichian, "The Role of the Ulama in the Politics of an Islamic State: The Case of Saudi Arabia," *International Journal of Middle East Studies,* vol. 18 (1986): 60.

38. *Muthakerat al-Nasihah* (The memorandum of advice), p. 2. It is worth noting that whenever I talked to Mas'ari, al-Faqih, or bin Laden's representatives, they referred me to the Memorandum of Advice as the frame of reference. In fact, I received three copies of the memorandum from the three of them as part of their packages to introduce me to their organizations. Unless otherwise stated, the following information and quotations are from the memorandum.

39. From the letter to Sheikh bin Baz that accompanies the Memorandum of Advice.

40. See Salman al-'Auda's letter of endorsement attached to the Memorandum of Advice.

41. Safar al-Hawali's letter of endorsement to the Memorandum of Advice.

42. As it will become obvious in the chapter discussing the sermons of Sheikh Salman al-'Auda, this criticism of the state information system and the restrictions the state imposes on the 'ulama are central to his message.

43. Other studies, namely that of R. Deckmajian, "Saudi Islamists," *Middle East Journal,* (Fall 1994) state that 107 men signed this document. My count is based on the original memorandum, which shows 108 signatures. Deckmajian also does not indicate the basis on which he broke down the Saudi Islamists in terms of education, region, and so on.

Chapter 2

1. For more on Hawali and his life, see Mamoun Fandy, "Safar Al-Hawali: Saudi Islamist or Saudi Nationalist?" *Journal of Islam and Christian-Muslim Relations,* vol. 9, no. 1 (1998): 5–21.

2. In his discussion of the Christian right in the United States, Hawali depends on Yousef al-Hassan's *Al-Bu'd al-Dini fil Siyasa al-Amrikiyya Tijah al-Sira' al-'Arabi al-Israili* (The religious dimension in American policy toward the Arab-Zionist conflict) (Beirut: Marakaz Dirasat Al-Wihda al-Arabiyya, 1990).

3. Hawali, "Filisteen Bayn al-Wa'ad al-Haq wal Wa'ad al-Muftara (Palestine between the true and false promise)," taped sermon, no. 1. Hereafter cited as "Palestine."

4. Hawali, "Mustaqbal al-'Alam al-Isalmi" (The future of the Islamic world), taped sermon.

5. Hawali, "Of Arab Constitutions," taped sermon, no. 1. This is part of four sermons.

6. "Palestine," taped sermon, no. 2. (Arabic)

7. "Of Arab Constitutions," tape no. 1.

8. "Palestine"

9. Hawali, "Satathkroun ma Aqul Lakum" (You will remember what I say to you), taped sermon, 1991.

10. Ibid.

11. Ibid.

12. Safar Hawali, *Haqa'iq Hawl Azmat al-Khalij* (Realities behind the Gulf crisis) (Cairo, Egypt: Dar Makka al-Mukarama, 1991), 5–6. Page numbers are given in text for further cites to this work.

13. See Hawali's review of Nixon's book in ibid., pp. 26–27.

14. "You Will Remember."

15. Ibid.

16. Ibid.

17. Interview, Kuwait, December 19, 1997.

18. Interview, Qatar, December 16, 1997.

19. "Realities Behind the Gulf Crisis," pp. 128–130.

20. Hawali's understanding of these evangelists comes directly from Grace Halsell's work; thus I will use the original of Halsell instead of retranslating it.

21. See Grace Halsell, *Prophecy and Politics: Militant Evangelists on the Road to Nuclear War* (Westport, CT: Lawrence Hill & Company, 1986), p. 74. For the quote in Arabic, see Hawali, *Filistin Bayn al-Wa'd al-Haq wal Wa'd al-Muftara* (Palestine between the real promise and the false one) (Ann Arbor, MI: Islamic Assembly of North America, 1994), p. 46.

22. Halsell, *Prophecy and Politics,* p. 141; and Hawali, *Palestine,* pp. 46–47.

23. Hawali, *Palestine,* p. 45.

24. Halsell, *Prophecy and Politics,* p. 163.

25. Hawali, *Palestine,* p. 47. All following quotations come from this work, unless otherwise specified. Page numbers are given in text.

26. Paul Findley, *They Dare to Speak Out* (Chicago: Lawrence Hill Books, 1989), p. 246. Also see Hawali, *Palestine,* p. 32.

27. Hawali, "Al-Hukm bi Ghayr ma Anzala Allah (Governance against God's revelations)," taped sermon, 1992.

28. Ibid.

29. This is from a taped interview with Sheikh Hawali, 1992.

30. Hawali, "Governance against God's Revelations."

31. These ideas are also repeated in a series of four taped sermons entitled "Ziyarat wa Ahdath" (Visits and Events), 1990.

32. Hawali, "Governance against God's Revelations."

33. This based on a review of two tapes: "Governance against God's Revelations" and "An Interview with Sheikh al-Hawali."

Chapter 3

1. Salman al-'Auda, "The Islamic Tape: An Assessment" (Arabic), taped sermon, Spring, 1991.
2. For more on the life of Sheikh Salman al-'Auda, see Mahmoud al-Rifaii, *Al-Mashrou' al-Islahi fil Saudia* (The reformist project in Saudi Arabia) (Washington, DC: n.p., 1995), pp. 17–18.
3. Salman al-'Auda and others, "The Sit-in in the Mosque," taped sermon, 1994.
4. Interview with Sa'd al-Faqih, London, June 12, 1997.
5. Interview with Sheikh bin Otheimeen, 'Uniyzah, July 19, 1997.
6. Interview with Sheikh Saleh al-Lihidan, Taif, Saudi Arabia, July 20, 1997.
7. Salman al-'Auda, "We Are Advocates of Peace and Unity," taped sermon.
8. Salman al-'Auda, "Al-Kalima al-Hurrah Dhaman" (Freedom of opinion), taped sermon, (Denver: Dar Mecca, 1994).
9. Salman al-'Auda, "Asbab Soqout al-Dewal" (Why do states disintegrate?), taped sermon, 1991.
10. Interviews, Riyadh, December 8, 1997.
11. The Cairo population conference and the United Nations came under attack in two sermons by al-'Auda: "The Sit-in in the Mosque" and "Islam and Human Rights."
12. This particular sermon has been popularized by MIRA.

Chapter 4

1. Author interview with Sa'd al-Faqih.
2. For more on the first document and reactions to it, see *Al-Jazeera Al-Arabia*, no. 29 (June 1993): 6–28.
3. Author interview with Muhammed al-Mas'ari, London, June 12, 1997.
4. Author interview with Sheikh Abdul Aziz bin Baz, Taif, June 18, 1997.
5. This is based on two interviews I conducted with Sheikh Saleh al-Luhaidan and Sheikh Salih al-Fawazation. Both are members of the Council of Higher 'Ulama.
6. Author interview with Mas'ari.
7. Ibid.
8. "Royal Mess," *The New Yorker,* November 28, 1993, p. 56.
9. For more on Khadiris, see Soraya Altorki and Donald Cole, *Arabian Oasis City* (Austin: University of Texas Press, 1989), p. 250.
10. Author interview with Mas'ari, London, June 13, 1997.
11. Ibid.
12. Ibid.
13. Ibid.
14. On loyal opposition, see William Zartmann, "Opposition as Support of the State," in Giacomo Luciani (ed.), *The Arab State* (Berkeley: University of California Press, 1990), pp. 220–26.

15. Author Interview with Mas'ari, June 13, 1997.

16. A collection of these essays has been published in book form. See Fahmi Howeidy *Al-Islam wal Dimocratiya* (Cairo: al-Ahram, 1995). Many of the ideas in this book informed the sermons and writings of Sheikh Hasan al-Saffar. Al-Saffar also told me that he is influenced by Howeidy. These points will be elaborated further in chapter 7.

17. CDLR, Communiqué no. 3, London, April 20, 1994.

18. This photo in fact inaugurated the group's monthly magazine *Ash-Shar'iyyah*. *Ash-Shar'iyyah,* no. 1, 1995.

19. One member of the royal family was furious over the government's "horrible mishandling of this case." He said they should have left Mas'ari to "fall victim for his own foolishness." Interview, Riyadh, June 26, 1997.

20. *Al-Huquq,* December 2, 1994.

21. These statements are based on my interviews with Sa'd al-Faqih.

22. Ibid.

23. Communiqué no. 2, Riyadh, May 26, 1993.

24. "Infijar Al-Riyadh Dilalatih wa Jizoorih" (The Riyadh explosion: Its implications and roots), *Ash-Shar'iyya,* vol.1, no. 6, (December 1995): pp. 3–6.

25. Muhammed al-Mas'ari, *al-Adellah al-Qat'iyya Ala 'Adam Shar'iyyat al-Dawla al-Sa'udiyya* (Evidence for the un-Islamic nature of the Saudi state) (London: Dar al-Shar'iyya, 1995), p. 233.

26. For the first in this series, see *al-Huquq,* no. 92, March 27, 1996. The last issue of this series of Saudi Arabia and Israel was published on May 29, 1996.

27. For more on this, see *al-Huquq,* no. 102, June 5, 1996, to no. 112, October 9, 1996.

28. For al-Mas'ari's views of the United Nations, see *al-Huquq* from June 5, 1996 to October 9, 1996.

29. For a sample of this series, see *al-Huquq,* nos. 117, 118, and 119 from December 18, 1997 to February 12, 1997.

30. "The Riyadh Explosion"

31. For a sample of this series, see *al-Huquq* nos. 117, 118, and 119 from December 18, 1997 to February 12, 1997.

32. Abdullah al-Hamid, *Huquq al-Insan bayn 'Adl al-Islam wa Jaour al-Hukkam (Human rights between the justice of Islam and the tyranny of the rulers)* (London: The Committee for the Defence of Legitimate Rights, 1995).

33. *Al-Huquq,* no. 90, March 13, 1996, pp. 1–2.

34. Ibid., p.1.

35. For a summary view of Taqi al-Deen al-Nabhani and Hizb al-Tahreer, see Fahmi Jedaane, "Notions of State in Contemporary Arab-Islamic writings," in Giacomo Luciani (ed.), *The Arab State (*Berkeley: University of California Press, 1990), pp. 263–283.

36. *Al-Huquq,* no. 90, March 13, 1996, p. 1.

37. This is part of an e-mail dated July 30, 1997, from CDLR@compuserve.com. The title of the dispatch was "The Oppression of the UN and Other International Organizations."

38. "Royal Mess," p. 72.

Chapter 5

1. Author interview with Sa'd al-Faqih, London, June 11–12, 1997. Unless otherwise indicated, all quotations are taken from this interview.
2. On the evolution of the Saudi political system, see David E. Long, *The Kingdom of Saudi Arabia* (Gainesville: University Press of Florida, 1997), pp. 40–57.
3. *Risalat al-Haraka*, no. 3 (no date given. This Risalat can be found on the movement's web page.)
4. For a theoretical discussion of this attitude toward the father in Arab society, see Hisham Sharabi's *al-Binyah al-Patrakiyyah* (Neopatriarchy) (Beirut: Dar al-Tali'a lil Tiba'at wal Nashr, 1987).
5. He said this in a response to an earlier draft of the chapter that I sent to him to check the accuracy of the quotes.
6. Author interview with al-Faqih, May 20, 1998.
7. Author interview with al-Faqih, January 18, 1998.
8. Al-Faqih told me this when I raised the issue of marginality with him in a telephone interview (May 25, 1998.)
9. Author interviews, Riyadh, December 20, 1997.
10. For more on the Wahhabi settlements and invasions of these areas, see Al-Sheikh Othman ibn Bishr, *'Inwan al-Majd fi Tarikh Najd* (The history of Najd) (Riyadh: Matbu'at Darat al-Malik Abdul Aziz, 1982), vol. 1, pp. 259–301.
11. *Risalat al-Haraka*, no. 2.
12. For more on the story of the Letter of Demands and the Memorandum of Advice and al-Faqih's role in these events, see Sa'd al-Faqih, *Zilzal al-Saud* (The Saudi earthquake) (London: The Islamic Movement for Reform, 1997).
13. Al-Faqih sent me this draft document entitled AMIRA's Political Program and Strategies for Change," on May 25, 1998. Most of the argument that follows is based on my reading of this 46- page document.
14. *Al-Islah*, no. 2, March 25, 1996, p.1.
15. Ibid., p. 1.
16. For more on this tape, see Sa'd al-Faqih, *The Saudi Earthquake*, pp. 77–87.
17. For examples of Western reporting on this tape, see Youssef M. Ibrahim, "Angry Islamist Aim a Taped 'Supergun' at Saudi Leaders," *The New York Times*, March 10, 1992; and Allen Philips, "Saudi Hunt for Secret Critic of the Royals," *The Daily Telegraph*, March 19, 1992.
18. *Al-Islah*, no. 3, April 1, 1996, p.1
19. See *Nashra*, no. 67, July 14, 1997, in *Wathaiq al-Haraka al-Islamiyya lil Islah, Ramadan 1416-Ramadan 1418* (London: The Islamic Movement for Reform in Arabia Publications, 1998), pp. 324–329.
20. Ibid., pp. 306–307.
21. *Risalat al-Haraka*, no. 1.

22. *Risalat al-Haraka,* no. 2.

23. When al-Faqih read a first draft of this chapter to check for the accuracy of quotes, he commented that this particular letter was "issued by al-Harakah al-Islamiyya and was published through us." He did not want to be associated with that letter. Nonetheless, MIRA published it. Thus one cannot dismiss this action as irrelevant despite al-Faqih's assertions.

24. *Al-Islah,* no. 1, April 16, 1996, p. 1

25. Transcripts of weekly broadcast, p. 18. These transcripts were provided to me by al-Faqih himself.

26. See Sa'd al-Faqih, *Kayf Yufakir Al Saud: Dirasah Nafsiyyah* (How do Al Saudi think: A psychological approach) (London: MIRA's publications, 1998). This book summarizes some of al-Faqih's opinions that he put out on the Web page and distributed by fax during the first two years of MIRA's work.

27. Ibid. Al-Faqih also repeated these ideas in my interviews with him. These ideas also dominate his broadcasting on the Internet.

28. For more on this point, see Sa'd al-Faqih, *al-Nizam al-Saudi fi Mizan al-Islam* (The Saudi system according to the Islamic scale) (London: MIRA's Publications, 1998).

29. Ibid., pp. 75–86.

30. Ibid.

31. Ibid.

32. Al-Faqih made this assertion as a response to a first draft of this chapter that I sent to him to check the accuracy of the quotes.

33. In its announcement MIRA makes it clear that the sources of this information is "its sources within the royal court." This particular announcement was made on March 3,1998. It was on the Web page (www.miraserve.com). Al-Faqih also faxed it to me and we talked on the phone about the ramifications of King Fahd's death for Saudi Arabia.

Chapter 6

1.One example of this is bin Laden's "I'lan al-Jihad 'ala al-Amrikiyyin al-Muhtaleen li Bilad al-Haramayn" (Declaration of war against the Americans who occupy the land of the two holy mosques), Afghanistan, August 23, 1996. This 22-page document distributed by the ARC office in London is analyzed below.

2. For more on the Wahhabi movement in India and Afghanistan, see Saiyid Athar Abbas Rizvi, *Shah 'Abd Al-Aziz; Puritanism, Sectarianism, Polemics and Jihad* (Australia: Ma'rifat Publishing House, 1982), especially chapter 7 on Sunni puritanism and jihad, p. 471–541.

3. "Bin Laden Special Report," NBC News, January 16, 1997.

4. Author interview, Riyadh, June 22, 1997.

5. Author interview by telephone with Khaled al-Fawaz, June 6, 1998.

6. Author interview, Riyadh, December 7, 1997.

7. For more, see Communiqué no. 4, "Indihar al-Shiyo'iyah fil Jazira al-Arabia" (The end of communism in the Arabian peninsula), ARC, London, July 11, 1994, pp. 1–2.

8. Communiqué signed by Usama bin Laden and publicized by ARC's London office on July 11, 1994.

9. Ibid.

10. For more, see bin Laden's "I'lan al-Jihad 'ala al-Amrikiyyin al Muhtaloon li Bilad al-Haramayn (Declaration of war against the Americans who occupy the land of the two holy mosques) Afghanistan, August 23, 1996, p. 10.

11. Interview with a Saudi opposition leader who refused to be quoted, May 27, 1998.

12. Interview with Mohammed bin Shaji', the head of the Wa'ila tribe, Al Quds al-Arabi, March 9, 1998.

13. Interview with Abdul Wahhab al-Ansi, Deputy Chairman of the Islah Party, San'a, November 11, 1994.

14. Author interview, Cairo, June 10, 1997.

15. Communiqué no. 17, August 3, 1995.

16. Bin Laden's "I'lan al-Jihad."

17. For more on this, see Communiqué no. 15, "Al-'Ulama' Warathat al-An-biya" (The 'ulama are the inheritors of the prophets), London, May 19, 1995.

18. Communiqué no. 5, "'Ulama' al-Quran fi Muwajahat al-Tughyan" (The Quranic scholars confront the tyranny), London, July 19, 1994.

19. "An Open Letter to Sheikh bin Baz Refuting His Fatwa Concerning the Reconciliation with the Jews," Communiqué no. 11, ARC, December 29, 1994, pp. 1–4.

20. "al-Risal al-Thaniyah to Sheikh Abdul Aziz bin Baz"(the second message to Sheikh Abdul Aziz bin Baz), ARC, January 29, 1995, pp. 1–4.

21. See bin Laden's "I'lan al-Jihad," p. 12.

22. He stated this in numerous interviews including the one he gave to CNN. April 7, 1997. The same theme is echoed in his interview with Al Quds al-Arabi, November 27, 1996.

23. See bin Laden's letter to King Fahd, ARC's Communiqué no.17, p. 4.

24. Bin Laden, "I'lan al-Jihad."

25. Ibid.

26. Al-Huquq, no. 124, May 14, 1997, p. 3.

Chapter 7

1. This assessment is based on my field notes during the summer of 1997.

2. Abdul Rahman al-Sheikh et al, Intifadat al-Mantiqa al-Sharqiya (The uprising in the Eastern Province) (London: Monazamat al-Thawra Al-Islamia, 1981), p. 33.

3. Richard F. Nyrop (ed.), Saudi Arabia: A Country Study (Washington, DC: U.S. Government Printing Office, 1984), p. 52.

4. *Human Rights in the Gulf and Arabian Peninsula,* Annual Report, 1989, pp. 39–50.

5. Interview with Sheikh Abdul Hameed al-Khati, a Shi'a judge, Qateef, July 27, 1997.

6. The Minnesota Lawyers International Human Rights Committee, *Shame in the House of Saud* (Minneapolis, 1992), p. 99.

7. Ibid., p. 102.

8. Ibid., p. 104.

9. Ibid., pp. 40–46.

10. *Al-Thawrah al-Islamiyya* (March 1985): 44.

11. Ibid. p. 47.

12. For more, see Sheikh al-Saffar, "al-Nizam al-Saudi Akthar al-Anzima Inti-hakan li Huquq al-Insan" (The Saudi regime is the worst violator of human rights), *al-Thawrah al-Islamiyya* (August 1988): 32–33.

13. In the early 1980s, members of the Saudi Shi'a movement had offices in Tehran. Although they were influenced heavily by the Ayatollah Khomeini's message, they refused to act at the behest of Iranians. Interview with a Shi'a leader, Washington, D.C., January 10, 1996.

14. See note 3 in Tawfiq al-Seif, "Nazrah 'ala Haq al-Ikhtilaf fil Islam," (A look at the right to differ in Islam), *al-Kalima,* no. 8 (Winter 1995): 88.

15. See for instance Fahmy Howeidy, *al-Islam wal Dimoqratiya* (Islam and democracy) (Cairo: Markaz al-Ahram lil Tarjama wal Nashr, 1993).

16. This judgement is based on a review of the 32 issues of *al-Jazeera al-Arabia* from its inception in January 1991 to its closure in August 1993.

17. See the interview with Sheikh Hasan al-Saffar, *Al-Jazeera al-Arabia* (June 1992): 18–21.

18. Interview with a Shi'a leader, Washington, January 19, 1996.

19. Interview with Sheikh Hasan al-Saffar, Qutif, Saudi Arabia, July 20, 1997.

20. Interview with Shi'a leader, Washington, December 10, 1995.

21. In addition to the history of the region, *al-Waha* also represents a dialogue between the Shi'a and the liberal forces in Saudi Arabia as well as between Shi'a and women. For instance, the third issue of *al-Waha* featured an arti-cle by Mohammed al-Ali, a well-known liberal cultural critic, entitled "Hawl Qira'at al-Turath" (Toward a reading of the tradition). Furthermore, the back cover included five paintings by five women, Kholoud al-Salim, Fathiya Zain al-Deen 'Afaf al-Jashi, Faiza la-Mas'oud, and Iman Mohammed Said al-Jashi. See *al-Waha,* no. 3 (December 1995).

22. Sheikh Hasan al-Saffar gave these three sermons to me during my field trip to Saudi Arabia in July 1997.

23. Human rights organizations have documented and repeatedly criticized op-pressive Saudi policies of discrimination against non-Wahhabis and non-Muslims. See *Amnesty International Report* (1992): 226–227; and *Human Rights Watch World Report* (1996): 306–312.

24. For the full text of the fatwa, see Mohammed Al-Hussein, "Al-Sheikh ibn Ji-breen Yafti bi Redat Almowatneen al-Shi'a wa Yafti bi Qatlihim" (Sheikh ibn

NOTES

Jibreen issues a religious decree that advocates the killing of Shi'a), *Al-Jazira Al-Arabia*, no. 11 (December 1991): 15–16.

25. Ibid., p. 15
26. See the texts of those religious decrees in ibid.
27. For more, see Jacob Goldberg, "The Shi'a Minority in Saudi Arabia," in Juan R. I. Cole and Nikki R. Kiddie (eds.), *Shi'ism and Social Protest* (New Haven, CT: Yale University Press, 1986), p. 235. Also see James Buchan, "Secular and Religious Opposition in Saudi Arabia," in Tim Niblock (ed.) *State, Society, and Economy in Saudi Arabia* (New York: St. Martin's Press, 1982), p. 118.
28. Mohammed H. al-Ghamari, "Haqa'iq al-Islam wa Abateel Al-Murjfeen" (The truth about Islam and the fables of the non-believers), *Al-Manhal*, no. 458 (October 1987): 128.
29. Minnesota Lawyers, *Shame in the House of Saud*, p. 103.
30. For detailed documentation on freedom of expression in Saudi Arabia, see *Silent Kingdom: Freedom of Expression in Saudi Arabia* (London: Article 19 Country Report, 1991).
31. This particular quote is taken from a book review by Ishaq Sheik Ya'quob, "Homeland and Citizenship," *Al-Youm*, June 26, 1997. The book was also reviewed earlier by another Saudi columnist. For more see Mohammed al-Soueigh, "Afkar wa Khawatir," *Al-Youm*, March 26, 1997.
32. Quoted in Roy P. Mottahedeh, "Toward an Islamic Theology of Toleration," in Tore Lindholm and Kari Vogt (eds.), *Islamic Law Reform and Human Rights* (Oslo: Nordic Human Rights Publications, 1992), pp. 35–36. Other than this passage all translations in this text are mine.
33. Ibid., p. 36.
34. Imam Malik ibn Anas is the founder of one of the main schools of jurisprudence in Sunni Islam.
35. On the question of freedom of belief, see Zakaria El Berry, *Man's Rights in Islam* (Heliopolis, Egypt: n.p., 1981), pp. 11–12.
36. Interview with al-Saffar, al-Qateef, July 26, 1997.
37. See al-Seif, "A Look at the Right to Differ," pp. 37–89.
38. For an English translation of the Cairo Declaration, see Appendix A in Minnesota Lawyers, *Shame in the House of Saud*, pp. 136–148.
39. Yousef al-Qaradawi, *Ghayr al-Muslimeen fil Mujtama' al-Islami* (Non-Muslims in an Islamic society) (Beirut: Mu'asasat al-Risala, 1983).
40. See the chapter entitled "No to Intellectual Terrorism," in Hasan al-Saffar, *Al-Ta'dudiya wal Huriya fil Islam* (Pluralism and freedom in Islam) (Beirut: Dar al-Bayan al-Arabi, 1990), pp. 125–141.
41. See Abdullah al-Yousef, "Haq al-Ikhtilaf wa Mashrou'iat al-Ra'i al-Akhar" (The right to differ and the legitimacy of the opposing viewpoint), *al-Kalima*, no. 6 (Winter 1995): 43–61; also see Abdullah al-Yousef, "Manahij Ta'seel Shar'iyat al-Ikhtilaf fil Fikr al-Islami" (The legitimacy of the right to differ in Islam: A methodological note), *al-Kalima*, no. 8 (Summer 1995): 42–69.

42. See al-Seif, "A Look at the Right to Differ," pp. 37–89.

43. Ann Elizabeth Mayer, *Islam and Human Rights* (Boulder, CO: Westview Press, 1991).

44. See notes to chapter 7 in ibid., pp. 235–239.

45. Mamoun Fandy, "Who Is Afraid of the Satellite Dish?" *The Christian Science Monitor,* December 15, 1993, p. 23.

46. Interview with Shi'a leader, Washington, DC, January 18, 1996.

47. Madawi al-Rasheed and Loulouwa al-Rasheed, "The Politics of Encapsulation: Saudi Policy towards Tribal and Religious Opposition," *Middle Eastern Studies,* vol. 32, no. 1 (January 1996): 96–119.

Chapter 8

1. Interview with Saudi official, Riyadh, July 12, 1997.

2. For more on the goals and objectives of the group, see "Mission Statement Page," http://www.saudhouse.com.mission.htm/.

3. Al-Auda, "The Islamic Tape."

4. For an analysis of these reforms, see Mamoun Fandy, "Saudi Arabia's Political Reforms Fall Short," *The Christian Science Monitor,* March 16, 1992. For a summary of the demands of the opposition as articulated in the Memorandum of Advice, see chapter 1.

5. Ibid., p. 50; also see the CDLR's weekly, *al-Huquq,* no. 95, April 17, 1996, p. 3.

6. *The Daily Telegraph,* January 5, 1996, p. 15.

7. The Saudi government has its home page maintained by its embassy in Washington, D.C. The address of the page is http://imedl.saudi.net/.

8. Author Interview, London, June 11, 1997.

9. Author Interview, London, June 12, 1997.

10. See MIRA's weekly newsletter, *al-Islah,* April 16 through December 9, 1996. Also see MIRA's homepage at http://www.miraserve.com/.

11. These tapes are popular in Egypt, Kuwait, and Jordan. In many cases taped sermons sell more than popular songs. For instance, Sheikh Abd al-Sabour Shaheen of Egypt sells 4,000 cassettes a week, each of which costs $1.50. One shopkeeper reported daily sales of 200 religious cassette tapes. For more, see Mirfat Dayab, "Religious Cassettes in Egypt: Half a Million Cassettes Preach Extremism," *Al-Majalla,* no. 874, November 10–16, 1996, pp. 20–24.

12. James C. Scott, p.16.

13. On the impact of mediation on hegemony, see Jesus Martin-Barbero, *Communication, Culture, and Hegemon: From Media to Mediations* (London: SAGE Publications, 1993).

14. Inderpal Grewal and Caren Kaplan (eds.), *Scattered Hegemonies: Postmodernity and the Transnational Feminist Practices* (Minneapolis: University of Minnesota Press, 1994).

15. Author Interview, Jeddah, June 19, 1997.

16. For more on Gramsci's notion of hegemony in a global context, see Robert W. Fox, "Gramsci, Hegemony and International Relations: An Essay in Method," *Millennium,* vol. 12, no. 2 (1983), pp.162–175.

17. Diane Singerman, *Avenues of Participation: Family Politics, and Networks in Urban Quarters of Cairo* (Princeton, NJ: Princeton University Press, 1995).

18. The case for the integration of Saudi Arabia into the global economy was made, though not shown by Chaudhry. See Kiren Aziz Chaudhry, *The Price of Wealth* (Ithaca, NY: Cornell University Press, 1997).

Index